T3-BSB-800

COMPARATIVE ADMINISTRATIVE CHANGE
AND REFORM

Comparative Administrative Change and Reform

Lessons Learned

Edited by

JON PIERRE AND PATRICIA W. INGRAHAM

McGill-Queen's University Press
Montreal & Kingston · London · Ithaca

BRESCIA UNIVERSITY
COLLEGE LIBRARY

© McGill-Queen's University Press 2010

ISBN 978-0-7735-3659-3 (cloth)
ISBN 978-0-7735-3660-9 (paper)

Legal deposit first quarter 2010
Bibliothèque nationale du Québec

Printed in Canada on acid-free paper that is 100% ancient forest free
(100% post-consumer recycled), processed chlorine free.

This book has been published with the help of a grant from the
University of Moncton.

McGill-Queen's University Press acknowledges the support of the Canada
Council for the Arts for our publishing program. We also acknowledge
the financial support of the Government of Canada through the Book
Publishing Industry Development Program (BPIDP) for our publishing
activities.

Library and Archives Canada Cataloguing in Publication

Comparative administrative change and reform: lessons learned /
edited by Jon Pierre and Patricia W. Ingraham.

Festschrift in honour of B. Guy Peters.
Includes bibliographical references.
ISBN 978-0-7735-3659-3 (bnd)
ISBN 978-0-7735-3660-9 (pbk)

1. Administrative agencies – Reorganization. 2. Civil service reform.
3. Public administration. 4. Comparative government. I. Pierre, Jon
II. Ingraham, Patricia W. III. Peters, B. Guy

JF51.C611 2010   352.3'67   C2009–906015–9

Typeset in Sabon 10.5/13
by Infoscan Collette, Quebec City

This book is dedicated
with affection, respect, and gratitude to

B. GUY PETERS

for his remarkable contributions
to the study of policy, administration,
and governance.

Contents

Preface

B. Guy Peters is the Maurice Falk Professor of American Government at the University of Pittsburgh. A native of Hopewell, Virginia, Professor Peters received his PHD from Michigan State University. He was an early leader in the analysis of public policy and the policy process. His classic text, *American Public Policy: Problems and Prospects*, is now in its seventh edition. He moved quickly to a companion interest in comparative politics, policy, and administration. *Comparative Public Administration: Problems of Theory and Method* was first published in 1988 and quickly became a touchstone for scholars and students who studied the role of administration in policy processes and administrative reform.

Guy Peters is the author or editor of over forty books that have been translated into a dozen languages. He has been a visiting professor or research scholar at over twenty-five universities around the world and has lectured at many more. His hundreds of published papers and research reports have informed virtually every aspect of public policy, administrative politics and policy, administrative reform, governance, institutionalism and institutionalist theory, and globalization, among other subjects. His perceptive analyses have made enormous contributions to these areas.

Perhaps of equal significance, Guy Peters' international network of colleagues and friends includes the leading scholars in the United States and Canada, the United Kingdom and Europe, Australia and New Zealand, Asia, and Latin America. Guy's work with Donald Savoie at the Canadian Centre for Management Development (now the Canada School of Public Service) created not only five important books but a lasting set of collaborations world-wide. Among his many contributions will be that the connections he provided have sparked some of the healthiest debates in academia and government.

Guy and his wife Sheryn, avid bird watchers, have traversed the globe several times in search not only of ever elusive species but also the ever elusive idea or concept that can move scholarly analysis forward. In his writing, his lectures, his students, and his unending energetic inquiry, Guy Peters is a model of the remarkably creative synergy that can exist between academics and the worlds they inhabit.

COMPARATIVE ADMINISTRATIVE CHANGE
AND REFORM

Ideas In Action: Why the Reality of the Administrative Reform Grinder Matters

PATRICIA INGRAHAM AND JON PIERRE

Public management reform was a compelling target of analysis and scholarly thought for much of the late twentieth century. The issues addressed by the reforms ranged widely, at some point including topics such as public sector productivity, public sector change, effective governance, and institutionalism. As disparate as these concepts might appear, there are complex interrelationships among them. Inherent in these relationships and connections is a growing body of evidence of the coming of age of public management, both as an empirical phenomenon and as an academic object of study. This is evident in the ever clearer difficulties of transposing private sector practices onto public organizations, in the similar difficulties of suggesting that reform ideas that may be appropriate in a Western setting may also be appropriate in a non-Western culture, and – most certainly – in assumptions that the elusive concept of "governance" is comparable across national and continental boundaries. An even more fundamental issue is that of defining the "public sector," a point made abundantly clear by Christopher Pollitt's discussion in chapter 4 of this book. In an earlier effort to examine the relationships among these different concepts and to explore possible integration of their alternative visions of change and reform, Guy Peters observed that, aside from the common factor of an often ill-defined desire for change, a look across the experiences of governments around the world indicated "piecemeal" and "unsystematic" approaches that had most frequently resulted in "disappointing" reform results (Peters 1996, 16).

Nonetheless, the reform experience – which now seems to have slowed substantially – has provided valuable lessons about the issues noted above, as well as about new ones that have emerged: accountability, political power, leadership, and citizen engagement. The many years of various national experiences have also produced a treasure trove of research questions for those who wish to pursue them. One sign of emerging maturity and development is that public management has now found its own niche, both among scholars and among practitioners. There are clearer demarcations between public and private management, just as there are now distinct differences between Weberian and neo-Weberian (Pollitt and Bouckaert 2002) ideas of public management and the more contemporary versions of that theory and practice. The cumulative knowledge gained, though incremental, has contributed to a much deeper understanding of the limits of institutional redirection and change, as well as to alternative definitions of effective governance.

There is now an extensive and continuous debate among both academics and practitioners on what characterizes good public management. Public sector organizations are multi-functional structures operating under some degree of political control and accountability (Christensen et al. 2007). Thus, public management is about more than maximizing efficiency and customer satisfaction; it is as much about upholding public sector norms such as legality, professionalism, and accountability. Good public management does not allow performance and results to take precedence over procedure; rather, it seeks to find the proper balance between a customer model and a citizen model of public service production and delivery.

There is also a growing understanding of the role of public management in democratic governance. Public management and emerging collaborative strategies are not identical processes or phenomena. However, they do suggest that both the processes of governing and those of managing public sector organizations share the challenge of opening up to the external environment, with all that entails in terms of handling complex contingencies. Traditional public administration did not have to concern itself very much with public-private partnerships, contract management, or network governance. But now, these challenges face contemporary public bureaucracies in most countries of this frequently more collaborative world.

In this setting, there is a growing awareness, or rediscovery, that while extensive collaboration and network management exist, there are also significant differences among the various partners – managing public organizations is something inherently different from managing a for-profit organization or an NGO. The organizational and procedural features that set a public organization apart from other types of organizations were to some extent seen as problems by the early public management theorists: they prevented public service organizations from emulating management and production strategies in the private sector. Today, there is a better understanding that public management theory and practice should not attempt to downplay or ignore those public sector peculiarities but rather to blend, to the extent possible, successful management practices from other sectors with the unique features of public organizations.

Taken together, all of this suggests that public management, having oscillated among several different intellectual and academic poles – business management, public administration, economics, organization theory, administrative law, and political science – gradually has found its own identity and role, as well as values, ideals, and discourse. Perhaps most importantly, public management has developed a position in the administrative reform process that combines close collaboration with and inspiration from practitioners, on the one hand, and the pursuit of an academic research agenda on the other. To put this slightly differently, there is now a balance between instrumentality and theory in public management research.

As an academic enterprise, public management is still the new kid on the block and, as such, must define and defend its turf from potentially hostile neighbours. Political scientists have often taken a tentative stance towards public management, trying to decide whether it should be taught in their own departments or in schools of public administration or business schools. Public administration scholars have viewed the emergence of public management with even greater suspicion, since public management represents a new way of looking at public bureaucracies, and this new perspective shakes many traditional foundations. Seen in a historical perspective, however, this juxtaposition of public administration and public management is an academic construct more than a real one. As Donald Kettl's work has elegantly shown (2002), the modernization of the public bureaucracy has drawn not on contrasting public administration and public management but rather on the synergy that exists between the two. The public bureaucracies of the twenty-first century face different tasks and operate in widely different environments compared to those of the nineteenth or even the twentieth century. To be sure, if there ever was a lesson that the public sector could learn from the world of private business, it would be that different organizational challenges call for different organizational and managerial solutions. Modern public management theory sits at the juncture between the constitutional continuity of public bureaucracies and the global, economic, and societal pressures for organizational change.

That said, we caution against believing that there are universal solutions to these contemporary challenges in public management. The chapters in this volume substantiate the historical and cultural embeddedness of public administration, as well as the enormous power of politics and political leaders. They demonstrate well the tensions and trade-offs – and perhaps even the cynicism – of critical actors who have made important reform choices. And they illustrate well the search for balance in modern governance choices. Again in Peters' words, "Any choice of paradigms for government and administration is unlikely to be Pareto optimal, but the benefits and sacrifices should be clear when making judgments about governance" (1996, 133). It is this very broad set of lessons and research questions that this book addresses.

HONORING GUY PETERS

This book honors and celebrates the scholarly contributions of Professor B. Guy Peters. His illustrious career has spanned many of the disciplinary divides and developments that we have outlined above. If the book seems to cover a wide array of topics and issues, it does so, at least in part, because it is an effort to portray the breadth of the scholarly inquiry that has marked Guy Peters' career. From his earliest work covering public policy, the politics of bureaucracy, and comparisons among governments broadly writ, Guy identified the topics that will captivate scholarly analysts for decades.

Guy Peters made significant contributions to the emergent body of public policy research but was also a leader in the preparation of textbooks that engaged undergraduate and graduate students around the world in better understanding the design, implementation, and evaluation (or lack thereof) of public policy (his text is in its seventh edition). With Professor Brian Hogwood, Guy explored not only the dynamics of public policy but what they termed the "pathology" of public policy as well. In this latter effort they carefully described the many ways in which "normal" policy processes can lead to dysfunctional and contradictory outcomes. At the same time, Guy Peters was leading the way in merging the study of public policy with the study of public bureaucracies and the roles they played in policy processes. This effort coincided with and complemented his early work in comparing public bureaucratic organizations.

In his important collaboration with Professor Donald Savoie and what was then the Canadian Centre for Management Development, Guy Peters began the systematic exploration of the cross-national dimensions of administrative reform. *Governance in a Changing Environment* (Peters and Savoie 1997), the first of the edited volumes to emerge from the collaboration, was in the vanguard of exploring the fundamental nexus between democratic government and efforts to reform its apparatus for governing. The collaboration also was reflected in the group of scholars who continue to be at the head of the contemporary research agenda on these issues. Many of these authors have written chapters for this book.

Guy Peters' breadth of inquiry and the ease with which he moves between public policy, public administration, public management, and governance research has facilitated cross-fertilization of ideas and fueled research advances in these areas. It has facilitated addressing issues such as the impact of collaborative strategies of governing on political institutions and public administration, the role of the public bureaucracy in shaping public policy, and the role of political institutions in governance.

Two additional aspects of Guy Peters' work are noteworthy. One is his involvement with growing the next generation of political scientists. As an undergraduate and graduate teacher, he has students all over the world. Christopher Hunold, Fiona Ross, Paul Taggart, and Tony Zito are among the many doctoral students who Guy taught and supported and who went on to successful academic careers. José Luis Méndez, from whom a chapter is included in this book, exemplifies the student who pursues both academic and practical governance roles.

Peters has also been an advisor on administrative reform to many nations. His work in this regard has departed from the traditional "global solution" models to provide, instead, very careful tailoring of recommendations to national administrative cultures. His work with the Finnish government deserves special mention; with Geert Bouckaert he developed highly original ideas that were later adopted by that government.

THE CHAPTERS IN THIS BOOK

This book covers many dimensions of complexity and the first chapters fully demonstrate its density and depth. Johan Olsen's compelling analysis of institutionalism and large-scale democratic change illustrates the tangle. He provides the critical institutional context for reform efforts and asks a fundamental question: "How in this complexity are we to understand change?" He notes again that the task of democratic governance is *not* to maximize change but to balance change and order. Debating and delineating the competitions and interactions among institutions and mechanisms promoting order, authority, accountability, and change, Olsen poses this question: "Under what conditions are institutions perfectly adaptive in changing themselves or their environments in ways that create a fairly stable order?" The question is at the heart of efforts to analyze administrative reform.

Chapters 2 and 3 engage a significant, but consistently thorny, dimension of change: the role of leadership in achieving it. Geert Bouckaert identifies critical challenges to effectively leading change in chapter 2. He contrasts these challenges (which include, for example, coordinating across governments and development of strong levels of trust and legitimacy) with emergent reform trends in OECD nations. Acutely observing that leadership is not an individual characteristic but a complex set of characteristics reflecting – and shaped by – institutional settings, he concludes that effective leadership is absolutely integral to effective change.

Continuing the argument in chapter 3, Ian Thynne examines types of political and administrative leaders in the reform equation and creates an exploratory framework for possible future comparative research. He links these types to different organizational settings and opportunities, as well as to potential modes of cooperation and conflict that may emerge when the leadership types (and organizational settings) are combined. The analytical dimensions he proposes also permit him to consider these interactions in different kinds of political systems. The result of his analysis is a fascinating set of possible research questions to be pursued in rigorous, comprehensive comparative research.

Chapters 4, 5, and 6 move the emphasis of reform analysis from leadership to management systems and other reform tools. In chapter 4 Christopher Pollitt describes and succinctly critiques international efforts to benchmark reform and governance. These efforts, utilizing composite measures to assess general properties of government, do not measure up, in Poliitt's view, in part because of the lack of comparability in the elements of the measures themselves, but also because their composite nature makes them very difficult to apply – or understand – in specific contexts. Pollitt argues, convincingly as usual, that international comparisons that are more limited in scope and intent are actually more useful to both practitioners and academics. He concludes: "If 'governance' means anything, then it means the inclusion of a wide range of actors in the process of public debate and decision. Paradoxically (these blunt measures) mean that only a few 'experts' can understand and use them."

Hood and Margetts engage the debate from a slightly different, but essential, perspective in chapter 5. Where, they ask, does the information that governments use in their decisions come from? They argue that information technology, which ought to be integrated into organizational and governmental processes if it is to provide guidance in decisions and evaluation, is in fact "ghettoized." It has, in effect, not felt the impact of reform and remains intact in an insular silo, prohibiting easy dissemination or understanding of critical data. It continues to stand apart from the core of public administration and public management.

In chapter 6, John Halligan returns to the broader issue of management reform and examines the extent to which reform activities have had any impact on better aligning management processes and other features of governing. This chapter clarifies the extent to which public management has "come of age," as Halligan discusses evolving conceptualizations of management and performance management. In a very useful conclusion, he sums up the core themes now evident across Westminster nations, which were among the first to adopt comprehensive reform packages. He identifies new emphases on horizontal collaboration among agencies and governments, additional delegation (but also some additional direction) from the centre to allow agencies better capacity-building ability, and new service delivery mechanisms and assessment of results.

Chapters 7, 8, and 9 examine the effect of reform in specific, non-Western nations. Doing so is important because many reform ideas and concepts originated in Western industrial nations. The descriptions of the processes as they unfolded should give the most dedicated policy diffusion theorists pause. In Chapter 7, José Luis Méndez describes the case of Mexico, whose reforms relied heavily on the creation of a professional civil service (in 2003) and on performance evaluation. He describes the rampant corruption that led to the discussion of civil service reform, the severe economic crisis that gripped Mexico, and the new support of advisors in the president's Office for Governmental Innovation as major influences on the adoption of reform. He also describes the difficulties of attempting to instill the idea of a civil service based on merit and open competition in a society long accustomed to spoils. In a very interesting argument, he argues that, to the extent that the reform (after many twists and reinterpretations) can be considered even a partial success, it can be attributed to the fact that creation of a civil service was not placed at the top of the presidential action agenda but was given an intermediate role. One of his major conclusions is also about reform in general: first, carefully construct the foundation of reform; add other reform elements only after the foundation is secure.

In chapter 8, John Burns discusses the intriguing case of reform in China. His absorbing and well-documented analysis examines both the wide variation in adoption strategies and the characteristics of the "reforms with Chinese characteristics" that resulted. Using Anthony Downs's typology of public officials and three case studies, Burns emphasizes that there were no "simplistic transfers" of Western models. Civil service reform (a fascinating case in the Chinese setting) came about largely as a result of top-down decision making. Performance management measures, on the other hand, were often the result of bottom-up pushing for reform. Burns links this model to the pursuit of self interest and promotion among local officials and others. Transparency reforms, on the other hand, resulted from both top-down and bottom-up pressures. In all cases, there was a process of selecting the elements of reform considered most compatible with the existing Chinese model and no wholesale adoption of a pattern from another nation.

In chapter 9, which focuses on Thailand, Bidhya Bowornwathana presents another example of reform policy diffusion, one linked very closely to international institutions and consultants. He also documents the critical relationships between the political environment and reform success. He links the role of academics and their support for accountability and transparency reforms to their adoption. Significantly, he outlines how private sector reforms moved easily and with little alteration into the public Thai domain. He also brings our attention to a seemingly obvious, but often overlooked, issue of reform: adoption of a reform is not in itself success. It is only step 1. He concludes, "It is difficult to reform bureaucrats and politicians if they are in charge of reforming themselves. As an old Thai saying goes, 'Don't let the cat guard the grilled fish.'"

In chapter 10, Alberta Sbragia demonstrates yet another dimension of reform in her analysis of the European Union. Describing the EU as existing in a "densely populated institutional universe," Sbragia explores the very complicated issues of a necessarily centralized, very powerful organization as it attempts to deal with member nation differences in capability and capacity and with a wide range of complex policy issues ranging from the environment to the economy. The "multi-level governance" model that the EU has necessarily adopted has created a very sophisticated architecture whose coexistence with national governments has created an unusual environment for reform – one that Sbragia chronicles in a very compelling way.

Finally, in chapter 11 Donald Savoie asks the ultimate taking-stock question: "So what?" His conclusions are not sanguine. He notes that politicians who have run against bureaucracy have been successful. But the question is, did they craft reforms that were successful as well? Has the capacity of the civil service become greater? Have governments increased their efficiency and their decision-making ability? Savoie answers, "No!" Many of the other chapters of the book would support that conclusion, or at least one that is along the lines of "Things haven't improved as much as we hoped they would."

At the same time, it is important to note that all the chapters discuss not a reform point or a reform time but a reform cycle. There have been lessons learned, corrections made, new directions taken. Governments are not tidy; neither are the processes and activities that seek to change them. Perhaps the issues now are as much about shaping expectations for reform as about reform components themselves. As Jon Pierre cogently notes in the concluding chapter of this book, to a large extent contemporary reform problems are also not necessarily problems of resources or of knowledge but of governance. Continuing to ask questions about how governments can better serve their citizens, act more nimbly, be better prepared for the future, and still honor democratic tradition and values remains an important part of the academic analysis tradition. It will also serve to further illuminate the important paths broken by B. Guy Peters.

PART ONE

The Ideas of Reform: Reforming Governance and Accountability

1

Change and Continuity:
An Institutional Approach to Institutions
of Democratic Government

JOHAN P. OLSEN

THE PROBLEM OF INSTITUTIONAL CHANGE

It is commonplace to argue that political institutions are a source of inertia and resistance to change. Institutions are seen as excessively static and likely to remain on the same path unless some effort is made to divert them. It is also a commonplace to claim that the "new institutionalism" as an approach to political life is not useful for making sense of institutional change, planned or not. The assumed inability to explain change is a result, because the new institutionalism is overly structuralist and does not grant purposeful actors a proper role. The approach does not deal adequately with political agency, conflict, and power asymmetries and can therefore not account for deliberate institutional design as a political instrument (Peters 1999a, b; Peters and Pierre 2005). Yet the label "new institutionalism" is used for a variety of approaches that understand change differently, and "most fundamentally, there is the question of whether or not change is recognized as an ordinary part of institutional life or as the exception to a rule of stability, and perhaps even hyperstability" (Peters 1999a, 147).

The aim of this chapter is not to take stock of competing approaches to institutional change. It is to use one specific institutional approach, with roots in studies of formal organizations, to explore how we may think about the mechanisms through which institutions arise, evolve, and decline and about how new institutions replace or supplement older ones. What conditions are likely to sustain or undermine change, and what is the significance of existing institutional arrangements?

This chapter calls attention to aspects usually neglected by approaches giving primacy to large-scale societal forces or to deliberate design. Within the first approach, institutional arrangements are determined by the external environment through competitive pressure and selection stemming from advantageous traits and differential survival and growth. Within the second, institutional arrangements are malleable and a matter of choice, and change is driven by actor strategies. In contrast, an institutional approach as understood here assumes that institutions are not pawns of external forces or obedient tools in the hands of some master. They have an internal life of their own, and developments are to some degree independent of external events and decisions. Change is an ordinary part of political life. It is rule-bound and takes place through standard processes, as institutions interpret and respond to experience through learning and adaptation. Yet such processes are not guaranteed to be "efficient" in reaching an enduring equilibrium, and sometimes change is discontinuous.[1]

In what follows I focus on the relations between institutional characteristics and change in governmental institutions in modern democracies. Accounting for how and why institutions emerge and change, however, requires a rephrasing of the questions an institutional approach should aspire to answer. The task of democratic government is not to maximize change but to balance order and change, and the scholarly challenge is to account for how and why institutions remain stable as well as for how and why they change.

Democratic government is, furthermore, made up of organized components with shifting relations to one another, and governing is structured collective action coordinating multiple actors, organizations, and resources. Knowledge about how formal organizations operate and change, therefore, is assumed to provide insight into the dynamics of governmental institutions. Formal organizations and formally organized institutions are conceived as collections of rules and standard operating procedures, pre-defined patterns of thought and action, including but not limited to legal rules and procedures, and resources.

First, the problem of change is reformulated in this chapter, and it is observed that institutions have a role in generating both order and change and in balancing the two. Second, the concepts of institution and institutionalization are elaborated. Third, institutional sources of change and continuity are explored. Fourth, some implications for how democratic change and order can be conceived are spelled out, and, finally, some future challenges are suggested.

NEITHER NEWTON NOR HERACLITUS

Portraying institutions as unable or unwilling to adapt to new contingencies and tasks has long historical roots. A standard argument has been that political institutions lag behind economic, technological, and social change – a claim that has been frequently repeated as a premise for reforms in the public sector during the last three decades. Contemporary societies emphasize the need for innovation and change, yet the main assumption, inspired by neoclassical economics, is that market competition is, and should be, the dominant mechanism of innovation (Fagerberg, Mowery, and Nelson 2005).

The argumentation seems inspired by Newton's first law, the law of inertia. Political institutions, like any material body that is at rest or is moving at a constant speed, will remain at rest or keep moving at a constant speed unless they are acted upon by an external force. External forces decide the direction and magnitude of change, and in the absence of external forces, political institutions will cling to the status quo, or there will be continuing and inevitable developments towards modernization, rationalization, democratization, bureaucratization, and so on.

Historically, however, political thinking has been as much concerned with the conditions for legitimate order, authority, and rule, as with change (Immergut 2006). Stability and ordered relationships have been viewed as precarious achievements, always threatened by disorganization, entropy, and chaos, which endanger life and property. The point of departure for this strand of analysis is closer to Heraclitus (540–480 BC) than to Newton. The indeterminacy of political life is emphasized. Everything is in flux under the pressure of shifting situations. Organizational arrangements are infinitely changeable and always in transition, and it is a Sisyphean job to create and maintain political order. Because it is as difficult to keep institutions constant as it is to change them, we need to explain continuity and smooth developments as well as radical transformations and abrupt breakdowns. Understanding order and change are two sides of the same coin and we need to know what processes and conditions may maintain or challenge the status quo.

Elements of Order

An institutional approach assumes that political life is neither deterministic (caused by external forces and laws) nor random (governed by the laws of chance) and that political institutions are neither completely static nor in constant flux. In contrast with the assumptions of the heirs of Heraclitus, institutions are assumed to create elements of order and predictability in political life. Institutions organize actors, issues, and resources in or out of politics, and they structure patterns of political struggle (Schattschneider 1960; Steinmo, Thelen and Longstreeth 1992; Egeberg 2006). They make less likely pure temporal sorting, where decision opportunities, actors, and problems and solutions flow together solely as a function of time (Cohen, March, and Olsen 1972, 2007). In contrast with the assumptions of the heirs of Newton, political institutions are assumed to have a dynamics of their own. The assumption that institutional arrangements persist unless external forces act on them underestimates both intra- and inter-institutional sources of change.

Imperfect Processes

Through what processes, then, do institutions emerge and change? To what extent are forms of government a matter of choice (Mill 1962, 1)? Are societies capable of establishing good government from reflection and choice, or are they forever destined to depend on accident and force (Hamilton, Jay, and Madison 1964, 1)? To answer these questions, students of political institutions have borrowed metaphors from both engineering and biology.

Political engineering and rational design assume that institutions are deliberately created and reformed in order to achieve substantive ends. Some actors have a vision of a better society. They diagnose problems and see institutions as partly causing them. They prescribe better ways of doing things and know how institutions should be changed in order to achieve better results. They also control the resources required to implement the prescription.

An alternative to rationalism – "the most remarkable intellectual fashion of post-Renaissance Europe" (Oakeshott 1991, 5) – is to see "living institutions" as social organisms that evolve over time as an unplanned result of historical processes. Institutions grow as artifacts of interaction, cooperation, and competition and embody the experience and normative and causal beliefs of a population. In this perspective the Parliament, for example, has been seen as "a product less of intention and design than of blind evolution" (Dahl 1998, 21). Actions may come before ideas and purposes. Ends and means may develop simultaneously, and evolving behavioral patterns may be described, explained, and justified post hoc, "frozen" into habits and traditions and formally codified. Surviving institutions are those that have proved their worth through the test of time.

Inspired by Mill's sarcastic comment that "it is difficult to decide which of these doctrines would be the most absurd, if we could suppose either of them held as an exclusive theory" (Mill 1962, 3), an institutional perspective conceives of political actors neither as engineers with full control nor as fatalists with no range of choice. Institutional developments are neither a direct product of will, planning, and design nor a mere haphazard by-product of chance events and an ecology of uncoordinated actions. Institutionalism emphasizes the endogenous nature and explanatory power of political institutions. It is assumed that the organization of political life makes a difference and that institutions have dynamics of their own. The theoretical challenge is to understand the shifting mix of deliberate design and adaptive behavior (March 1981; March and Olsen 1989, 2006b; Brunsson and Olsen 1998).

In the literature it is often assumed that institutions survive and flourish because they are well adapted to their functional (Goodin 1996; Stinchcombe 2001) or normative environments (Meyer and Rowan 1977; Scott, Meyer, and Associates 1994). There is, however, no reason to believe that processes of adaptation are always perfect in a context of large-scale governmental organizations. Political institutions have historically shown robustness facing comprehensive societal change; institutional stability is possible in situations with high external pressure (Héritier 2007, 242), and it has even been asked whether government organizations are immortal (Kaufman 1976) – suggesting that the external environment has a limited and varying ability to select and eliminate political institutions. Likewise, in spite of accounts of the role of heroic founders and constitutional moments, democracies have a limited capacity for institutional design and for achieving the intended effects of reorganizations (March and Olsen 1983, 1989; Olsen and Peters 1996; Offe 2001).

In contrast with standard equilibrium models, institutionalism holds that history is "inefficient."[2] "Historical inefficiency" implies that institutions rarely are perfectly adapted to their environments and that the matching of institutions, behaviors, and contexts takes time and has multiple, path-dependent equilibria. The receptivity to external pressure varies: consequently, adaptation is less automatic, continuous, and precise than is assumed by equilibrium models (March and Olsen 1989).[3] Institutions affect the rate of change by the ways in which they adapt their internal structures and processes, by creating actors and providing them with premises of action, and by ignoring or modifying external pressures and influencing environments – and thereby influencing future environmental inputs. There is, for example, no guarantee that surviving institutions represent an efficient response to external environments, because the rate of external change may outpace the rate of institutional adaptation and because institutions sometimes speed up and sometimes delay or impair external impulses and decisions.

While institutionalism assumes that change and order are generated by comprehensible processes that produce recurring modes of action and patterns of change (March 1981), the possibility of inefficiency in standard processes requires detailed knowledge about how historical experience is incorporated into institutional structures and processes (DiMaggio and Powell 1991, 33). The key behavioral mechanisms encoding experience into rules and routines are history-dependent, and in a world of partly autonomous institutions we need to move our focus from a single dominant, coherent, and efficient process to observations of how institutional properties mediate between inputs and outcomes by influencing several "imperfect" and possibly disjointed processes of change. The observation and interpretation of experience, targets and aspiration levels, memories, the retrieval of information, capabilities, and responses are all affected by the organization and legacy of institutions (March and Olsen 1989, 1995).

Institutionalists therefore need to identify processes and determinants that increase or hamper the ordering effect of political institutions and make history more or less inefficient, and they need to attend to how such processes themselves are stabilized or destabilized (Olsen 2008a). Because a well-designed institution "is not a stable solution to achieve, but a developmental process to keep active" (Nystrom and Starbuck 1981, xx), democracies face a grand balancing act between exploitation and exploration. Exploitation involves using rules, routines, and knowledge that are known to work. Exploration involves a willingness and an ability to experiment with rules, routines, and knowledge that might, but often do not, provide improvements. The elimination of exploitation will make an organization obsolete in a dynamic world. Continuous experimentation will prevent the organization from realizing the potential gains of new discoveries. What is less obvious is the optimal balance between the two (March 1991).

To elaborate this approach, we need to specify in more detail what is meant by "institution" and "institutionalization."

INSTITUTIONALIZATION, DE-INSTITUTIONALIZATION AND RE-INSTITUTIONALIZATION

Formally organized political institutions, such as the legislature, the executive, public administration, and the judiciary, have for long been important research sites for students of politics. Institutionalism, however, is a specific approach that aspires to make sense of how such institutions emerge, function, and change. What makes an approach to government and politics "institutional" (Peters 1999a, 18)? As already argued, the simple answer is that an institutional approach assigns more explanatory power to the organization and legacies of institutions than to properties of individual actors and the broader societal contexts.

A parliament, a ministry, or a court of law, like any formal organization, can be conceived of as a rational instrument for a dominant centre or entrepreneur that creates, reforms, and eliminates institutions; as an arena for struggle and bargaining among contending groups; as an artifact of environmental forces; or as a transformative institution. Each conception demands different kinds of knowledge. An instrumental perspective and an arena perspective require knowledge about the preferences, beliefs, resources, and strategies of (respectively) the dominant decision maker(s) and the participants negotiating and re-negotiating the terms of order. An environmental perspective demands knowledge about broad economic, technological, and social forces and movements. An institutional perspective requires knowledge about the internal success criteria, structures, procedures, rules, practices, career structures, socialization patterns, styles of thought and interpretative traditions, and resources of the entity to be in focus.[4] An institutional perspective also requires concepts of "institution" and "institutionalization" that go beyond everyday language.

Rules, Reasons, and Resources

Institutionalism conceives of an institution as a relatively enduring collection of rules and organized practices embedded in structures of meaning and resources that are relatively invariant in the face of the turnover of individuals and changing external circumstances (March and Olsen 2006b). Constitutive rules and repertoires of standard operating procedures structure institutional behavior and developments by prescribing appropriate behavior for specific actors in specific situations. Structures of meaning, involving standardization, homogenization, and authorization of common purposes, reasons, vocabularies, and accounts, give direction to, describe, explain, justify, and legitimate behavioral rules. Structures of resources create capabilities for acting. Resources are routinely tied to rules and worldviews, empowering and constraining actors differently and making them more or less capable of acting according to behavioral codes.

Institutionalism involves purposeful human agency, reflection, and reason-giving, as well as rules. Yet in contrast with models assuming a logic of consequentiality and strategic action, where actors maximize their (self-) interest, institutionalism assumes that the basic logic of action is rule-following. Behavior is governed by standardized and accepted codes of behavior, prescriptions based on a logic of appropriateness and a sense of obligations and rights derived from an identity, role, or membership in a political community and the ethos and practices of its institutions. Actors do not simply please others by acting in accordance with their expectations. Rather, rules are to some extent self-enforcing, because actors have internalized the belief that some actions are appropriate, natural, and legitimate (March and Olsen 1989; 2006a,b). Members of an institution observe and are the guardians of its constitutive principles and standards. Nevertheless, they can take purposeful action based on rule interpretation, including the ability to develop and modify normative criteria and identities through collective processes.

The scopes and modes of institutionalized activity vary across political systems, policy areas, and historic time (Eisenstadt 1965;

Berger and Luckmann 1967). Over time political life achieves or loses structure, and the nature of order changes. At some periods in some areas of politics and policy, politics is organized around well-defined boundaries, common rules and practices, shared causal and normative understandings, and resources adequate for collective action. At other times and places, politics is relatively anarchic. Boundaries are less well defined, relations are less orderly, and institutions are less common, less adequately supported, and less involved (March and Olsen 1998, 943–44).

Institutionalization

Institutionalization is both a process and a property of organizational arrangements. Institutionalization as a process implies that an organizational identity is developed and that acceptance and legitimacy in a culture (or subculture) is built. It involves

1 Increasing clarity and agreement about behavioral rules, including the allocation of formal authority. The standardization and formalization of practice reduce uncertainty and conflict concerning who does what and when and how. As some ways of acting are perceived as natural and legitimate, there is less need for using incentives or coercion in order to make people follow prescribed rules.
2 Increasing consensus concerning how behavioral rules are to be described, explained, and justified, with a common vocabulary, common expectations, and common success criteria. There is also a decreasing need to explain and justify why modes of action are appropriate in terms of problem solving and normative validity.
3 Increasing shared conceptions of what are legitimate resources in different settings and who should have access to or control common resources. The supply of resources required to act in accordance with behavioral prescriptions becomes routinized and taken as given. It takes less effort to get the resources required for acting in accordance with prescribed rules of appropriate behavior.

As a corollary, de-institutionalization implies that existing institutional borders, identities, rules, and practices, and existing descriptions, explanations and justifications, and resources and powers are becoming more contested and possibly even discontinued. There is increasing uncertainty, disorientation, and conflict. New actors are mobilized. Outcomes are more uncertain, and it is necessary to use more incentives or coercion to make people follow prescribed rules and to sanction deviance. Re-institutionalization implies either retrogression or a transformation from one order into another, constituted on different normative and organizational principles.

Since institutions are human products, they exist only because a sufficiently high number of citizens believe that they exist (Searle 1995). Institutions require continuously renewed collective confirmation and validation of their constitutive rules, meanings, and resources. Yet all institutions experience challenges, and some turn out to be fragile and unable to reproduce themselves. The basic assumptions on which an institution is constituted and its prescribed behavioral rules are never fully accepted by the entire society (Eisenstadt 1965, 41; Goodin 1996, 39). Institutions may recede into oblivion because trust is eroded and rules are not obeyed. Institutions may also be resisted and overthrown because they are discredited as being illegitimate, inefficient, immoral, or exploitative. There may be rationally motivated dissent and change (Habermas 1996, 36) and "revolutionary violence may contribute as much as peaceful reform to the establishment of a free society" (Moore 1966, 20).

Institutionalization, therefore, is not an inevitable, irreversible, unidirectional, or monotonic process, and institutionalization, de-institutionalization and re-institutionalization can follow a variety of patterns (Weaver and Rockman 1993; Rokkan 1999; Bartolini 2005). Can, then, knowledge about intra- and inter-institutional properties contribute to an improved understanding of how formally organized governmental institutions mirror and maintain a certain kind of order but nonetheless change?

INSTITUTIONAL SOURCES OF CONTINUITY AND CHANGE

Organized Democracy

Theories of political development have to take into account that modern democracies are "organized democracies" (Olsen 1983) and that institutions are markers of a polity's character, history, visions, and identity. Institutions give order to social relations, reduce flexibility and variability in behavior, and restrict the possibilities of a one-sided pursuit of self-interest or drives (Weber 1978, 40–3). Democratic government, however, consists of a conglomerate of partly autonomous and powerful large-scale formal organizations that operate according to different repertoires of relatively stable rules and standard operating procedures (Selznick 1957, 1; Allison 1971, 67).

Governmental organizations do, often on their own initiative, what they are trained to do and know how to do, and government can, at least in the short run, deliver only what large-scale organizations (military, police, administrative, health, and educational systems, etc.) are capable of and motivated to do. Understanding what feasible alternatives organizational routines and repertoires provide is, in particular, important in complex situations that require coordinated action by a large number of individuals, organizations, technologies, and resources. Government actions and institutional developments can then be understood by uncovering how organizations enact standard operating procedures. It is necessary to know which organizations government consists of, how tasks and responsibilities are allocated among them, and what standard operating programs and repertoires different organizations have (Cyert and March 1963; Allison 1971; March and Olsen 1995).

Rules and standard operating procedures define satisfactory performance (targets, aspiration levels) and organize attention, interpretation, recruitment, education and socialization of personnel, resource allocation, action capabilities, and conflict resolution. Governmental organizations also avoid uncertainty by stabilizing relations to other significant actors; for example, through developing shared understandings about turfs, jurisdictions, and budgets. There is normally limited flexibility in organizational targets and aspiration levels, frames and traditions of interpretation, total budgets and internal allocations, and external relationships. Resistance to change increases the more organizations are institutionalized, so that structures and processes have value and symbolic meaning beyond their contributions to solving the task at hand, and change is seen as threatening institutional identities, the sense of mission, and emotional attachments (Selznick 1957, 17; March and Olsen 1983, 1989).

Institutions are, nevertheless, not static. Rules and practices are modified as a result of positive and negative experience and organizational learning and adaptation (March, Schultz, and Zhou 2000). Routines, identities, beliefs, and resources can be both instruments of stability and vehicles of change; institutions of government do not always favor continuity over change. In democracies change is usually incremental, but it can also be path-breaking, with a sharp departure from existing practice. The question is when, how, and why routines are challenged and how institutional characteristics affect institutional developments and the likelihood of comprehensive change.

Rules

In institutionalized contexts foundational rules affect the mix of continuity and change. Constitutions, treaties, laws, and institution- and profession-specific rules are carriers of accumulated knowledge. They define fairly stable rights and duties, regulate how advantages and burdens are allocated, and prescribe procedures for conflict resolution. Institutions may, however, carry the seeds of their own reform. There are rules for constitutional amendment and for who is responsible for initiating and implementing reforms; for example, specific departments for planning and organizational development. Change can also be driven by explicit rules institutionalized in specific units or subunits, rules prescribing routine shifts within an existing repertoire of rules (March and Simon 1958).

For example, constitutional rules protect *Rechtsstaat* values and limit the legitimacy of sudden, radical change. However, constitutional rules and routines also facilitate and legitimate change, such as the transfer of power from one government to another, and the instrumental strand of democratic theory holds that citizens and their representatives should be able to fashion and refashion political institutions at will. Founding assemblies, lawmakers, and governments are assumed to provide a dynamic element, making statecraft through institutional design and reform an important aspect of political agency and an assertion of human will and understanding and the power to shape the world (March and Olsen 1995; Heper, Kazancigil, and Rockman 1997; Goodin, Rein, and Moran 2006, 3). Change is furthermore supported by the institutionalization of critical reflection and debate, legitimate opposition, and rights of citizens to speak, publish, and organize – including through civil disobedience – against the incumbent government. The mix of rules constraining and facilitating change varies across political systems, and the more heterogeneous a polity the more likely it is that priority is given to rules protecting individuals and minorities (Weaver and Rockman 1993).

Identification

Institutionalists see identification with and the internalization of accepted ways of doing things as a key process for understanding rule following. Institutions affect individuals, their normative and causal beliefs, and not only their environments. Rules are followed because they are seen as legitimate and not solely because of external incentives, and belief in a democratic order and commitment to democracy's institutions may be generated through socialization, education, and participation. Humans are born into a world of institutions where normative and causal beliefs are handed down from generation to generation, and the main institutions of the culture are (at least for a time) taken for granted. Humans are prepared, and prepare themselves, for different offices and roles. They may be recruited to specific positions on the basis of their normative and causal beliefs, which are fashioned through on-the-job training and selective exposure to information (Simon 1957; March and Simon 1958; March and Olsen 2006a).

People's habits of mind, including their beliefs in legitimate political organization and rule, may be more difficult to change than formal rules and incentives. However, cultures and subcultures may inculcate respect for traditions or emphasize innovation and change, and some institutions, for example the university, are organized around skepticism about existing knowledge, beliefs, and practices. Even a Weberian bureaucracy, designed to be effective and independent of environmental variation and change and usually seen as rule-bound and inflexible, is founded on beliefs in legitimate change as new knowledge and insights become available, governments shift, and courts of law (re)interpret existing rules.

How individuals are differently selected and fostered can also be a source of change as well as continuity. Like all organizational processes, recruitment, socialization, education, participation, and identification are more or less "perfect" in the sense that to different degrees they successfully select or mold people's mindsets. There is great variation across institutional settings and over time in what and in who controls such processes. Socialization agencies are weak or strong, and institutional cultures are more or less integrated. Participants are "social but not entirely socialized" (Wrong 1961, 191), and non-conformity is always possible. People also often have more than one identity, and change depends on which identity and rules of appropriateness are evoked in different contexts.

Socialization is, for example, affected by organizational growth rates, internal careers, the length of apprenticeship for top positions, the frequency of promotions and rewards, the turnover of personnel, and the ratio of veterans to newcomers (Lægreid and Olsen 1978). Institutional identities and memories are enhanced by a permanent civil service, in contrast to a spoil system such as exists in the public administration of the United States, where identities are weakened, memory is removed, and the ability to learn from experience is reduced because many key actors leave with changes in government (Peters 1996).

Interpretation and Search

The impact of rules and identities depends on how they are interpreted. The core assumptions within the tradition of "bounded rationality" in organizational studies are that all humans act on the basis of a simple model of the world and that the office one holds and the organizational setting in which one acts to a large extent provide the premises for action (Simon 1957; March and Simon 1958). Existing meaning systems, frames, and traditions of interpretation can be a source of inertia. However, thoughtful and imaginative reasoning about current and historical experience and the meaning of behavioral codes, causal and normative beliefs, and situations can also generate change – even a reinterpretation of an institution's mission and role in society (March and Olsen 1995). External impulses may also be interpreted in ways that increase or constrain their impacts. For example, global prescriptions of administrative reform have consistently been interpreted and responded to differently depending on national institutional arrangements and historical traditions (Christensen and Lægreid 2007).

Change can follow from shifting institutional attention. An organization will usually enact the program believed to be most appropriate for the case at hand among the repertoires of options available. Most of the time actors attend to the tasks, targets, and task environments they are responsible for. Bounded rational actors do not constantly attend to institutional issues if that is not their specific responsibility. Because time, energy, and attention are limited, some challenges are not faced, some opportunities are not realized, and competency traps reduce experimentation and produce "lock-ins" (Arthur 1989). The organization of attention, then, affects whether pressure for change accumulates, so that sudden change may follow from an internal refocusing of attention. The better democratic politics and organizational routines work as feedback mechanisms, ensuring collective learning and continuous adaptation to feedback, the less need there is for comprehensive reform and the less likelihood of sudden breakdowns (Olsen 1997).

Institutional routines are developed for fairly well-structured and recurring problems and situations and may look inappropriate when applied to ill-structured and non-recurring problems and situations. Searches for alternatives, innovations, and change are initiated when available standard operating procedures are perceived to be unsatisfactory for solving problems, resulting in search in the neighborhood of problems or current alternatives (Cyert and March 1963). Search and innovation can be driven by internal, aspiration-level pressure caused by enduring gaps between high institutional ideals and self-decided targets and actual practices (Broderick 1970). An example is provided by unattainable democratic ideals that are never completely fulfilled in any society (Dahl 1998, 31). Institutional ideals can also be deliberately mobilized for change, as illustrated by the development of the European Parliament. While the EP started out with few of the functions and competencies usually found in national parliaments, the vision of "Parliament" has been used in particular in crises situations to enhance the status and power of the EP (Héritier 2007).

Search and innovations can, furthermore, follow because people gradually lose faith in institutional arrangements or as a result of sudden performance failure. There can be not only external but also internal disenchantment, discontent, and a loss of faith in the institution and the authoritative interpreters of its mission, history, and future. Typically, taken-for-granted beliefs and arrangements are challenged by new or increased contact between previously separated entities that are based on different normative and organizational principles. Institutionalized beliefs can then be threatened by realities that are meaningless in terms of the beliefs on which an institution is founded. Unexplainable inconsistencies and incoherence cannot be dealt with by standard operating procedures, and change follows from efforts to reduce inconsistency and generate a more coherent interpretation of existing difficulties (Berger and Luckmann 1967, 103, 107–8). An important aspect of such processes is change in beliefs about what is inevitable and what it is possible to do. For example, for citizens and political leaders to imagine that they could apply reason and will to remake institutions, they had to begin to believe that institutions expressed the will and interests of humans and to discard the medieval belief that institutions reflected the creation and will of God, that institutions had existed since time immemorial and that they would persist into perpetuity (Lathrop Gilb 1981, 467).

Resources

Under ideal democratic conditions all citizens have equal influence. In practice, the ability to comprehend, implement, and enforce rules, identities, and beliefs and to punish deviance depends on the resources available for action. Institutions are defended by insiders and validated by outsiders and cannot be changed arbitrarily. Institutional resources can be mobilized to inhibit externally induced efforts to change, as well as to amplify such impulses or to initiate change (March and Olsen 1989, 1995; Offe 2001).

Institutionalists, therefore, have to attend to the standard procedures through which institutions allocate and reallocate resources and to how the internal redistribution of resources, authority, and power may affect change. How much authority and power results from winning a majority in popular elections (Rokkan 1966)? How much influence is located in specific positions and roles and, in particular, what are the resources available for those who occupy institutional command posts (Wright Mills 1956)? Resourceful, organized groups in society may initiate change and overwhelm and capture political institutions. Foreign influence, for example externally induced or assisted institutional change, is also well known from colonialism to today's reform programs of the World Bank and the International Monetary Fund (Nef 2003, 529). Institutions, however, are to varying degrees vulnerable to external changes in available resources, generating budgetary bonanzas or enduring austerity where expectations and demands are excessive compared to available resources.

Slack institutional resources may work as shock absorbers against environmental change and contribute to continuity. However, slack resources may also create surpluses that generate search, innovation, and change. Slack resources may, furthermore, support institutional autonomy so that the inconsistencies and tensions of everyday life are buffered by specialization, separation, sequential attention, and local rationality. Budgetary starvation or reduced slack are likely to generate demands for joint decisions and coordination, and such demands tend to make conflict and change more likely (Cyert and March 1963).

Arguably, the mechanisms of institutional specialization, separation, and autonomy help democracies cope with tensions that create conflicts and stalemates at constitutional moments. Constitutional decisions often generate struggles over the identity of the polity or a specific institution. Owing to their catch-all character, constitutional decisions easily become "garbage cans" for a variety of ill-structured issues, characterized by competing or ambiguous goals, weak means-end understanding, and fluid participation (Cohen, March, and Olsen 1972; Olsen 2003). Simultaneously, the demands for consistency and coherence become stronger. Institutional routines are challenged, and it is more difficult to make joint decisions. Therefore, one hypothesis is that democratic systems work comparatively well *because* their political orders are not well integrated. Rather than subordinating all other institutions to the logic of one dominant centre, democracies reconcile institutional autonomy and interdependence. Problem solving and conflict resolution are disaggregated to different levels of government and institutional spheres, making it easier for democracies to live with unresolved conflict (Olsen 2003, 2007, chap. 9).

Unresolved Conflict

Institutions are not merely structures of voluntary cooperation and collective problem solving that produces desirable outcomes, and institutional change is not necessarily an apolitical, harmonious process. It cannot be assumed that conflict is solved through social integration and shared values, political consensus, or some prior agreement and "governing text" (constitution, treaty, coalition agreement, or employment contract). Except at the level of non-operational goals, most organizations most of the time exist and thrive with considerable latent conflict (Cyert and March 1963, 28, 117). Change processes assuming a single, unitary designer with well-specified objectives therefore have to be supplemented with processes involving conflict and unequal power (Knight 1992). Tensions and change may follow, because those deciding, implementing, and being affected by rules are not identical (Farrell and Héritier 2007; Héritier 2007) or because the dynamics of rules, beliefs, and resources are not synchronized.

Conflicts over the form of government and how society is to be constituted politically can be destructive as well as a source of innovation and improvement. Key questions are under what conditions democracies are successful in channelling discontent and protest into institutionalized conflict resolution and how different institutions influence how disputes are coped with. For example, political processes produce more or less clear winners and losers, and losers are often supposed to mobilize politically and demand change (Clemens and Cock 1999). "Winner-take-all" systems are then more likely to generate institutional oscillation with shifting political majorities, while incremental change is more likely in political systems that routinely aim at sharing benefits and costs, including compensation for the losers.

While much of the literature attends to how conflicts between political parties and societal groups are dealt with and how mass mobilization through social movements produces change, institutionalists also have to study how intra- and inter-institutional conflicts within government may drive change. De-institutionalization is seen as creating "institutional chaos" and an "institutional vacuum" (Ágh 2003, 541). Destroying the *ancien régime* is perceived as a precondition for clearing the way for a new set of institutions (Moore 1966, 16), and in market economies "creative destruction," generated by entrepreneurs and competition, is seen to guarantee continuous change, as new ways of doing things eliminate outmoded and less efficient and profitable organizational forms and technologies (Schumpeter 1994).[5]

This view, however, has to be supplemented with the possibility that destruction is less complete. Democratic politics are generally uneasy about excessive change and the uneven distribution of gains and losses following from "creative destruction"; they usually try to reach compromises that modify the pace of change, compensate losers, and maintain social peace. European processes of transformation also suggest that there may be an asymmetry between institutionalization and de-institutionalization. New institutionalization has taken place at the European level without the predicted de-institutionalization (non-viability, withering, and demise) of the nation-state. Rather than "creative destruction," the main pattern has been that new institutions have supplemented, rather than replaced, national institutional arrangements. The European state has been under strain, but it has endured as a key political institution and contributed to its own transformation (Hurrelmann et al. 2007). Loosely coupled polities with partly autonomous institutions may in particular generate new institutions and keep old ones. Rather than a general "creative destruction," there may be processes of sedimentation, making new and old institutions co-exist even when they are constituted on partly inconsistent principles (Sait 1938; Christensen and Lægreid 2007; Olsen 2007).

Tensions within and among institutions, nevertheless, provide a potential challenge to coherence and stability, as institutions organized upon competing principles and rules create problems for each other. While "political order" suggests an integrated and coherent institutional configuration, polities are, as already argued, never perfectly integrated and monolithic. No democracy subscribes to a single set of doctrines and structures, and no grand architect has the power to implement a coherent institutional blueprint. Institutional arrangements are usually a product of situation-specific compromises. They fit more or less into a coherent order, and they function through a mix of co-existing organizational and normative principles, behavioral logics, and legitimate resources.

Even a Weberian bureaucracy, the prototype of hierarchical organization, harbors competing claims to authority and logics of appropriate behavior. Bureaucrats are supposed to follow commands rooted in a formal position and public mandates generated through competitive elections. They are expected to be governed by rules, laws, and *Rechtsstaat* principles, and they are assumed to be dictated by professional knowledge, truth claims, and the democratic doctrine of enlightened government. The three competing claims are also embedded in different institutional contexts, i.e., elected government, courts of law, and institutions of higher education and the professions (Olsen 2008b). Likewise, diplomats face competing claims because diplomacy as an institution involves a tension between being the carrier of the interests of a specific state and being the carrier of transnational principles, norms, and rules maintained and enacted by representatives of the states in mutual interaction (Bátora 2005).

Polities, then, routinely face institutional imbalances and collisions, and some of the fiercest societal conflicts have historically been between carriers of competing institutional principles. Transformative periods have been characterized by major institutional confrontations and resource mobilization (Weber 1978). The raison d'être of an institution may be questioned, and radical intrusions and attempts to achieve external control over the institution may arise. Stern institutional defenses against invasions of alien norms may also occur, combined with a re-examination of the institution's ethos, codes of behavior, primary allegiances, and pacts with society (Merton 1942; Maassen and Olsen 2007). Sometimes such collisions generate radical change in internal as well as external relationships.

However, while disagreement over inter-institutional organization may be a source of change, change is unlikely to take the form of an instant shift from a paricular coherent equilibrium to a new one (Olsen 2004, 2007; Orren and Skowronek 2004; Hurrelmann et al. 2007). For example, strong relationships with other institutions make it difficult to redesign institutions (Peters 1999b), and in tightly coupled systems, change is likely to involve several institutional spheres and levels of government. The more loosely coupled a political order, the more likely are institution-specific processes of change. In fragmented systems innovation may take place in partly autonomous communities, where deviant ideas can be insulated long enough to mature before they are confronted with dominant ideas (March 2004). Institutions may then be transformed as participants learn from local experience and adjust local linkages, rather than being transformed as a result of global rationality achieved through some singular grand process, such as deliberate choice, experiential learning, or competitive selection. Adaptation may be myopic, meandering, and "inefficient" (March 1999), and "designs" may be local (Goodin 1996, 28–9).

The long list of relevant mechanisms and factors suggests why it has been difficult to build simple models that explain institutional change and continuity. The difficulties are general – institutionalism does not relate solely to institutions of democratic government. It may, nevertheless, be of value to explore in more detail possible implications for how democratic development is conceived, particularly in a period when students of formal organizations primarily address business enterprises and economic organization and the innovation literature largely ignores democratic debate, competition, and institutions as a source of innovation and change (Fagerberg, Mowery, and Nelson 2005).

DEMOCRACY AS A COMPLEX ADAPTIVE SYSTEM

An institutional approach calls attention to one of democracy's great mysteries: how is it possible that a huge number of potentially chaotic decisions by "sovereign" individuals generate a fairly stable order and a political community capable of making and implementing binding collective decisions? The discussion above suggests that to answer the question it may be useful to see democracies as examples of complex adaptive systems, i.e., self-renewing institutional arrangements that learn from experience. In relatively simple terms, self-organizing local relationships modify existing forms, generate new ones, and create an order with properties that each component part does not have. Adaptation based upon a small set of standard rules and procedures generates systems of surprising complexity, so that the system persists while individual components change, and the interaction between the components is responsible for the persistence of the system (Holland 1995, 1998; Axelrod and Cohen 1999).

Unfinished Democracy

When "democracy" is used as a fixed category – to describe a specific form of government classified according to stable properties, in the taxonomic tradition of Aristotle and Linnaeus – making sense of change implies understanding how non-democratic systems become democratic and vice versa. In a dynamic perspective, however, democracies are being made continuously through processes of institutionalization, de-institutionalization, and re-institutionalization. The nature of democracy is to be unfinished and in the process of becoming, rather than static.

Historically, democratic institutions have waxed and waned as citizens and their leaders have developed and redefined (often unattainable) normative doctrines and organizational principles of good government towards which rulers and the ruled are supposed to orient their behavior. The idea of democracy has been redefined as it has been linked to the city state, the nation state, emerging regional polities such as the European Union, and cosmopolitan democracy. There has been a succession of democratic forms and an open-ended series of institutional origins, transitions, and breakdowns. In many parts of the world there is a gap between citizens and their institutions; and electoral volatility, a reduced number of party members, new political parties, and new alliances indicate weaker institutions and also less predictability in developed democracies (Mair 2007).

A customary starting point for making sense of democratic development is to see democracy as government by and for the governed. The people are "the only legitimate fountain of power" (Hamilton, Jay, and Madison 1964, 11), and political institutions reflect the will of the people, understood as equal citizens. Governing, nevertheless, includes responding to citizens' demands and societal change, as well as initiating and driving change through forecasting and planning. Then what kinds of institutions does democracy require (Dahl 1998)? Historically, different conceptions of democracy have been reflected in competing institutional prescriptions. Today there is no stable consensus concerning ideas about appropriate ways of organizing government, and there is huge variation among what are in everyday language called democracies with regard to how the will of the people is established and implemented in practice.

Until the middle of the nineteenth century democracy was regarded as an unstable and dangerous form of politics that was incompatible with personal security and the right of property.[6] Since then, democracy has come to be considered as more legitimate. However, its meaning has been lost in "the cacophony of competing interpretations," and contemporary democracies lack meaningful concepts for describing, criticizing, and defending political institutions and practices (Hanson 1987), including the relationship between democratic norms and other legitimate normative standards. Normative political theory and practice provide incomplete answers – a loose framework rather than clear guidance – and there is an ongoing "belief battle" over democratic ideas (Sartori 1969, 87) and the desirability of particular political institutions. The democratic belief that political institutions should and can be designed and implemented to achieve preconceived goals also lives side by side with the observation that it is difficult to establish a firm theoretical basis for institutional design (Olsen 1983, 9).

Do democracies, then, have a unique ability to learn from experience and to adapt to shifting circumstances? If so, through what institutional mechanisms is learning and adaptation taking place? How do democracies adapt to and also adapt environmental circumstances? How do they fit themselves to changing environments and also fit external environments to themselves? Arguably, understanding democracy as a complex adaptive system can supplement accounts that give primacy to learning through a centralized authority and organizer, as well as to individual learning through decentralized, voluntary exchange and competition.

Between Centralization and Decentralization

Democracies are usually seen as organized around making collectively binding rules, executing and applying those rules, sanctioning deviance, and adjudicating rule disputes (Rothstein 1996). Democratic organizational thinking, however, has a bias. Primacy is given to formation of opinion and will in civil society and to legislative supremacy. "The authorization of rule is derived from elections" (Przeworski 2006, 312), and the contestation of will and power and the selecting and legitimating of government take place in the electoral channel through the competition for people's votes. That is, the demos exercise power through public debates, electoral systems, competition among political parties, votes, and legislatures. Within this frame one centre (usually the legislature) acts authoritatively on behalf of society and fashions institutions such as bureaucratic organizations and competitive markets through legal acts (Habermas 1996, 75, 171).[7] It is the task of elected leaders to make "the state apparatus" an efficient and smooth-running machine, to exercise control over agencies and agents, and to counteract usurpation and arbitrary use of public power.

    In contrast, Lindblom, relying on economic theories of competitive markets, argues that political science has an "overriding disposition" towards centrality. The "intelligence of democracy" – rationality, coordination and efficiency – is, however, achieved through the dispersion and fragmentation of power and mutual adjustment. Actors "have an eye on each other" and there is coordination without a central organizer, common purpose or identity, or detailed rules (Lindblom 1965, 3, 305). New forms evolve and disappear without a deliberate act of design. The resulting system is an artifact, evolving through competition and struggle for advantages and existence among self-interested individuals. When the incentives are right, human actors will follow their selfish interest and at the same time further the common good. Within such decentralized, market-inspired approaches the primary function of democracy is to aggregate pre-determined preferences and resources. Democracies are held together by individual calculations of utility and expediency.

An institutional perspective does not deny that the electoral channel is important and that a central authority sometimes has considerable organizing power or that individual autonomous adjustment is significant in contemporary democracies. Nevertheless, in contrast with decentralized approaches, institutionalism assumes that institutions can be integrative (March and Olsen 1986). A core task for democratic institutions is to translate a heterogeneous and pluralistic society into a viable political community and to provide long-term systematic arrangements and agreed-upon principles and procedures that have normative value in themselves. Institutions provide a framework for policy-making that affects but does not determine outcomes, and non-deterministic institutions may even be a precondition for legitimacy and compliance (Pitkin 1972; Di Palma 1990).

To be a member of a political community, a *citoyen* rather than a *bourgeois*, implies that collective life is to some degree governed by socially validated and individually internalized rules, norms, and understandings. Democratic politics is a fundamental process of interaction and reasoning that involves a search for collective pur-pose, direction, meaning, and belonging. Citizens discuss how they want to live together, what rules to follow, what the common good is, and what resources are legitimate in different institutional spheres – reasoning that may generate a belief in legitimate authority and order and develop empathy and trust (March and Olsen 1986; Viroli 1992). Democratic governing and politics involve not only shaping history but also shaping citizens' understanding of it and their will-ingness to accept it (March and Olsen 1995). Citizens are educable, and preferences, measures of success, and identities evolve over time. Democracy's challenge is "to construct institutions and train indi-viduals in such a way that they engage in the pursuit of the public interest ... and at the same time, to remain critical of those institu-tions and that training, so that they are always open to further interpretation and reform" (Pitkin 1972, 240).[8] New beginnings are possible when people have a "hypothetical attitude" toward existing institutions and forms of life (Habermas 1996, 468).

In contrast with centralized approaches giving primacy to the electoral channel, institutionalism assumes that modern democracies are characterized by institutional *differentiation*. Over time new institutional spheres have split off from older ones and developed their own identities: spheres of politics, economics, administration, law, civil society, religion, science, art, and the family. Partly autonomous institutions are constituted on different normative and organizational principles, defining different actors, behavioral logics, arguments, resources, and distributional principles as legitimate. What is appropriate in one institutional sphere is inappropriate in others.

Normatively the idea of centralized, monolithic power in a single branch of government has been attacked as the very definition of majority tyranny and electoral despotism, and demands have been raised for institutions to provide "inefficiencies" in adaptive processes in order to protect individuals and minorities. Limited government, the separation of powers, checks and balances, making decision makers responsive to different constituencies, constitutions, the rule of law, bills of inalienable rights, and an independent judiciary have been prescribed as instruments for protecting individuals and minorities from the misuse of political power and securing representation of all, and not only the majority (Hamilton, Jay, and Madison 1964, nos. 47, 48). Modern democracies aspire to balance effective problem solving and the protection of rights, and shifting conceptions of the appropriate mix are reflected in organizational arrangements.

While centralized approaches link learning and power to the formal decisions of a lawmaker and while they are less interested in how formal-legal decisions are executed and turned into outcomes and effects, there is in practice huge variation across polities and over time in the role and capabilities of overall coordinating institutions in relation to legitimate public entities with resources of their own and allies in society. It is, however, unrealistic to assume a priori that some aspects of governing (e.g., making formal decisions) are political while others (e.g., preparing and implementing formal decisions) are apolitical.

For example, while partially independent courts of law are usually acknowledged, public administration is considered a non-political instrument – a rational structure established to achieve coordination and maximize pre-determined purposes. This view is not totally without merit, but as a general description it "must be rejected as empirically untenable and ethically unwarranted" (Long 1962a, 79;

also Selznick 1957).[9] Public administration is not a mere instrument for elected leaders. Over the last few years there has been a growth in the number of non-majoritarian, regulatory agencies, kept at arm's length from politicians (Majone 1996), and in the literature public administration is portrayed as a core institution of modern government, staffed with professionals with their own ethos, standards, and rules of appropriate behavior. Administrators have substantial discretion, control vast resources, and exercise power. They are active participants in the preparation, formulation, implementation, and enforcement of public policy. Public administration is a major point of contact between citizens and the state and a target of citizens' influence; it is important in creating an image of government in the popular mind. Public administration also has a constitutive dimension: explicating collective interests; protecting values such as universality, equality, and legal security; providing fair implementation of laws and policies; securing predictability, accountability and control; and reducing corruption and favoritism (Peters and Pierre 2003, Olsen 2008a).

A Complex Institutional Ecology

An institutional perspective, then, holds that democracy is a form of ordered rule involving an institutional sphere with the specific task of governing a territory and population. Political institutions have some autonomy from other spheres of society, absorptive and adaptive capabilities, and internal differentiation and coordination of offices and roles with specified authority and responsibility (Huntington 1968; Weber 1978). Political institutions are, nevertheless, embedded in a larger historical-institutional order, enabling and constraining individual institutions in different ways. Modern democracies form a complex ecology of partly autonomous yet interdependent and interconnected institutions with separate origins, histories, and traditions and different internal and external organization (March and Olsen 1989, 170). There are many often "inefficient" and not necessarily synchronized and coordinated institutionalized processes of will formation, decision-making, experiential learning, and adaptation. Therefore, the whole configuration of institutions across levels of government and institutional spheres has to be taken into account (Pierson 2000; Pierson and Skocpol 2002; Olsen 2007). Understanding change requires information about how different types of institutions fit together, how they are interdependent and how they interact (Powell and DiMaggio 1991; Scott 1995), and how change in one institution is linked to change in other institutions.

One hypothesis holds that in routine and calm periods learning and adaptation largely take place in parallel, fairly autonomous institutional spheres, yet in the shadow of somewhat shared basic understandings or political pacts. Different institutions interpret and respond to external impulses through a set of standard operating procedures and bounded rational models of the world, taking into account only selected parts of the environment. Institutionalized behavioral rules, understandings, and available resources are incrementally modified on the basis of experience, and individual institutions have a reservoir of rules and procedures, and therefore sources of internal variability. However, feedback from the environment is in particular important when large-scale failures and performance crises generate demands for more coordination. Then institutional developments are more likely to be influenced by the interaction, collisions, conflicts, meta-rules, and power struggles between several institutional spheres adapting to each other, and then it becomes less fruitful to study learning and adaptation in each sphere in isolation.

Consequently, we need to understand the organizational processes through which compromises and victories in political battles are "frozen" into institutions, sustaining a lasting legacy (Lipset and Rokkan 1967; Thelen 1999, 390). An example of such institutionalization is provided by the processes taking place after "the birth of an organization," i.e., after a formal decision has been made to establish an entity and provide it with legal competences, offices, staffs, and budgets. Then the organization has to find its place in a larger institutional order, and its identity is shaped as it becomes aware of and adapts structures and practices to opportunities and constraints in the internal and external environments (Simon 1953; Selznick 1957; Laffan 1999).

Studies of institutionalization, de-institutionalization, and re-institutionalization, however, require long-term perspectives. For example, the institutionalization of the European state as the key modern political formation took centuries as administrative and military capacity was built and these capacities were legitimated through nationalization and culture-building, legalization, democratization and mass mobilization, and the development of the welfare state and social citizenship (Rokkan 1999; Bartolini 2005). Likewise, the emergence of the European Union as a multi-level and multi-centred polity and as a possible new stage in the development of the European state and democracy illustrates the need to take an extended historical perspective. The EU is also an example of a political order with properties that the component parts (member states) do not have. The new order has evolved through complex interaction between supra-national, intergovernmental, and trans-national processes producing outcomes that are difficult to predict precisely, even if the postwar trend has been towards more cooperation and integration. Because new institutions have arisen without older ones disappearing, political life has tended towards increasing complexity, and the balancing of order and change has been affected by the increased intercourse among member states (Olsen 2007).

Mea culpa, ideas about complex adaptive systems have in this chapter been used in a loose fashion. The literature on complex adaptive systems has so far not taken much interest in the emergence of democratic political institutions, and we have far to go before (if at all) the mechanisms and factors that influence such phenomena as the emergence of the European Union are well understood. Nevertheless, an institutional approach and studies of complex adaptive systems, in particular those looking at organizational implications and conditions for harnessing complexity (Axelrod and Cohen 1999), share many assumptions and puzzles. Therefore, ideas about complex adaptive systems may be useful for understanding democratic order and change in an institutionally differentiated polity, useful as a supplement to models assuming a single dominant central learner and organizer and to market-inspired models assuming decentralized, individual learning and adaptation.

MUCH REMAINS ...

It is easy to agree that "new institutionalists should specify more rigorously the factors that change institutions and explicate the links between these factors and institutional change" (Gorges 2001). There are many unanswered questions. Why are institutions what they are, how do institutions matter, and why do some matter more than others (Rothstein 1996)? When do routines stop being routine (Immergut 2006, 241)? How do institutions unleash processes of stability and change simultaneously (Greif and Laitin 2004, 636)?

Which institutional collisions are likely to be consequential (Thelen 1999, 397)? Is change in some institutions dependent on continuity in others (March, Schultz, and Zhou 2000)? What is the relationship between incremental adaptation and radical change and between the decline of one institutional order and the rise of another (Olsen 1997, 2007)? What is the role of intention, reflection, and choice in the development of institutions (Hamilton, Jay, and Madison 1787–88; Mill 1861)?

It can be difficult to distinguish between competing explanations that give similar predictions and disentangle the impact of institutions (Immergut 2006, 249; Przeworski 2006, 325; Caporaso 2007), and processes of change can be linked to each other in complex ways. For example, civil service reform may emerge as part of efforts to solve a specific problem, but the diffusion of the reform may be part of a growing legitimacy of these efforts (Tolbert and Zucker 1983). Patterns also co-evolve and co-dissolve. Party systems, for example, may become de-institutionalized and break down because voters become more critical and less predictable in their preferences and behavior. Yet voters may also lose their identities and shift their predilections because they can no longer make sense of party systems (Mair 2007, 152).

It has been argued that "it is a dismal science of politics (or the science of a dismal politics) that passively entrusts political change to exogenous and distant social transformations" (Di Palma 1990, 4). Nevertheless, the belief in the explanatory power of political institutions among students of politics has varied over time. The connections between human agency, institutional design, and change have remained "bafflingly complex" (Moran 2006, 158), and today there is no agreed-upon theory explaining how institutions affect change. While scholars of different persuasions tend to agree that change and continuity depend on both institutional and non-institutional properties and that different approaches starting out with different privileged explanatory factors give partial insight, theorizing is frustrated by the need to reconcile the mutual influence of partly autonomous institutions, human agency, and macro-historical forces. All of them, and the relationships between them, matter, but there is no agreement on the conditions under which one matters more than the others.

Institutionalism simply claims that relationships between political agency, large-scale societal processes, normative democratic prescriptions, existing institutional arrangements, and institutional development are complex and that knowledge about the functioning of formally organized institutions adds to our understanding of continuity and change in democratic contexts. In contrast with the view of recent reform ideology, democracy's problem in this paper has been seen as balancing stability and change, institutionalization and de-institutionalization, rather than maximizing change. It has been argued that mainstream normative democratic theory is incomplete and has a biased "institutional theory." Institutions and actors have been seen to mutually constitute each other, and contrary to conventional wisdom, it has been shown that an institutional approach can deal with institutional dynamics, political agency, conflict, and power differentials.

This chapter has concentrated attention on how intra- and inter-institutional properties may affect the processes through which institutions emerge and change, rather than addressing the huge literature on deliberate reform and broad societal processes, including revolutions and wars. Routine processes of rule application, identification, interpretation, attention, search, resource allocation, and conflict resolution have been used to explore possible "inefficiencies" in processes of change and how institutions may enable and constrain human agency and modify external impulses. While ideas about complex adaptive systems have some promise with regard to democratic dynamics, the aspiration of discovering a limited number of principles and laws generating complex systems has certainly not been met in this chapter. Rather, in terms of parsimony and clear predictions, the many mechanisms and the probabilistic and context-dependent trajectories of change that have been found to be relevant may be discouraging. An institutional approach, nevertheless, assumes that institutional developments are better understood by analyzing the basic underlying processes than by specifying a (long) list of factors for a comparative static analysis of change.

However, "institutional change and order" is probably too heterogeneous a phenomenon to be captured by any simple theory based on a few grand generalizations and a dominant mechanism of change. An institutional approach invites further exploration of the processes through which institutional structures affect human behavior and change and of how human action is translated into change in governmental institutions. We need to specify in more detail the latitude of purposeful institutional reform, environmental effectiveness in eliminating sub-optimal institutions through competitive selection, and the abilities of institutions to adapt spontaneously to deliberate reforms and environmental change in modern democracies (Olsen 2001, 2008a; March and Olsen 2006 a,b). Under what conditions – if any – are environments perfect enough (little friction, perfect knowledge, easy entry, many actors, no externalities) to eliminate non-competitive governmental institutions? For which institutions are there clear, consistent, and stable normative standards and adequate understanding and control so that institutions can be deliberately designed and reformed and so that actors can achieve desired effects? Under what conditions are institutions perfectly adaptive, changing themselves or their environments in ways that create a fairly stable order?

NOTES

This chapter is a mildly edited version of Johan P. Olsen, "Change and Continuity: An Institutional Approach to Institutions of Democratic Governance," *European Political Science Review* 1 (1): 3–32. European Consortium for Political Research.

1 March and Olsen (1984, 1989, 1995, 1998, 2006a, b). Thanks for useful input from Åse Gornitzka, Ruth Johnson and Karin Lillehei (Akasie), Per Lægreid, Peter Mair, James G. March, Maria Martens, B. Guy Peters, Jon Pierre, and two anonymous reviewers.

2 "Equilibrium" refers to the relationship of a set of institutional arrangements to the features of their environments. Key assumptions are that strategic actors, maximizing their preferences, operate within a perfectly competitive context and that survival is determined by evolutionary fitness or rational adaptation. In equilibrium it is rational for all those with an ability to change an institution to follow the prescription of institutional rules. That is, no individual or group with the power to change the institution has an incentive to do so. Change follows when some (powerful) actor has an incentive to challenge existing arrangements because they think an alternative arrangement will provide more benefits or entail fewer costs (Shepsle 2006, 1033, 1038).

It is, however, not obvious that institutions have any independent explanatory power if they are mere descriptions of the equilibrium strategies of rational actors: "There is, strictly speaking, no separate animal that we can identify as an institution. There is only rational behavior, conditioned by expectations about the behavior and reaction of others. When these expectations about others' behavior take on a particular clear and concrete form across individuals, when they apply to situations that recur over a long period of time, and especially when they involve highly variegated and specific expectations about the different roles of different actors in determining what actions others should take, we often collect these expectations and strategies under the heading institution. This is not to say that institutions do not exist. Rather, it is to say that there are no institutional 'constraints' or 'preferences' aside from those arising out of the mutual expectations of individuals and their intentions to react in specific ways to the actions of others, all in an attempt to maximize utility in a setting of interdependency. Institution is just a name we give to certain parts of certain kinds of equilibria" (Calvert 1995, 73–4).

3 While the approach used here assumes rule-driven actors and inefficient history, historical institutionalism usually assumes strategic actors, yet sees institutional developments as path-dependent and embedded in temporal societal processes. Institutions develop as products of struggle among actors with unequal resources, and institutions "rarely look like optimal solutions to present collective action problems" (Pierson and Skocpol 2002, 706, 709). The standard model of punctuated equilibrium assumes discontinuous change. Long periods of institutional continuity, where institutions are reproduced, are assumed to be interrupted at critical junctures of radical change, where political agency (re)fashions institutional structures (Krasner 1988; Steinmo et al. 1992; Pierson 1996, 2004; Thelen 1999, 2004; Streeck and Thelen 2005).

4 The distinction between seeing a legislature as a "transformative institution" and as an "arena," based on the legislature's independence of outside forces, was made by Polsby (1975, 277–96).

5 For Schumpeter, entrepreneurs are the engines of change in capitalism. Innovation is a fairly independent process "that incessantly revolutionizes the economic structures *from within*, incessantly destroying the older ones, incessantly creating a new one" (1994, 83).

6 One reason why democracy was seen as an inherently unstable form of government was a perceived threat to private property. Universal suffrage and capitalism were seen as incompatible, and democracy was expected to breed more social and economic equality than it has done. However, the probability that a democracy will survive rises steeply with per capita income, and survival depends on achieving an income distribution that is

sufficient for the poor and not excessive for the rich who have the capacity to overthrow the regime (Przeworski 2006).

7 In contrast, the behavioral revolution in political science downplayed the importance of constitutions and laws compared to socio-economic "underlying conditions." One of the key figures argues that "most of the basic problems of a country cannot be solved by constitutional design. No constitution will preserve democracy in a country where the underlying conditions are highly unfavorable. A country where the underlying conditions are highly favorable can preserve its basic democratic institutions under a great variety of constitutional arrangements. Carefully crafted constitutional design may be helpful, however, in preserving democratic institutions in countries where the underlying conditions are mixed, both favorable and unfavorable" (Dahl 1998, 139). Arguably, the behavioral reaction against conceiving an institution in terms of legal rules may have contributed to underrating the importance of rules in general, written or un-written. In European Union studies, however, constitutions and legal rules have had a renaissance as explanatory factors.

8 This view borrows from Mill's developmental view of human nature. Humans are malleable, and the quality of government depends on the quality and activity of the human beings comprising the society over which the government is exercised. The first element of good government is to promote the virtue and intelligence of the people (Mill 1962, 30, 32). In comparison, the Federalists have a more static view. Neither rulers nor the ruled are angels. If they were, no government or controls of government would be necessary. Therefore human nature has to be controlled through external incentives (Hamilton et al. 1964, 122–3).

9 Long argues that "the lifeblood of administration is power" and that "there is no more forlorn spectacle in the administrative world than an agency and a program possessed with statutory life, armed with executive orders, sustained in the courts, yet stricken with paralysis and deprived of power. An object of contempt to its enemies and of despair to its friends" (Long 1962b, 50).

PART TWO

The Ideas of Reform:
Leaders and Change

2

New Public Leadership for Public Service Reform

GEERT BOUCKAERT

Increasingly, countries are coping with new challenges that will require improved mechanisms to take the lead in guiding, controlling, and evaluating societal reforms. In this chapter I describe six competencies that governments will need in order to cope with volatile environments and that will require new leadership to foster public service reform and to interconnect with other leaders in public management and public governance. Reform will require not just new models for governing (Peters 1996) but also new types of political, administrative, and citizen leadership.

SIX COMPETENCIES FOR GOVERNMENTS IN A VOLATILE ENVIRONMENT

In an OECD report, *Government of the Future* (OECD 2000), the question, "Why public management reform?" is answered in three ways. First, governments need to be more responsive to society by providing better, faster, and more services. Second, trust in government needs to be re-established. A third reason for reform is that government's role is changing under new pressures, including the loss of the government monopoly, greater competition, and the opening up of societies and international structures. It is clear that public sector reform, as part of public service reform, is a response to common new challenges in the Western world, challenges that result in an equally common list of about six competencies required by governments and their administrations in volatile environments (Bouckaert, Ormond, and Peters 2000, 7–16). The "way forward"

for the public sector is to "modernise" (OECD 2005), including modernising its leadership (OECD 2001b; Van Wart 2005; Denhardt and
Denhardt 2006), especially since leadership in the public sphere should
not be weaker than leadership in the private or societal sector. Renewed
leadership is therefore both a condition and a consequence of reform.

SIX CHALLENGES AFFECTING THE LEADERSHIP QUESTION

Administrations need to focus on integration and co-ordination
across governments and within the public sector. Governments need
to address issues that respect no organisational boundaries in an
effective cross-governmental way (Verhoest and Bouckaert 2005).
The creation of many new autonomous entities in the public sector
has triggered a centrifugal momentum for agencies vis-à-vis their
ministries/departments that needs to be reversed into perhaps a
centripetal project. This change will require organisational leadership
between levels of government and between a range of organisations
in policy fields, especially if networks are to provide the guiding
principle for coordination and consolidation.

Vision and the capacity to develop a balanced strategic view of
the public interest are also required. That is, short-term projects
need to be seen in a longer-term perspective, in the context of
budget realities, and the views of civil society and individual citizens
need to be connected. Pressures to realise operational objectives as
a stepping-stone to realising strategic objectives have fostered leadership behaviors that are driven by "quick wins," "indicators,"
and "benchmarks." They have triggered a perverse tendency to
focus on the short term, on gaming and tactics. Leadership is therefore required to establish a hierarchy of performance in a long-
term perspective.

A third challenge is to foster effective organisations and policies
that are economical and efficient by drawing on a much wider set
of methods and networks or relationships in order to implement
public programs successfully and achieve desired outcomes (Bouckaert
and Halligan 2008). There is currently a tendency to focus on the
manageable and measurable, that is, on economy and efficiency,
rather than on effectiveness. Thus, new leadership is required to
move from performance administration to, ultimately, performance
governance, which will put effectiveness and participation first.

Fourth, the challenge of internationalisation requires adapting domestically and influencing others in order to produce mutual benefits. As barriers get lower, smaller countries have relatively more to gain by timely organisational and economic adjustment, while external co-ordination affects all government activity. A crucial issue is what mechanisms of coordination, what new or renewed mechanisms of (institutional and organisational) hierarchy or of the market, and what networks are applicable. Leadership should master all three mechanisms and be able to combine them in a functional way. This conclusion also applies to transnational and cross-border relationships, especially in multilateral interactions.

The fifth challenge is to foster trust and a sense of legitimacy in order to build new relationships (Van de Walle and Bouckaert 2003). Although some countries are better placed than others, no country is immune to a decline in trust. Avoiding this problem requires anticipatory action by governments to bring about a responsible engagement of citizens and to make them confident that their public institutions cater to their needs. While there has been leadership for quality management, perhaps even for satisfaction management, the new public leadership will need a capacity for trust management. Leadership easily turns into misleadership, especially when political leaders seem to prefer distrust management or even fear management as a political priority in an era of terrorism (Gore 2004).

Finally, the sixth challenge is to develop responsiveness in adapting to change. More than ever, an unpredictable environment requires governments to continuously look ahead, detect trends, and think creatively about ways of shaping policies and institutions to respond to new challenges. Increasingly, rapid responses are required when dominos are falling quickly (e.g., in the banking crises) and when consultations are required. The leadership, especially in a governance context, should take stakeholder management on board.

Four possible reform strategies (4M's) can meet these challenges: maintaining (incremental changes), modernising (i.e., focusing on performance for all management functions), marketising (i.e., using market type mechanisms within the public sector, mechanisms such as, e.g., compulsory competitive tendering, market testing, benchmarking, vouchers), and minimising (i.e., contracting out, active and passive privatisation) (Pollitt and Bouckaert 2004). It is not obvious so far, either theoretically or empirically, to what extent results have been obtained (Pollitt and Bouckaert 2002). The question about the effectiveness of leadership could simply amount to a question about the effectiveness of the leadership of reform. Reform requires leadership to integrate and co-ordinate, to develop clear strategic views, to focus clearly upon improved performance, to build trust as social-capital, and to respond consistently. However, to succeed, renewed leadership also requires an effective and sustainable reform program. Thus, new public leadership (NPL) becomes both a condition and a result of public sector reform: in other words, it is both an independent and a dependent variable. Responding to the six challenges of a volatile environment can only result in trends toward reform.

TRENDS IN PUBLIC MANAGEMENT IN OECD COUNTRIES

Three new trends are changing the focus of public management in OECD countries. First, there is more pressure for performance. The implicit assumption is that big administrations and big bureaucracies do not change by themselves and need pressure on their "black boxes" in order to focus more on performance and its improvement. The guideline is therefore as follows: more internal pressure results in better performance. The key questions then become, what kind of pressure is required at what level, and under what circumstances will this pressure result in improved performance? Internal pressure operates in several ways. Strategic plans are translated into operational plans and are used to define responsibilities and accountabilities, which increases pressure and helps to focus on results. Financial cycles are therefore transformed, resulting in performance budgets, double bookkeeping (or accrual accounting) and cost accounting, and performance audits. These changes appear to provide strong leverage for emphasising results. New trends in personnel functions include performance-based contracts, promotions, hiring, and firing. Finally, organisational relations are also determined by performance-based contracts.

All these institutionalised instruments should help to guarantee a permanent focus on results. However, some commentators consider them to be insufficient and think that internal pressure should be complemented by external pressure. Market type mechanisms (MTM) should be established (for example, vouchers, competitive tendering, and benchmarking), in order to increase pressure. Obvious questions, of course, are concerned with the level and type of external pressure, its timing, and the conditions that must be met for it to be functional, since pressure may of course become dysfunctional. It may be too high, or it may be the wrong type of pressure. The timing may be wrong, or it may operate under suboptimal circumstances, causing unintended negative effects. Consequently, new leadership needs to organise, institutionalise, and channel legitimate pressure for performance that is functional, sustainable, and, in turn, legitimate. These remarks are about legitimate pressure for performance both within and between organisations and levels of government.

A second trend is to define autonomous units as specialised and separate organisations. It is part of a strategy to better define responsibilities and to facilitate accountability. Specialisation also requires a context of co-ordination to realise the gains arising from it. Another type of change focuses on responsibility and accountability in a context of managerial autonomy. Redefining mechanisms of allocating responsibilities, by using contracts, is complemented by redefining mechanisms of accountability and expanding (internal and external) performance audits and evaluation. This combined redefinition assumes as a consequence a better focus on performance. NPL will have to focus explicitly on co-ordination. Since a range of mechanisms are used, such as hierarchy type mechanisms, market type mechanisms, and network type mechanisms, this leadership will require a mixture of hierarchy-based, market-based, and network-based leadership profiles. Consequently new leadership will need to take responsibility and be accountable for a performing system that consists of specialised and (hierarchical, market, and network) consolidated entities. New leadership will need to be capable of combining hierarchy leadership, market leadership, and network leadership.

A third type of reform includes the increasing involvement and commitment of different actors in society. Citizens as customers, users, payers, or clients become actively involved. Citizenship turns into an activity, rather than remaining simply a status (Kymlicka and Norman 1995). Citizens become active partners of government itself (OECD 2001). Citizens and civil organisations, but also private companies, become active parts in a societal chain that creates added value. This chain is part of a wider governance system for which government in the narrower sense of the word is still ultimately responsible. The wider system requires leadership to coordinate the design of strategies, to make decisions, to implement policies, and to evaluate results, with all the relevant stakeholders as partners (Pollitt et al. 2006). It is quite clear that many OECD

countries are shifting to an almost common performance agenda
in a governance context.

STUDYING LEADERSHIP: SOME ANTECEDENTS

The purpose of this chapter is not to provide an overview of all
studies of leadership. However, it is useful to understand in general
what has been covered, and what not.

Studying leadership has been a varied exercise, within and between
disciplines (Van Slyke and Alexander 2006), to the extent that there
are almost as many definitions of leadership as there are persons
who have attempted to define the concept (Stogdill 1974). There is
a range of opinions on how leadership and management are related.
Leadership may be part of management functions (Minzberg 1973);
leadership and management functions may even be identical to
management, or leadership and management may be seen as two
distinct, complementary categories that may even be in conflict
(Zaleznik 1977). According to Yukl (2006) leadership is a process
of influencing others to understand and agree about what needs to
be done and about how to do it, and it is a process of facilitating
individual and collective efforts to accomplish shared objectives.

Theoretical and empirical research has been focusing on different
elements or aspects of leadership. A first stream of research has studied the features and skills of leaders and has resulted in lists of
various lengths. Stogdill (1974) prepared the first one just after the
Second World War. A second stream has investigated the behaviour
of leaders. The focus here has been on task orientation or on people
orientation and the tensions between them (as contradictory or
dependent) (Hersey and Blanchard 1977). This research has produced typologies of leaders such as that of Blake and Mouton (1964).
Another stream has focused on interactions between leaders and
collaborators. Leader-member exchange theory (LMX), which appeared
in the mid–1970s (Dansereau et al. 1975; Graen and Cashman 1975),
is one example. According to some researchers this theory identified
a life-cycle type of interaction (Northouse 2003) or a path-goal type
(House 1971). Another set of studies has focused on contingencies,
taking "substitutes" and "neutralizers" into account, in order to
look for the absence of or alternatives to leadership.

One issue that remains to be studied is the behaviour of "followers"
(Hersey and Blanchard 1977). We also need to investigate new types

of leadership that are shifting from transactional to transformational strategies (Burns 1978; Bass 1985), thereby triggering a debate concerning to what extent these types are mutually exclusive.

This brings us to the debate about the differences between leadership in the public and in the private sector (see also Van Wart 2003, with his "leadership action cycle"). It results also in a debate about the relative value of a more entrepreneurial vision of leadership or one that focuses more on stewardship (Denis et al. 2005). Leadership in the public sector needs to take into account dual leadership (political and administrative) and the primacy of politics in this type (Rainey 2003). The complexity of networks, especially within a governance context, derives from the sharing of powers. Obviously the multiplicity of objectives within a broad range of rules and regulations creates specific requirements for leadership. Finally, the need for transparency and accountability also affects the leadership itself.

These requirements create a challenge to redefine leadership in the public sector. They raise questions about how, for example, to develop more public officials who can draw others into a strong spirit of public service geared to the needs of contemporary society and thereby make their services to government and to the citizens more effective (OECD 2001; Paarlberg et al. 2008; Vandenabeele 2008). It has given rise to "leadership for results." The profile for this set of leadership competencies, originating in the United Kingdom, focuses on the following dimensions: thinking strategically, getting the best from people, learning and improving, focusing on delivery, giving purpose and direction, and having a personal impact (see also Horton and Farnham 2006). Another model, which was developed by Bryson and Crosby (2005), focuses on "leading in a shared-power world" and includes elements such as leadership in context, personal leadership, team leadership, organisational leadership, visionary leadership, political leadership, ethical leadership, policy leadership, and leadership for the common good.

A final issue concerns the integration of these theories and practices into "integrative leadership." Integrative leadership perspectives argue that effective leadership is not "a free-floating phenomenon but must be specifically linked to organizational abilities and performance ... The creation of a sustainable institutional base is as important to public leadership as is leadership style and/or behavior" (Ingraham 2001).

There has also been some research on outcomes of leadership, which means, predominantly, research on goal achievement, group maintenance, organizational alignment, and, recently, service to the end customers, to "the people," to society, and to the public interest (Van Wart 2003). Current research on leadership seems to connect all current concerns with leadership issues: ethical issues and leadership (Adams and Balfour 2008), performance issues and leadership (Fernandez 2008; Moynihan 2008), institutionalism and leadership (Boin and Christensen 2008), and motivation and leadership (Perry and Hondeghem 2008; Newman et al. 2009). What is missing in this literature is the interaction of leaders. Leaders interact not just with followers but predominantly with other leaders: political, administrative, and civic. These interactions are the focus of the next part of this chapter.

NEW PUBLIC LEADERSHIP (NPL) FOR PUBLIC SECTOR REFORM (PSR)

Leaving a leadership legacy is becoming increasingly important (Gibbs 2007). According to the OECD, "the most important role of public sector leaders has been to solve the problems and challenges faced in a specific environment. When we say we want more leadership in the public sector, what we are really looking for are people who will promote institutional adaptations in the public interest. Leadership in this sense is not value neutral. It is a positive espousal of the need to promote certain fundamental values that can be called *public spiritedness*" (OECD 2001b,7).

Based on this definition the report describes three general trends in leadership development: developing comprehensive strategies, setting up new institutions for leadership development, and linking existing management training to leadership development. There are many typologies of leadership. Fairholm (2004) distinguishes between five types (scientific leadership, excellent management, values leadership, cultural-trust leadership, and "whole-soul" spiritual leadership). All typologies have a shared assumption. According to Ingraham et al., "leaders are the glue" (2000, 57) of systems. Their article puts leadership in a broader context of governance and links it to the modernisation agenda. For that purpose it is indispensable to let leaders lead – and sometimes to make leaders lead.

The point of departure is a double triangle (figure 2.1) that is corroborated by new or renewed procedures or instruments that

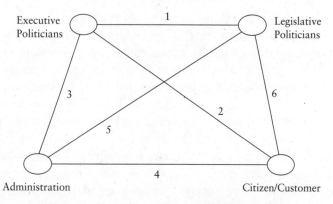

Figure 2.1   Renewing six traditional relationships to build new public leadership.
Adjusted from Bouckaert (2003), Bouckaert and Halligan (2008).

have emerged in the last decades. The traditional triangle consists of the executive politician, the administrator, and the citizen as customer. These three interactions are framed in renewed or even new settings. Politicians and administrators define their relationships in contracts or mandates or agreements, and in all of them, competences, resources, and results are linked. Politicians also frame their relations with citizens as customers in charters. This has occurred in the United Kingdom, France, Belgium, and Portugal. More detailed charters between administrators and their customers have also been established in specific sectors or specific institutions, resulting in six relationships that need to be renewed to develop new public leadership, as presented in figure 2.1.

In the United States, the Volcker Commission (the National Commission on the Public Service) stated that only two actors were relevant to an effective management of government: "the two components of that system, political appointees and career executives, must work together in a partnership; neither alone can run the executive branch" (1989, 167). Ingraham et al. concur: "The responsibility of leaders and top managers for the performance of their employees and their organizations must be recognized. Leaders are part of an organization's culture, its reward structure, and as such define the clarity of goals and objectives. If leaders abdicate this responsibility, the performance effort is moot" (2000, 57). However, the double triangle consists of politicians (executive and legislative) and administrators and citizens as customers, all of whom are an integral part of public sector reforms, and therefore of its leadership.

The six traditional relationships have been supported or amended by new types of instruments or procedures that refer explicitly to the reform agenda of public management itself. The link between executive and legislative politicians is redefined in performance budgets and performance audits. Some countries have made concerted efforts to improve this relationship, as, for example, in the case of Canada, with its Improved Reporting to Parliament Project (IRPP). The extent of performance coverage and the method of covering (percentage-wise) budget resources by indicators differs between countries. However, despite the differences, the general approach has become an increasingly accepted standard of interaction. Obviously, the general nature of the relationship between parliament and the government is determined by the relationship between the opposition and the majority within parliament. It is, of course, usually the opposition's duty to oppose the majority. So a key question is how the legislation on performance budgets and audits, which has usually been accepted unanimously, has affected the majority and the opposition leadership. This remains unclear. There is also an increasingly gray zone between program evaluation and audit, whether internal or external.

In the case of the relationship between administrators and the legislative branch, parliamentary commissions have required administrators to explain their responsibilities and also to be accountable for certain matters that, in many cases, are defined in the contracts between administrators and executive politicians. Further, citizens/customers have renewed relationships with the legislative branch. Of course, some Scandinavian countries already had a long tradition of ombudsperson functions, but the renewed link is sometimes defined as the second or third line of defence for citizens, where the first line is quality control inside the administration (with a possible appeal). Also, direct electronic contact between MPs and citizens has brought politicians closer to their electors and hence increased the pressure on them to take responsibility and be accountable.

These changes have resulted in six new or renewed relationships between four actors. Table 2.1 describes these relationships and mentions some leadership implications.

Table 2.1
Contents of New Public Leadership for Each Interaction

Content	Leadership Cluster One	Leadership Cluster Two
1 Performance budgets and audits	**Executive Leadership** Generate explicit strategic objectives Take performance audits into account Stimulate open, documented debates Accept grounded budget re-adjustments Strengthen parliament	**Legislative Leadership** Focus debates on explicit strategic objectives Participate in open, documented debates Instruct the audit office to conduct broad reviews Propose grounded budget re-adjustments Support or oppose executive leadership based on its performance
2 General charter	**Executive Leadership** Release sufficient performance-based information Involve citizens as customers in all stages of the policy cycle Redirect service provision towards functional participation Trust citizens and customers	**Citizen Leadership** Stimulate open and fair service perception Develop reasonable service delivery expectations Accept reasonable price/quality ratios Accept some limitations in solving problems
3 Contracts	**Executive Leadership** Accept an open debate between principal and agent Choose between market state and state of law Focus on outcomes as a context for outputs Define reasonable levels of responsibility Steer for goal convergence between principal and agent	**Administrative Leadership** Reduce information asymmetry Focus on outputs as contributing to outcomes Accept a functional level of responsibility Take an accountability attitude Reduce goal divergence with other agents and with the principal
4 Specific charters/ service-level agreements	**Administrative Leadership** Release sufficient information for a functional and open debate Involve citizens as customers in different stages of design, decision, implementation, and evaluation Redirect services accordingly	**Citizen Leadership** Stimulate open and fair perception Develop reasonable expectations Accept reasonable price/quality ratios Guarantee constructive co-production commitment Accept partnerships as co-design, co-decision, co-implementation, and co-evaluation

Table 2.1   (Continued)

Content	Leadership Cluster One	Leadership Cluster Two
	Legislative Leadership	*Administrative Leadership*
5 Responsibility/ accountability hearings	Focus on outputs and outcomes Focus on quantity and quality Distinguish between political and administrative responsibility	Guarantee transparency Distinguish between political and administrative accountability
	Legislative Leadership	*Citizen Leadership*
6 Ombudsperson	Choose general interest and principles of the state of law	Reject self-interest of group capture Emphasize public interest/ principles of the state of law

A critical discussion of the six public leadership relationships results in the following analysis.

Relationship One: Performance Budgets and Audits between Executive and Legislative Leaders

Performance-based budgets are documents voted on in parliament in which the legislature authorises the executive to spend money for a particular purpose in the coming year. Budgets should answer the question, what will happen next year? Doing so requires leadership from the executive side, which prepares and defends the proposed documents. Generating explicit objectives in order to stimulate a debate on policies aiming to achieve particular future results requires a new type of leadership. On the other hand, the legislature should focus on the main policy themes and on policy objectives and get sufficient information from the available auditors to allow it to do so. In a system of countervailing powers this goal requires parliamentary leadership, since, as a consequence of these discussions, there may obviously be an increase or a decrease in funding for certain programs. Thus, in general, leadership requires guidance (authorising expenses), control (monitoring), and evaluation (auditing) to facilitate the interaction between the legislative and the executive branch. A key question will be, to what extent has the interaction resulted in a new equilibrium between the two powers?

Relationship Two: General Charters between the Executive and the Citizen Leadership

The link between the executive and the citizenry is under pressure. Measures of trust seem to demonstrate that citizens have many second opinions in matters of executive political leadership. Also, more and more citizens are giving voice to their reactions or exiting the system. Extreme and volatile voting behavior, terrorism, hooliganism, or migration is more visible in Western systems. Even if general charters or renewed Magna Charta's will not solve this problem, this behavior may actually be an expression of a renewed pact between citizens and their executive powers. For that reason a citizen partnership requires executive leadership that includes transparency about policies and service delivery and the deliberate involvement of citizens, as customers and more generally.

In the United Kingdom, there was an effort to institutionally redesign local governance to strengthen leadership. According to Prime Minister Blair "the heart of the problem [was] that local government need[ed] recognised leaders if it [was] to fulfil a community leadership role" (Blair 1998, 16, as quoted in Hambleton and Sweeting 2004, 474). Such a change may mean that services or policies are redirected. On the other hand, citizens (whether separate or clustered) or their organisational expressions (whether for-profit or non-profit) should develop reasonable expectations, stimulate and accept open and fair perceptions and reporting on what happens in the public sector, and accept reasonable price/quality ratios. This desideratum applies also to the media. Citizen leadership should include all these responsibilities.

Relationship Three: Contracts between Executive and Administrative Leadership

The interaction between executive politicians and administrators has always been complex and has also depended heavily on the politico-administrative systems. Because they are guided by contracts, "the roles of the political and administrative leadership are more separated, making the relationships more formal and creating potential tensions and problems of flow of information and trust" (Christensen

2001, 462). Also, "the division of politics and business through structural devolution generally undermines the central political control, weakening the executive political leadership and strengthening the leaders of the state commercial units" (467).

Nevertheless, executive leadership in this context means that there must be a critical debate before a decision can be made by principal and agent. Transparency of modelling is also important. Choosing a market state or a state of law defines the role models and the rules of the game. Executive leadership should also focus on the outcomes that result from outputs, which are negotiated in contracts. Goal convergence should be a key concern for executive leadership. On the other hand, a major responsibility of administrators is to reduce information asymmetry and focus on outputs in a context of projected outcomes. Subsequently, administrative leadership should pursue accountability and facilitate goal convergence since "contracts do in fact give the political leaders a potent control instrument, making it easier for them to fulfil political goals and priorities." However, there are "other, more typical effects of the use of contracts, which lead to an undermining of political control and increased influence of administrative and institutional leaders." These effects result in tension, a lack of trust, ambiguous accountability, and reduced involvement of administrative leaders, rather than the opposite (Christensen 2001, 472; see also Christensen and Laegreid 2001).

Christensen and Laegreid conclude that it is not entirely clear that political control of the core civil service is strengthened, that there is a transformation of the administrative leadership role to a more typical managerial role, with more discretion built in, which is therefore more powerful but probably also more vulnerable (Christensen 2001, 473–4; see also Christensen and Laegreid 2001).

Relationship Four: Specific Charters or Service-Level Agreements between Administrative and Citizen Leadership

Specific charters link administrators and citizens. This requires administrative leadership, which includes sufficient information for citizens and direct and active involvement of those citizens in the whole cycle of design, implementation, and evaluation. This may result in redirecting services. On the other hand, citizen leadership, including the media, should take a positive attitude towards co-production, stimulate open and fair perceptions, develop reasonable expectations, and accept a fair price/quality ratio. These requirements are rather complex, since there is a range of different and sometimes conflicting citizen and customer roles, such roles as that of the beneficiary, consumer, producer and consumer, user, buyer, payer, and decider. Sometimes these roles are played by the same person, but not necessarily. For example, a doctor may decide, an insurance company may pay, a private nurse may produce, a child may consume, and parents may benefit. Shifts are taking place whereby, in a never-ending process, citizens turn from passive listeners to active learners, even as proactive partners with a longer-term perspective and an openess to other partners (Wallis et al. 2007, 158–68).

Relationship Five: Defined Responsibility and Accountability Agreements between Administrative and Legislative Leadership

Administrative leadership should be willing to guarantee transparency and to positively distinguish between political and administrative accountability. On the other hand, legislative leadership should focus on outputs and outcomes and on quality and quantity and it should also distinguish between executive and administrative responsibility.

Relationship Six: The Interaction between the Citizen Leadership and the Legislative Leadership

In its interaction with citizens the legislative leadership will have to choose explicitly for the general interest and for the legal principles of the state. On the other hand, the citizen leadership should reject positions based on self-interest that damage the general interest and should behave in a civic way.

Consolidating Leadership Roles: Some Preliminary Conclusions and Remaining Questions

This chapter differs in four ways from the traditional leadership literature in general and from the leadership study of the OECD (2001b) in particular. Contrary to the OECD analysis, it has analysed public sector leadership in a governance context, which is broader than that of the public sector *sensu stricto*. Civic society, in shorthand defined as consisting of citizen-customers, should be seen here in its broadest context as including private companies and non-profit organisations, as well as ad hoc citizen groups and individual citizens. A specific actor on this side of the double triangle mentioned earlier is the media, which has a major responsibility in renewing leadership in society.

A second difference with the traditional literature is that leadership as it is understood here is not just a feature of an individual but also a characteristic of a relationship between actors in an institutional setting. Individual and personal leadership with followers becomes also multilateral institutional leadership with other leaders. Creating circumstances to "let leaders lead" or "make leaders lead" should be imbedded in public sector reform policies. They should take into account the variety of interactions that depend on hierarchy type mechanisms, market type mechanisms, and network type mechanisms and that require the matching of combined types of hierarchy, market, and network leaders.

A third difference is that this chapter advocates connecting leadership requirements to the precise managerial instruments that have been installed in the context of public sector reform. Opportunities and threats may result from the reform, since it may affect the balance of power, and opportunities may turn into threats if the leadership circumstances are not fully understood. If marketisation is used as a mechanism to enhance performance but insufficient levels of autonomy are granted to adjust management to policies, then traditional leadership may collapse, which may result in a rebalancing of power in society.

Fourth, this chapter considers new public leadership as an essential part of public sector reform itself. New public leadership should be located at the level of a second loop in the learning process and at meta-learning (learning about learning levels of reform). Leadership becomes a difficult variable in the reform strategy, since it is both the cause and an effect of reform: it is a condition and an outcome of the reform process itself.

Renewed public leadership therefore consists of three components that should interact in a renewed way: new political leadership, both executive and legislative; new administrative leadership; and new citizen leadership.

Many questions still remain: answering them would require almost a separate research program. What has not been touched on, let alone covered, in this contribution is the issue of how e-government is affecting leadership, how the new "praetorian guards" of consultants and advisors are affecting leadership and the balance of power within the double triangle. Finally, the whole issue of crisis management and leadership in times of crisis also affects leadership in times of routine (Boin et al. 2006).

3

Leaders and Leadership in Administrative Reform

IAN THYNNE

INTRODUCTION

Leaders and leadership clearly matter. This proposition is no less relevant to administrative reform than it is to most other aspects of governance, politics, and management. It recognizes that when we seek to understand the reform of administrative systems, structures, and operations, there is definite merit in considering the contributions of senior politicians and administrators. For, whatever the context, political and administrative leaders determine the focus, scope, and extent of reform. Accordingly, any study of reform ideas, initiatives, and results, both within and across national boundaries, needs to appreciate the nature and significance of leaders and their involvement.

The leader-leadership feature of reform is usefully addressed in terms of identifiable types of political and administrative leaders in the reform equation. Here, three couplets of contrasting types are canvassed. They are *integrators* and *autonomisers*, *architects* and *builders*, and *mobilisers* and *restrainers*. Each type has its own agendas and commitments, with each leader in practice being one or more of the types working alongside or against others involved in reform activity.

These types of leaders in reform are influenced by policy and organizational analyses, both old and more recent (e.g., Lindblom 1959, 1979; Downs 1967; Aberbach et al. 1981; Wettenhall 1984; Peters 2001; Pollitt and Bouckaert 2004; Thynne 1998, 2003a; Thynne and Wettenhall 2004). They are sketched below and thereafter aligned with organisational examples. They are then considered according to governance and institutional thinking, leading to selected research questions and concluding comments.

The underlying assumption is that reform is normally the result of consciously determined activity, with senior politicians and administrators being key players, consistent with the types of leaders portrayed below. As the types are fleshed out, structural and operational arrangements are referred to for illustrative purposes, but they are not the main concern. The focus is firmly on leaders and the value of considering their preferences and initiatives when studying and assessing reform in practice.

In essence, an exploratory framework is established as a possible basis for comparative research. The leader-leadership crux of the framework, with reform as an activity involving both content and processes, serves to highlight the people dynamics of reform. It indicates inevitable tensions and competing interests that need to be accommodated as reform is planned and as it occurs. In doing this, it appreciates that structural and operational arrangements, as tangible products of reform initiatives, are static and listless in the absence of leaders who affect their form and substance.

THE TYPES SKETCHED

Integrators and Autonomisers

The distinction between integrators and autonomisers lies largely in the content of reform. These types are interested in various forms of organization with reference to their apexes, power, functions, and responsibility involving centralization, decentralization, coordination, specialization, control, and accountability. They have differing preferences concerning the structural and operational manifestations of these matters.

Integrators favour multi-functional organizations that are each centralized by being headed by a political office-holder in whom the power of the organization is formally vested. They consider these features of organizational life to be essential to the responsible management of public affairs. The multi-functionalism seeks to ensure that logically related activities are performed by a range of specialists whose contributions are coordinated within a unified structure, rather than having to be managed across structural boundaries. The centralized

political leadership aims to guarantee political control and accountability, with the head accepting responsibility, politically and publicly,
for what is, or is not, done and achieved by the organization.

Autonomisers recognize that while politically led, multi-functional
organizations certainly have their place and value as centralized entities, they need to be complemented by other, decentralized forms of
organization. The forms are potentially varied and diverse but have
a fundamental characteristic in common. Thus, as alternatives to being
politically led, they are each headed by a non-political office-holder
or by a board, committee, council, or the like, in whom or in which
the power of the organization resides. As such, they can still be subject
to political oversight and direction but are able to operate as semi-
independent entities, as is suited to their respective functions.

Integrators and autonomisers alike appreciate the need for organizational specialization, coordination, control, and accountability,
but from different perspectives. As already indicated, integrators
consider these matters to be best provided for within unified structures, subject to immediate political responsibility. Autonomisers,
on the other hand, see merit in a variety of arrangements, in keeping
with their commitment to organizational diversity. In general, they
support decentralized organizations each having limited and quite
focused functions so that they are able to specialize in functional
performance. A consequence is that the coordination of related functions has to be managed on an inter-organizational basis. This affects
the nature of control and accountability, with control needing to be
both intra-organizational and inter-organizational, accompanied by
multi-directional forms of accountability and subject to overall political responsibility.

All of these arrangements involve the management of organizational relationships, be they upward, downward, outward, inward,
sideways, or the like, with different modes of management being
applicable. In this regard, integrators view organizations as internally
contained networks of people, power, and responsibility that need
to be locked firmly into the executive – and, accordingly, they attach
importance to command and control. Autonomisers, by contrast,
focus on organizations both as networks within themselves and as
entities within networks, and thus appreciate the significance of
complementing command and control with exchange and associa-
tional means of negotiating organizational commitments and pathways. These differences in thinking and approaches are influenced

by the particular centripetal and centrifugal forces, both vertically and horizontally, to which integrators and autonomisers need constantly to respond.

Architects and Builders

While the distinction between integrators and autonomisers rests largely in reform content, that between architects and builders is largely process-based, involving differing alignments in the formulation, implementation, and evaluation of reform initiatives. Formulation is either design-oriented or action-oriented. Implementation is by imposition as a top-down strategy or by disposition as a strategy of co-facilitation. Evaluation is summative or formative, depending on whether it occurs at the end of the reform process or throughout the process. These alternative arrangements are relevant to architects and builders, respectively.

Architects view formulation, implementation, and evaluation as related but separate stages or phases over which they need to retain control. They are especially interested in reform design and, accordingly, concentrate on developing a design with the aim of getting it right. Once they are satisfied that this has been achieved, they are eager to oversee and direct its implementation to ensure its content and integrity are maintained. Only when they believe its implementation has been completed successfully are they happy for the results to be evaluated.

Builders, by contrast, see formulation, implementation, and evaluation as being intertwined. They, too, are interested in controlling the process, but they do so in conjunction with others involved. Their particular focus is on reform action, with action, design, and review effectively being fused. Thus, through the coming together of formulation, implementation, and evaluation, action is designed, taken, assessed, and recast by them as an ongoing iterative process of creation and adjustment.

Architects are committed to a rational-comprehensive, theory-driven approach, the strengths and limitations of which are forever on their minds. Most notable is their interest in the reform design–reform action relationship in terms of the preconditions for "perfect implementation" (e.g., Hood 1976; Hogwood and Gunn 1984). This means that, in determining and acting on a reform design, much of their time is devoted to addressing external forces, competing objectives, uncertain cause and effect equations, complex

dependency relationships, the sequencing of tasks, resource constraints, obstacles to effective communication and coordination,
and issues of compliance.

Builders also have to grapple with these matters, but in a less detailed
and concentrated way because of their more pragmatic incrementalist
approach, the basis of which is the fusion of action and design from
the outset of the reform process. But this, in turn, poses challenges
for them. Of particular importance is their need to maintain the focus,
direction, and momentum of reform, which usually requires their
astute balancing of proactive initiatives and reactive recastings, with
willing and meaningful inputs constantly being secured from all whose
contributions are necessary to reform success.

Architects and builders alike can be either integrators or autonomisers, with the converse obviously also being the case. The basic
reasoning is that objectives and strategies pursued by integrators and
autonomisers involve initiatives that, in general, have either to be
designed afresh, with architects as key contributors, or to comprise
adjustments to existing arrangements, with the contributions of
builders being of central significance.

Mobilisers and Restrainers

The distinction between mobilisers and restrainers is also largely
process-based, as with that of architects and builders. The emphasis
of mobilisers and restrainers is, respectively, on the fostering and on
the stalling or dampening of reform through a combination of formulation and implementation activity, with evaluation featuring
when suited to their particular stances and causes. Especially significant for them are key "decision points" and associated "clearances"
by relevant contributors (Pressman and Wildavsky 1974). They need
to approach these matters through the skilful exercise of power, for
an inability to control or influence them can make or break what
they want to accomplish.

Mobilisers are drivers joined by supporters, with political-
administrative relationships in reform potentially comprising an
array of driver-supporter alliances when the political mobilisers hold
executive office (Thynne 2003a). The possibilities include politicians
as drivers, drawing on the support of administrators; as well as the
converse, with administrators requiring the support of politicians.
There can also be instances where politicians are the publicly visible

drivers, while being driven by and, in turn, both supporting and being supported by administrators operating out of the public gaze. In all such alliances, the ideal is for those involved to possess complementary knowledge, competencies, and capacities geared to creating opportunities, understanding and managing systems, generating acceptance, advancing initiatives, and achieving results. These are essential ingredients of effective collective mobilization in reform.

Restrainers, as stallers or dampeners of reform, seek to be effective "veto players" (Tsebelis 2000). The most committed restrainers tend to be those politicians who are in formal opposition to a government. They are normally well placed to raise issues and voice concerns in the course of making maximum use of any veto power that is available to them. In doing this, they, too, can enhance their capacity to act and achieve results by forging alliances within and beyond a legislature, often with unions where employment matters are of reform significance, but not with administrators, unlike political mobilisers in executive office.

On occasion, administrators might well see value in slowing politically inspired reform, altering its direction, or changing its focus, but the professional response in such circumstances is to tender appropriate advice to those who are politically responsible and then to accept and act on the decisions taken. This response accords with their being there to work closely, competently, and loyally with the government of the day. It is not for them to be restrainers by working against reform to which a government is committed.

Mobilisers can be integrators or autonomisers, and also architects or builders, with the converse being so in both cases. Restrainers can be, or can assist, integrators in countering the activities of autonomisers, just as they can be, or can assist, autonomisers in countering the activities of integrators.

THE TYPES AND ORGANISATIONS

Integrators and Autonomisers as Architects and Builders

While integrators and autonomisers and architects and builders are distinguishable and also interrelated along the lines sketched above, they inhabit arenas that are more complex and multi-dimensional than a simple "one or the other" configuration involving organizational integration, on the one hand, or organizational autonomy, on the other. There are several aspects to this, comprising initiatives that integrators and autonomisers can, and do, take as architects and builders in the reform process.

Fundamentally, the consequences of organizational integration and autonomy can be both positive and negative, often beyond the control of integrators and autonomisers, irrespective of whether they are architects or builders. Cooperative interaction as a positive of integration can quickly turn to subjugation as a negative. Similarly, dynamic self-management as a positive of autonomy can easily lead to isolation as a negative – to an organization being left out in the policy and administrative cold (Thynne 1998, 2000).

These positives and negatives of integration and autonomy can sometimes be compounded by organizations being both integrated and autonomous at the same time, as affected by the pushes and pulls to which they are subject (Thynne 2006a). A relevant example is an organization with regulatory responsibilities. Such an organization, as an initiative of autonomisers as architects, is likely to be structured and resourced to operate with a high degree of autonomy from political control. As a result, however, it could possibly in time be captured by, and thus essentially become integrated into, the entities that are being regulated by it, at the expense of its legitimacy, integrity, and effectiveness. In response, integrators and autonomisers, as builders, will similarly want to negate its captivity, but by taking contrasting remedial action. Integrators will seek to rein it in and reduce its autonomy, while autonomisers will aim to strengthen its autonomy by means that will protect it from capture, both beyond and within government.

The pulling and pushing activities of integrators and autonomisers, whether as architects or as builders, often result in organizations which are "this and that" or "this but that." These are dualistic organizations in the sense of their being established in one form but treated, at least in part, as though they were in some other form. An example is when autonomisers secure the formation of a semi-autonomous statutory body with considerable power to perform its service delivery functions free from close political control, and integrators respond by ensuring that its staffing and financing are brought within the scope of central personnel and financial authorities in the same ways and to the same extent that departments are at the core of government. Another example is when autonomisers move to create a statutory body or government company to pursue commercial objectives as a semi-autonomous public enterprise with entrepreneurial flair, and integrators counter this by adding a requirement that it also meets significant community service obligations as directed or contracted by the politician responsible for it at no direct cost to those who benefit from the obligations. Such arrangements are all quite legitimate, but they do increase the stresses and strains of the organizations in ways that need to be fully appreciated by integrators and autonomisers in their reform endeavors.

These examples of integrators and autonomisers at work as architects and builders involve organizations that are created to operate as semi-autonomous decentralized entities but are then subject to integrative forces that act to centralize them in ways that restrict their operational freedom. Equally legitimate dualistic organizations, in converse form, emerge when integrators are active in establishing or recasting departments as entities subject to direct political control but are prepared to concede a little to autonomisers by allowing units within the departments to enjoy a degree of functional independence. An example is a department that has a business division with significant discretion to maximize its commercial interests, while in all other respects being managed as an integral component of the department.

Whatever the importance of the integrative and autonomising forces in the above examples, all of the organizations involved are intended to be, or to remain, wholly in government-public hands. A variation on this underlying feature of "governmentness-publicness" is encountered when a privatization initiative is taken. An example is when autonomisers move to divest the ownership of an organization and integrators respond by making sure that the divestment is only partial, the result thus being a mix of public and private ownership. Again there will be stresses and strains. New expectations of control and accountability will assume considerable significance. This is largely because the private owners are bound to be a combination of individual and institutional investors, the former of whom might also include employees of the organization, in addition to their still being public owners through continuing government-public ownership of the organization.

All of the above examples are of integrators and autonomisers acting with regard to the one organization in each case. Their respective inputs need to be synchronized as meaningfully as possible, lest the organizational outputs of their efforts are, or become, unmanageable and untenable. They need to recognize this and be willing to self-correct any overly zealous commitment to a preferred objective and strategy, especially as architects, but also as builders, as reform initiatives are taken.

As an alternative to concentrating on the same organization, integrators and autonomisers are often able to work in tandem by focusing on separate, but functionally linked, organizations. The main options for them include the organization-based decoupling of policy formulation and policy implementation and of service funding and service provision. The formulation-implementation split sees integrators centering the formulation of policy above and within departments, and autonomisers locating its implementation in decentralized bodies with a degree of independence from political-departmental oversight and control. The funding-provision split similarly has integrators subjecting the funding of services to close political-departmental control, and autonomisers ensuring that the services involved are provided by semi-independent entities. The underlying reasoning in these cases is that "steering" and "rowing" and "facilitating" and "delivering," while directly interrelated and thus in need of effective coordination, can benefit from the enhanced levels of specialization that their separation is likely to ensure (Osborne and Gaebler 1992; Kettl 2000; Thynne and Wettenhall 2004).

With regard to these inter-organizational arrangements, as with the intra-organizational ones, integrators and autonomisers alike, initially as architects and later as builders, need to understand the nature and significance of principal-agent relationships (e.g., Lane 2005). There is a sense in which integrators aim to protect and promote the interests of politicians as principals, and autonomisers to safeguard and advance the interests of administrators as agents, with the public being the ultimate principal in both cases. The reality is often more variable and uncertain, with the relationships themselves sometimes being complicated by mixed arrangements, such as when some private owners of a partially divested organization are employees of the organization, as mentioned above. These owners can be principals in their private-individual capacities as well as in their public-collective capacities as taxpayers, while also being agents as employees.

Where principal-agent relationships exist as key elements of organizational alignments, integrators and autonomisers as architects and builders tend to favour contracts as means of both locking

in, and freeing up, activities on terms and conditions that are acceptable to those directly involved (e.g., Boston 1995; Hood 1997; Lane
2000). The negotiation and exchange bases of contracts can make
them suitable for a variety of relationships – within government,
often as an internal market arrangement, as well as beyond government, with both for-profit and not-for-profit entities. In all cases, a
challenge for integrators and autonomisers is to prescribe appropriate
degrees of rigidity and flexibility, without which contracts have significantly reduced value in the management of organizational alignments and activities.

Integrators as Mobilisers with and without Restrainers

Integrators are often successful mobilisers in winning acceptance
of contracts to manage political-administrative (principal-agent)
relationships at the apexes of departments and also the relationships
between politicians responsible for decentralized organizations (as
principals) and the top office-holders or boards of the organizations
(as agents). A few autonomisers might seek to be restrainers by
arguing against contracts in these circumstances, but they are
unlikely to have much impact. Most autonomisers will appreciate
that contracts, if astutely negotiated and worded, can serve to
protect and promote the significant interests and needs of those
immediately involved – again, so long as rigidity and flexibility are
effectively balanced.

Integrators tend to be effective mobilisers when it comes to the
restructuring of departments and the re-allocation of departmental
functions – possibly, but not necessarily, with the aim of further
centralizing political-executive power. These matters can usually be
determined and acted on by a government without reference to a
legislature, other than where they depend on specific appropriations.
Accordingly, while there could well be restrainers in the legislature
who are opposed to the developments, they will have few meaningful
opportunities to influence what the government does.

This situation of legislative restrainers being kept at bay by government initiatives is altered when integrators have reform objectives
and commitments that require legislative involvement. Notable cases
are when integrators see the need for public employment legislation
and public finance legislation to be amended, overhauled, or designed
afresh in accordance with centralizing interests and forces. These are

situations that restrainers can seek to exploit, with relevant counter-responses from integrators as mobilisers.

The efficacy of legislative restrainers in these and other circumstances considered below depends particularly on political-party configurations and government-legislature relationships in parliamentary-executive systems and presidential-executive systems alike. These factors affect the inclination and capacity of a legislature to influence the timing, content, and continuity of legislation. They are addressed below when considering issues of power and responsibility.

Autonomisers as Mobilisers Circumventing Restrainers

Autonomisers as mobilisers frequently favour the fostering of decentralized organizations in non-statutory form. Their reasons include the perceived need to circumvent likely legislative restrainers both in the establishment of the organizations and in their subsequent operation. They can usually realise this need, at least partly, by endorsing the formation of organizations such as non-departmental executive bodies, government companies, and government trusts – all without significant legislative involvement.

These organizations are sometimes subject to specific legislation, in addition to public sector, company, and trust legislation, but the legislation is not the instrument by which they are established in each case (Thynne 1994, 2003b). For non-departmental executive bodies, the instrument is an executive-administrative decision, order, or the like. For companies, it is their own constitution that, on registration, is complemented by a certificate of incorporation. For trusts, it is a deed of trust. These instruments are at the immediate disposal of a government. They are normally beyond legislative action, unlike statutes as legislative enactments.

Autonomisers need to appreciate that non-departmental executive bodies, while potentially having a degree of operational independence, are examples of quite weak decentralization. Their power is often only delegated from the politicians responsible for them, rather than vested in them through a process of devolution. Where this is so, the power remains open to revocation – and, thus, to re-centralization – as a simple and swift matter of administration, in contrast to the combined executive and legislative action required to revoke devolved power.

Government companies and trusts are examples of stronger decentralization than non-departmental executive bodies are, despite their also being amenable to central control. Their legal form guarantees them considerable operational independence. Indeed, as incorporated, free-standing legal entities it is possible that they can sometimes perform functions that a government as their owner or settlor is not, itself, legally empowered to perform (Thynne 2003b). Autonomisers have to recognize this and constantly seek to maintain the "governmentness-publicness" of the organizations.

Autonomisers as Mobilisers Courting Restrainers

While autonomisers as mobilisers frequently move to circumvent legislative restrainers, they often adopt the converse tactic of courting such restrainers in support of their objectives. On these occasions, they focus on statutory bodies rather than on non-statutory options, as addressed above. In doing so, they put faith in legislative restrainers being able to ensure the retention of these bodies over time, as opposed to arguing against their establishment or critiquing their activities on a regular basis.

This faith in restrainers is based on a belief that statutes, as the output of a formal legislative process, provide degrees of certainty and protection from pre-emptive and behind-the-scenes action by a government that are greater than that provided by non-statutory instruments (Thynne 2006a; cf. Yesilkagit 2004). In essence, the legislative process is both political and public. As such, the required legislative action not just to establish bodies by statute but also later to alter them in any way can put those responsible in the spotlight, if not the hot seat, politically and publicly. It is this feature of the process that is especially appealing to autonomisers as mobilisers. Their hope is that, if properly courted, restrainers will effectively oppose any action that is, or could be, to the detriment of the bodies in terms of their independence, resources, and continued existence.

Autonomisers have long appreciated that the certainty and protective potential of statutes make statutory bodies well suited to audit, ombudsman, tribunal, and other review activities that need to be distanced from a government and linked to the legislature or aligned with the exercise of judicial power by the courts. They have also considered them to be attractive for regulatory purposes, the pursuit of commercial objectives, and a range of service delivery functions – for which a balance of operational independence and policy control is usually essential. In all cases, the statutes seek to structure and empower the bodies in ways appropriate to their work that, especially for review and regulatory bodies, include measures aimed at ensuring their impartiality and the public's confidence and trust in them. Where the bodies continue to be justified and effective, restrainers committed to the cause of autonomisers need to be vigilant vis-a-vis any counter-initiatives by integrators.

THE TYPES, GOVERNANCE, AND INSTITUTIONALISM

Warranted Governance and Constitutive Institutionalism

In pursuing reform, integrators and autonomisers, variously as architects and builders and as mobilisers and restrainers, operate within political systems comprising complex governance and institutional arrangements. The systems affect their capacity and opportunities to make a mark and to achieve results. Significant aspects of the systems are usefully synthesized by the notions of "warranted governance" and "constitutive institutionalism."

Warranted governance raises issues of power and responsibility. For something to be warranted, it can be either, or all, of the following: authorized, justified, and vouched for. All three are applicable to the establishment and operation of organizations as means of governance. The processes and decisions involved need to be based on the exercise of legitimate power as "legal-rational authority." The reasons for the decisions need to be clear, relevant, and sustainable. The results, in the form of structures, activities, and achievements, need to be supported by institutions and people who are able and prepared to stand up and be counted for them (e.g., Weber 1973; Pierson 1996; Mulgan 2003; cf. Lienhard 2006).

Constitutive institutionalism complements warranted governance by recognizing that organizations are usually the formative products of an amalgam of factors – just as they themselves can, and do, influence such factors. Convincing explanations of their existence and operation seldom lie in a single theory. They are more likely to be found in an array of theories embracing constitutional-political structures and processes, historical circumstances, cultural norms and values, motivational interests, and salient ideas – as portrayed by "old institutionalism" and several variants of "new institutionalism" (esp., Selznick 1957, 1996; Hall and Taylor 1996; Hay and Wincott 1998; Schmidt 2006).

These matters inevitably affect the who, what, why, and how of organizations and reform. The implications are clear for all involved, as influenced by the particular systems and contexts in each case. Of significance here are the interplay of power and responsibility, the spread of ideas, the possibilities of self-interest, and the hopes of institutionalization.

Power and Responsibility

Architects and builders are important power brokers, with the power of design and the power of action at their disposal. They are the levers of reform in terms of its shape and advancement. Whether as integrators or as autonomisers, they are responsible for the integrity and efficacy of what is proposed and put in place. As such, they become the custodians or stewards of reform, with a concentration on the legitimacy and consequences of reform initiatives.

A challenge for architects and builders is to ensure that the organizations they form or mould have a sound underpinning. One requirement is that power distributed in the public interest be exercised and reviewed in accordance with that interest. Another is that structures, practices, and procedures certainly do matter – as means, but not as ends in themselves. A third is that acceptable ends, as outputs and outcomes, are crucial and need to be measured, assessed, and accounted for in logical and meaningful terms.

Mobilisers and restrainers naturally are also power brokers, as affected by key features of the political systems involved, including political party configurations and the extent to which governments are able to dominate legislatures (Thynne 2003a). These matters are interrelated, and often inter-dependent, with legislative activity being necessary especially for reform requiring legislation and appropriations.

In all systems, actually or essentially, politics can be either a one-party, a two-party, or a multi-party affair, irrespective of whether the systems have parliamentary executives or presidential executives. In a one-party system, a government can dictate the work of a legislature by controlling most, if not all, of its seats. Where two parties exist, a government can normally dominate a legislature by controlling a majority of its seats, or at least a majority of the seats in the lower house if it is a bi-cameral legislature. Where there are several parties, a government, usually as a coalition of parties, is often unable to exercise any sustained influence over a legislature.

These contrasting arrangements suggest that the work of mobilisers becomes more difficult as the number of parties increases, just
as that of restrainers becomes easier. In one-party systems, senior
politicians and administrators tend to be an integrated elite who, as
mobilisers of reform, have little need to generate public support and
even less to manage a legislature – which, anyway, is unlikely to
comprise any or many effective restrainers. In two-party and multi-
party systems, on the other hand, senior politicians, as mobilisers,
have to articulate and move reform agendas forward in public and
also in or through the legislature when legislation and appropriations
are required. This opens up avenues and opportunities for restrainers
who, especially in multi-party systems with parliamentary executives,
can often be active not only in the legislature but also within the
government as members of a loosely formed governing coalition.

While restrainers are likely to limit reform in multi-party systems,
the absence of restrainers in one-party systems is unlikely to lead to
reform initiatives surpassing those in both multi-party and two-party
systems. The political-administrative elite in one-party systems is
usually conscious of pursuing reform that, far from being radical, is
simply progressive enough to ensure a continuing hold on power.
This contrasts with the more strident reform that can occur in two-
party systems whenever an opposition becomes the government by
promising reform, only to be replaced some time later through the
ebb and flow of the electoral cycle. As this occurs, mobilisers and
restrainers can wax and wane, architects can come to the fore, followed by builders, and integrators can give way to autonomisers,
and vice-versa.

Ideas

Architects and builders have differing interests in reform ideas, with
architects focusing on the latest research and new lines of inquiry
both at home and abroad, and builders concentrating more on
immediate practical thoughts about how existing arrangements at
home can be enhanced. This difference is consistent with their respective reform design and reform action orientations. It has implications
for whether or not their commitments as integrators or autonomisers
result in significant, innovative initiatives in organizational centralization or decentralization. It also has implications for whether or

not their activities as mobilisers, responded to by restrainers, are informed by theoretical insights and perspectives.

The spread of reform ideas globally has affected reform within and across countries and systems over time (e.g., Pollitt and Bouckaert 2004; Raadschelders et al. 2007). Relevant is the extent to which architects in particular, but also some builders, whether as integrators or as autonomisers, have contributed to the international convergence of reform, with "discursive convergence" potentially leading to "decisional convergence," "practice convergence," and "results convergence" (Pollitt 2001). In this respect, there has been much discussion internationally of a similar array of ideas about reform. But, not surprisingly, the decisions taken, practices adopted, and results achieved have varied, often considerably, from one country to another, as influenced by the systems and contexts involved. This suggests, at least in part, that while architects have held sway over ideas as a basis of reform design, builders have been effective in determining the shape and significance of reform action.

The respective influence of architects and builders on ideas and consequent decisions, practices, and results raises the issues of when, and how, they can best make their mark in the reform process. An important factor is whether or not they are also integrators or autonomisers, or are closely aligned with integrators or autonomisers, whenever there are calls within a system for greater centralization or greater decentralization. This duality or alignment of types is likely to be crucial for the timely achievement of desired outcomes.

Self-interest

Integrators, as a matter of political or administrative self-interest, sometimes promote the formation of semi-autonomous organizations (Thynne 2006a). This seemingly paradoxical situation occurs when they want strategically to control an area of activity but at some distance from themselves or from others. An example is when politicians see political merit in having a statutory body to perform, safely at administrative arm's length but under firm policy control, a publicly sensitive task such as the setting of fees in the provision of health services or public transport. Another example is when administrators wish to buffer a commercial function from immediate political control and thus argue for a statutory body or government company that is then brought conveniently within the scope of their administrative responsibilities and oversight.

Autonomisers can also, for self-interested political or administrative reasons, foster arrangements that initially appear to be contrary to their commitment to decentralized organizations. An example is when, as politicians or administrators, they seek to ensure the autonomy of a function essentially by hiding it within a department rather than giving it to a semi-independent entity. Their aim is to shield the function especially from oversight and interference beyond government as a means of giving themselves increased flexibility in the management of the function. A commercial function is again a possible case, as illustrated by the reasonably extensive use, until quite recently, of departments or divisions within departments as trading entities.

Integrators and autonomisers can both be committed to divestment, with integrators viewing it as a means of embedding organizations and functions in the market, and autonomisers seeing it as a way of freeing organizations and functions from government restrictions. Self-interest considerations are again relevant (Thynne 2006b). For example, it is often believed that, as a result of divestment, the self-interested propensities of public-turned-private enterprise managers will be kept in check by the disciplines of the market and the active scrutiny of shareholders. This is a belief usually held by politicians who, not surprisingly, can themselves be self-interested in their support for divestment. They can be influenced by its vote-winning potential in terms of generating resources for electorally popular activities, including the possible off-setting of timely tax cuts.

These examples of integrators and autonomisers being motivated by self-interest can also involve self-interested architects and builders, as well as self-interested mobilisers and restrainers. Such mixes of self-interest can be a potent force in reform. They need to be kept in check by measures based on the pre-eminence of the collective-public interest, complemented by appropriate forms of control and accountability.

Institutionalization

Integrators and autonomisers alike, whether as architects or as builders, undoubtedly hope that, in practice, their favoured organizations will quickly evolve, in each case, from being "an expendable tool, a rational instrument" into "a responsive, adaptive organism." To evolve in this way, the organizations have to be "infused with value," so as to acquire "a distinctive identity." In essence, they need to become "institutionalized" and, thereby, transformed into truly legitimate, purposeful entities capable of working effectively in an ever-changing and often unstable environment (Selznick 1957, 1996; cf. Powell and DiMaggio 1991).

Any transition from organization to institution in this cultural-contextual sense of institutionalization is largely a naturally occurring phenomenon, with value infusion and legitimacy effectively being won rather than planned and actioned. This creates special challenges for integrators and autonomisers, but it is not beyond some degree of control. Thus, while they remain unable to guarantee an organization's institutionalization in any way, they are able to adopt strategies that affect its ongoing existence as a recognizable free-standing entity.

Integrators like to use containment and conflation as strategies of organizational survival. Containment serves to fence in possible organizational competitors or other immediate threats, if not to internalize them through a process of "cooptation" (Selznick 1949), so as to reduce their independence and thus limit their force and significance. Conflation takes the process a step further by removing competitors or other threats altogether by way of organizational fusion or amalgamation on terms that are fully advantageous to the organization invoking the strategy.

Autonomisers, by contrast, see value in cooperation and collaboration as strategies of managing organizational interaction without jeopardizing organizational independence. Cooperation usually comprises one-off, but possibly repeated, relationships that address specific needs and objectives at a particular time. Collaboration, on the other hand, tends to be longer-term, with the relationships involved being based on goodwill and often requiring operational adjustments to increase the efficacy of joint activities, while maintaining organizational separateness.

An issue underlying these aspects of organizational life and relationships is whether institutionalized entities are innovatively integrated or creatively autonomous in relation to the environments of significance to their work (Thynne 2006c). An associated issue is whether – and, if so, the extent to which – value infusion and legitimacy as bases of institutionalization affect the dynamics of organizational integration or autonomy on a day-to-day basis. These issues have implications for organizational performance involving resources, processes, outputs, and outcomes.

THE TYPES AND RESEARCH QUESTIONS

Leader Level

The discussion thus far suggests a number of researchable questions about political and administrative leaders in the reform equation, whatever the political systems involved. These are leader-level questions. They include the following:

- To what extent are political and administrative leaders readily distinguishable from one another in terms of the types?
- What mixes of personal knowledge, capacities, and interests result in political and administrative leaders each being only one of the types – or being more than one type?
- Where political and administrative leaders are each only one of the types, with which other types are alliances most needed, and also most readily formed, by those leaders?
- Where political and administrative leaders are each more than one type, what mix of types is most apparent – and, again, with which other types are alliances most needed, and also most readily formed, by those leaders?

These questions recognize the possibility, or maybe the inevitability, of political and administrative leaders being of different, contrasting types by reason of their respective positions and responsibilities. They appreciate that the personal attributes of leaders clearly influence, if not determine, their type or combination of types. They also appreciate that alliances associated with individual or combined types are, or can be, important features of leadership in reform.

System Level

Leader-level questions are appropriately complemented by questions concerning the reform-related leader-type consequences of different political systems. The latter are system-level questions. They include the following:

- To what extent do one-party, two-party, and multi-party
  systems, respectively, foster political and administrative leaders
  of a particular type – or a particular combination of types?
- How significant is a government's relationship with a legislature
  in fostering a dominant type, or dominant types, of political
  and administrative leaders?
- How significant are differences between parliamentary-
  executive systems and presidential-executive systems in
  fostering a dominant type, or dominant types, of political
  and administrative leaders?

These questions address the leader-type effects of political party
configurations and government-legislature relationships in different
political systems. The effects are likely to be conditioned by whether
the systems have parliamentary executives or presidential executives.
An understanding of the effects would make it possible to refine or
extend the types from one system to another.

CONCLUDING COMMENTS

Leaders and leadership in governance do matter in numerous ways,
including the administrative reform-related ways suggested by the
leader types, alignments, thinking, and questions canvassed above.
Personal attributes influence whether a leader is a single type and
remains true to type – or, alternatively, is a mix of types with the
ability to combine or straddle types as circumstances permit or dictate. Personal preferences, in turn, affect organizational arrangements,
such that leader initiatives in keeping with preferences are likely to
result in distinctive forms of organization through reform activity.

These aspects of leaders and leadership are significant and need
to be appreciated and studied in relation to reform content and
processes. They pose important analytical challenges, conceptually
and empirically, concerning the validity, relevance, and consequences
of leader types as key elements of reform. The challenges are there
to be met, ideally through comprehensive comparative research that
explores the leader dimensions and dynamics of reform in various
political systems and contexts.

PART THREE

The Ideas of Reform: Management Systems and Other Reformed Tools

4

Simply the Best?
The International Benchmarking
of Reform and Good Governance

CHRISTOPHER POLLITT

INTRODUCTION

Government Effectiveness Scores, 2006

Denmark	+2.29
Finland	+2.08
UK	+1.83
USA	+1.64
Italy	+0.38
Afghanistan	−1.39
Somalia	−2.19

Source: World Bank Worldwide Governance Indicators. Scores range between theoretical maxima of +2.5 and minima of −2.5.

So there we have it: the ultimate comparison. Of the 212 countries compared, Denmark is the most effectively governed country in the world, and Somalia is the worst. And those Italians – well, what would you expect? Such magical figures could threaten to put old-fashioned comparativists like Guy Peters out of business. No longer does one need to wade through all those pages of description and analysis (and associated caveats): now there are these powerful, convenient, summary statistics. As their chief architects say, "a useful role of the aggregate indicators is that they allow us to summarize in a compact way the diversity of information on governance available for each country, and to make comparisons across countries and over time" (Kaufmann et al. 2007, 16).

The sheer weight of data going into these aggregate indicators may well reassure their customers. For the 2006 round, data was taken from 33 different sources provided by 30 organizations, adding up to 310 individual variables (Kaufmann et al. 2007, 4). But wait a minute. *"Disclaimer: The data and research reported here do not reflect the official views of the World Bank, its Executive Directors, or the countries they represent. The WGIs are not used by the World Bank to allocate resources or for any other official purpose" (http:// info.worldbank.org/governance/wgi2007/;* accessed 20 November 2007, original italics).

This seems odd. First, these numbers do look tremendously useful and, especially if one sees the huge amount of work that has gone into them (Kaufmann et al. 2007), it seems curious that the World Bank would make such a big investment of time and skill and then not use the product. (In fact they do use another set of indicators, the Country Policy and Institutions Assessments (CPIAS), full details of which have not – unlike the WGIs – been in the public domain.) Second, other actors in the development aid world seem perfectly willing to factor the WGIs into their decision making, including the U.S. Millenium Challenge Account (MCA) (Arndt and Oman 2006, 41–6; Johnson and Zajonc 2006). Certainly a Google over "World Governance Indicators" on the web will reveal much journalistic interest and no shortage of lesson-drawing of various kinds. Yet, third, in mid–2007, despite this apparent usefulness, nine of the World Bank's twenty-four executive directors wrote to its new president arguing that the bank should reconsider whether it ought to be producing this kind of analysis at all (Guha and McGregor 2007).

THE FOCUS OF THIS CHAPTER

This apparent puzzle – a set of indicators that are expensively acquired and widely used but that, it is claimed, are not used for any official purpose by their own originating institution – should alert us to the fact that measuring good governance is both an influential and a controversial activity. In this chapter I will explore the growing debate around comparative governance indicators, with a particular focus on the issue of what kind of practitioner decisions and scholarly analyses these indicators are useful for. In the contemporary management jargon, where and how do they add value? In common language, what can they do?

To address these questions, I will need to say something about the technical, conceptual, organizational, and political aspects the indicators. I will not spend much time on the technical issues, because they have already been very competently dealt with by other scholars (Arndt and Oman 2006; Arndt 2008; Van de Walle 2006; Van de Walle and Roberts 2008). Nevertheless, it is necessary to say some-. thing about those before coming to the other, as yet less well-articulated, aspects.

This is, of course, only one perspective on governance indicators. It is a largely external perspective – an analysis of what we know from documents and speeches and academic research. Other aspects remain unexplored. There is room, for example, for a closer study of the "bureaupolitics" of the WGIs. Why did they appear when they did and who is for them and who is against them inside international organizations (for some useful hints, see Arndt 2008)? It would also be useful to have some systematic attempt to assess the impact of the WGIs in different countries. How does the relationship between donor agencies, national governments, and the media work out on the ground? Unfortunately neither these nor other interesting directions can be pursued very far in this chapter.

GENERAL BACKGROUND: THE GROWTH OF
INTERNATIONAL BENCHMARKING
OF GOOD GOVERNANCE

It is important to understand that the WGIs are but one manifestation of an already large and rapidly growing new industry – that of measuring and comparing aspects of government and governance between different states. It is now a quarter of a century or more since various "quality tools" first claimed to be able to measure and compare operations in different companies and different sectors all over the globe. Tools such as Total Quality Management (TQM) spread from manufacturing industry to the service sector and from the private to the public sector (Pollitt and Bouckaert 1995). Today such systems continue to be applied, and in Europe the European Foundation for Quality Management (EFQM) approach and the Common Assessment Framework (CAF) are particularly popular (Pollitt, Bouckaert, and Löffler 2007). Further, in the early 1990s, ideas of benchmarking became popular, and these have survived and, indeed, to some extent linked up or merged with the quality movement. Again, they migrated from the corporate sector to the public sector. In all these cases what was being offered was a generic conceptual scheme, implemented by a measurement system, that, in principle at least, could be applied to almost any kind of organization. Thus, a set of categories, such as "leadership," "human resource management," "customer results," etc., can be applied to the activities of almost any organization. Occasionally they have been used for international comparisons of particular public agencies (Next Steps Team 1998). More commonly, however, the main focus would normally be on one organization and on how far it met prescribed standards/criteria for each of these activities. So even if these generic frameworks *can* be used to compare one organization with another, that has not usually been their primary aim, at least in the public sector. The primary intention has usually been to use them formatively, as vehicles for self-improvement, focusing on quite detailed sets of criteria (Gaster 2003; Jenei and Gulácsi 2004).

In parallel, however, a different kind of comparison began to gain in popularity. We have seen many attempts, some of them well-publicized in the media, to compare specific public services across countries. The most notable and sophisticated attempts have tended to be in education and health care (e.g., Programme for International Student Assessment 2007; World Health Organization Europe 2005), but one can also find international comparisons of tax collection, crime clear-up rates, and many other aspects of public services (e.g., Van Dijk et al. 2005). These types of comparison are sector and subject specific: they do not use generic methods to rate different types of organization against predetermined criteria (as with TQM or CAF) but rather develop measurement systems tailored to the specific service: standardized reading ability for eleven-year-olds or survival rates for particular types of cancer. Here the main purpose tends to be comparison itself – to find out who is best and who is worst, and why – rather than the self-improvement of individual organizations.

In the twenty-first century we have begun to see a third type of international comparison. It involves the use of *composite* measures to assess very *general* properties of governments, such as "bureau-cratic quality" or "good governance." wGIs are an example of this new fashion, and it is with this type of measure that this chapter will principally concern itself. In 2006 Arndt and Oman estimated that there were 140 user-accessible sets of internationally com-parative data to choose among (2006, 30), and a year later the Inter-American Development Bank claimed to offer 400 governance indices on its website (Inter-American Development Bank 2007; see also Besançon 2003, 11–32, and Social and Cultural Planning Office 2004). The purpose cited for such composite measures has usually been the improvement of general attributes such as "transparency" and "accountability," although their precise use – as we shall see – is not always entirely clear (Van de Walle and Roberts 2008).

Paradoxically, perhaps, this new industry for monitoring govern-ments is heavily, if not dominantly, based in the private sector. For-profit consultancies and NGOs collect, package, and sell data, and the media, both mass and specialist, pay them a good deal of atten-tion. If we take the particular example of e-government, a recent article notes that there are four current regular international bench-mark series, two of which are produced by management consultan-cies, one by an American university and one by UNPAN (Bannister 2007). In the case of the wGIs themselves, as we shall see, the World Bank depends heavily on data drawn from a variety of private as well as public sector sources.

One noticeable feature of this recent upsurge of international comparisons is therefore the increasing prominence of *composite* indicators. Simple indicators may measure one or two relatively understandable variables – the number of doctors per 1,000 popula-tion, or the percentage of the total workforce that is employed in the public sector. Even here there are frequently significant technical problems where categories differ from country to country. However, indicators that yield scores for "good governance" or "bureaucratic quality" or "e-government" are aggregate measures made up of all sorts of contributory measures of different concepts or aspects. As Bannister (2007, 173) observes, "there are usually no fixed or agreed rules for this," and there may well be quite serious difficulties in understanding what the resulting composite measure actually means (see also Jacobs et al. 2006). The wGIs are amongst the most intensely composite/aggregated indicators yet produced.

SPECIFIC BACKGROUND: THE NATURE OF THE WORLD BANK'S WGIS

The "government effectiveness" indicators shown at the beginning of this chapter constitute only one of six of the World Bank's "dimensions of governance":

· Voice and accountability
· Political stability and the absence of violence
· Government effectiveness
· Regulatory quality
· Rule of law
· Control of corruption

WGIS giving scores on each of these dimensions are published in most years, and the series goes back to 1996 (it was probably not a coincidence that that was the year in which the World Bank policymakers began publicly to move away from the previous "Washington consensus" and rediscovered the importance of a strong public sector). I will focus mainly (though not exclusively) on the WGIS because they are, by common consent, the most carefully thought-out and presented indicator set. They are also one of the most widely cited and used (Arndt and Oman 2006, 28; Van de Walle 2005, 439; Van Roosbroek 2007, 3). Therefore, problems with them are also likely to be present, often to greater degrees, in most other "governance" or "government" or "bureaucratic quality" indicator sets.

So – to take the dimension we started with – what is "government effectiveness" in the view of the World Bank? It is a mixed bag of characteristics, including data relating to government instability, the quality of government personnel, progress with e-government, the quality of bureaucracy and the amount of excessive red tape, the composition of public spending, the quality of general infrastructure, the quality of public schools, satisfaction with public transportation, with roads and highways, and with the education system, policy consistency, and forward planning (Kaufmann et al. 2007, table B3, 72). The World Bank authors sum this up as "*Government effectiveness (GE)* – measuring the quality of public services, the quality of the civil service and the degree of its independence from political pressures, the quality of policy formulation and implementation, and

the credibility of the government's commitment to such policies"
(Kaufmann et al. 2007, 3).

CRITICISMS

Now let me attempt quickly to summarize the six main features of
the WGI that have attracted criticisms – continuing to bear in mind
that the WGIs are among the *best* of the composite international
governance indicators.

NO THEORY OF GOVERNANCE

Ideally, such an indicator set would grow out of a theory of
governance. The theory would predict which factors were most
likely to improve or undermine governance, and the measures
would then measure changes in these factors. Evidently there is
no such theory behind the WGIs (Arndt 2008). They are oppor-
tunistic measures, aggregating what a range of other bodies are
already measuring.

NO OPERATIONAL DEFINITION OF GOOD GOVERNANCE

The failure to provide an operational definition of good governance
is a slightly different point. The WGIs are not based on an explicit,
coherent, and operationalizable definition of good governance,
although one implicitly emerges from the six-dimensional structure.
The World Bank authors do make an attempt. They say that governance is comprised of "the traditions and institutions by which
authority in a country is exercised" (Kaufmann et al. 2004, 3). The
trouble with this is that "such a definition is just about as broad
as any definition of 'politics'" (Rothstein and Teorell 2008, 168).
Conceivably, the lack of a sharper definition might not be a problem
if the concept in question was one where there was already a broad
agreement about its meaning within the relevant community of
discourse. Notoriously, this is not the case for "governance." It has
almost as many versions as there are authors writing about it.
Bovaird and Löffler describe the attempts to develop the concept
as like trying to "nail a pudding on the wall" (2003, 316). A standard text opens with two experts offering, respectively, five and
seven different meanings for the term (see chapters 2 and 3 in Pierre
2000). An international handbook of public management charts

endless, complex differentiations among governance scholars (Frederickson 2005).

LACK OF CLARITY AND STABILITY OF MEANING

Each of the six dimensions gives rise to a composite index figure (such as those in the table in the introduction to this chapter). However, although the aggregating and weighting process is openly specified by the World Bank authors, the sheer complexity of this process is such that it is virtually impossible to give a clear meaning to any of the indicators. In some cases users even aggregate the six separate WGI dimensions into one score, despite the World Bank's own clear advice not to do so. Arndt and Oman (2006, 45) describe very vividly what this illegitimate procedure results in: "it is to aggregate the quality of apples and oranges: if the quality of apples is very bad and the quality of the oranges is very good, saying the quality of the fruit is satisfactory would mask the respective quality differences."

But even within a single indicator domain, such as our chosen one of government effectiveness, the fruit is pretty mixed, and it is not at all clear what "Finland = 2.08" actually means. If one looks back at the definition of government effectiveness given above one can see what a potpourri of things it is – and is not. It includes inputs ("the quality of personnel"), processes (time spent by senior management dealing with government officials), and outcomes (public satisfaction with roads and highways). It covers some policy sectors but not others. It includes measures that attempt to capture complex and ambiguous concepts (the "quality of bureaucracy," "the quality of public schools") and then submerges these in a weighted, composite index of even greater complexity. If one reads the technical explanations of the indicators given by their creators, it soon becomes clear that even if these composite indicators were highly valid and reliable, their precise meaning could be understood only by a few experts – and not by many of the politicians, public servants, and media professionals who actually use them. Take, for example, their explanation of how the data from different sources is given differential weights in order to make up an aggregate indicator score: "The aggregation procedure we use in effect first rescales the individual indicators from each underlying source in order to make them comparable across data sources. It then constructs a weighted average of each of these rescaled data sources to arrive at an aggregate indicator of governance. The weights assigned to each source are produced by the unobserved components model" (Kaufmann et al. 2007, 11).

Ironically, the obscurity of the basic concepts can have advantages. In a paper on the Millenium Challenge Corporation two Harvard academics comment as follows on the MCC's use of World Bank indicators:

> Some of the indicators, most notably those which measure civil liberties, political rights and trade policy, are simply too opaque to plausibly be subject to manipulation. Scores on these indicators are set by a panel of independent anonymous experts according to guidelines only vaguely described by the organization responsible for compiling the indicators. With little clue as to what specific aspects of governance these experts base their evaluations on, countries would be hard-pressed to find an easy shortcut to a higher score. (Johnson and Zajonc 2006, 19–20)

In the case of survey data, or even of expert opinions drawn from experts from different countries, there is also a possible set of problems with different cultural responses. To begin with, there may be different understandings of some of the keywords or concepts (Schedler and Proeller 2007). Furthermore, there is evidence that different respondents from different groups and cultures behave in different ways when faced with the choice of "extreme" or "middle" box markings (Rice et al. 2008). There may also be different cultural predispositions with respect to the use of the "don't know" category. As one of the most experienced researchers in cross-cultural comparisons for management purposes put it of his own work: "Working through many different people in so many different cultures means a large number of sources of error" (Hofstede 2001, 48; more generally, see 43–58). In the case of the WGIs the World Bank has to rely on a number of surveys carried out by other organizations under conditions and methods that the World Bank does not control. It would be safe to assume that the problems referred to by Hofstede, Rice, and Co. would therefore multiply further. As yet, little work seems to have been done on this in the WGI case. There is therefore at least the possibility that cultural variations may lessen the comparability of the responses.

LACK OF TRANSPARENCY

Transparency may be distinguished from clarity in meaning in that the latter can eventually be puzzled out (because the data is there, although obscurely expressed) whereas the former cannot (because relevant data is concealed or simply absent). Although the World Bank authors have done much to improve transparency, they are ultimately limited by the fact that some of the data from some of the commercial sources they use is not freely accessible (indeed, some are very expensive). Furthermore, there is no comprehensive listing of the criteria all the sources have used to arrive at their own country scores (Arndt and Oman 2006, 72; Arndt 2008, 7).

POSSIBLE BIAS TOWARDS BUSINESS AND AWAY FROM ORDINARY CITIZENS

Many critics note that the aggregation procedure seems routinely to give greater weight to the opinions of business experts and commercial risk-rating agencies than to the perceptions of ordinary citizens. The technical detail of this debate is dense but admirably summarized in Arndt and Oman (2006, chap. 4). On the one hand, the World Bank has here been a prisoner of the fact that most of the available comparative sources *were* business-oriented and that setting up new comparative surveys of citizen opinion is both complex and expensive. On the other, thus far, their attempts to beef up the citizen side have been weak – Arndt records that much was made of the recent inclusion of a particular international household survey (the Gallup World Poll) but that in fact the aggregation procedures meant that this new element was given no weight on two of the six dimensions, only marginal weight on two more, and "not applicable" to the remaining two (Arndt 2008, 14). If we look specifically at the indicator for government effectiveness we find that of the 1845 data points included in the measure 46 percent come from "commercial business information providers," 20 percent from "surveys of firms or households," and 17 percent from "public sector organizations" (Kaufmann et al. 2007, table 2, 28). What is more, the complicated weighting system used for the aggregation gives a preponderance of the aggregate score to business-sourced data. Thus, for example, in the composition of government effectiveness, the data from Global Insight Business Conditions and Risk Indicators is accorded a weight of 0.148, while the main household survey (Gallup World Poll, as mentioned above) is weighted at 0.005 (Kaufmann et al. 2007, table 3, 29).

WGIS are constructed using a technique (the "unobserved compo-nents model") that gives less weight to perception data that diverges from the dominant majority perceptions. Arguably this devalues the very variance that we should be interested in, as extreme values may well express different perspectives or concepts or values. Of course, the whole idea that one should exclude values that "deviate" "too much" from some underlying and objective state of "true governance" would be regarded as both reificatory and indefensibly positivistic by many interpretive and social constructivist scholars (see, e.g., Hawkesworth 2005; Bevir 2005). Kaufmann et al. refer to the unob-served components method as "quite standard" (1999, 2), but this sidesteps the larger point of whether it is appropriate to this purpose, and to such a slippery and contested concept as governance.

CHANGES OVER TIME

Despite the originators' claims to the contrary (see the Kaufman et al. 2007 quotation in the introduction, above), WGIS "cannot reli-ably be used for monitoring changes in levels of governance over time" (Arndt and Oman 2006, 67), partly because the sources used to compose each indicator vary from one year to the next, so one is not comparing like with like (Arndt 2008, 7). More generally, a change in a particular index figure over time may imply one or more of the following four possibilities:

1 There has been an actual change in "government effective-ness," "voice and accountability," or whatever.
2 There has been a change in the perceptions held by the people surveyed, but this does not reflect an underlying change (and the key people – for reasons indicated above – will usually be business advisers and risk experts).
3 The ratings of other countries have changed. Because WGIS are designed so that the global average and standard deviation will remain constant, changes in one or more countries' rat-ings usually change all countries' ratings.
4 There has been a change in the number and composition of the sources from which the data are drawn.

Kaufmann et al. defend themselves against these criticisms by arguing that large changes in the index scores are likely to reflect that some-thing real is going on (Kaufmann et al. 2007, 18–21). I will refer to this argument again a little later on.

WHAT MIGHT THESE INDICATORS BE USED FOR?

Let us begin by making a (possibly over-simple) distinction between scholars and practitioners, assuming that they have somewhat different needs and purposes. Comparative governance scholars want to make scholarly analyses such as cross-country comparisons, cross-time comparisons, cross-level comparisons, and cross-policy comparisons (Peters 1988, 1–8). They want to use these comparisons to answer theoretical questions such as what best explains significant differences between countries, or how far and why developmental trajectories over time converge or diverge? As academics they also want to test their key concepts (including governance) against empirical evidence to see how clear, powerful, and discriminating these concepts can be.

Practitioners are more numerous and have different needs. They aim at actually improving governance by drawing attention to problems and at improving the effectiveness of development aid by directing it towards countries whose governments stand some chance of making appropriate use of it. They may also want to know whether previous programs or projects are working and should be re-enforced, or dropped. At the same time investors need to assess how far governance regimes may put their investments at risk.

At national and local levels, indicators of performance have become central to a very wide range of public management reforms, in developed and developing countries alike (Batley and Larbi 2004, 87–8; Pollitt and Bouckaert 2004, 90–3). They are part of a broad movement towards "steering at a distance" or "steering not rowing" (see the best-selling Osborne and Gaebler 1992). The philosophy is that the central authority sets measured targets and the operational level has management freedom to achieve these targets in flexible and innovative ways. As "indicators" the WGIs have been able to ride on the back of this widely promulgated way of thinking.

Unfortunately, as the foregoing discussion has made clear, the WGIs are unsuitable for many, if not all, the purposes referred to in the foregoing paragraphs. Their opaqueness and hyper-composite nature means they are certainly not suitable for "steering." Table 1 summarizes the problems for academics, table 2 for practitioners.

Table 4.1
Usefulness of WGIs for Answering Core Academic Questions

Purpose	WGIs Useful?	Comment
Cross-country comparison	Unlikely – perhaps sometimes as a first pass in cases where not much is known. Added value therefore marginal.	Although WGIs have sometimes been used in this mode, their use as a sole or main prop for comparison appears vulnerable to serious misinterpretations. Certainly, they are no replacement for a detailed knowledge of each country concerned.
Cross-time comparisons (diachronic)	Not useful.	Database changes too much over time. And scores change relative to other countries rather than to change in own-country.
Cross-policy/sector comparisons	Not useful.	Far too aggregated. Much more sector-specific data would be required.
Refinement of key concepts such as "governance," "effectiveness," etc.	Not useful.	Far too aggregated. Meaning of measures extremely hard to disentangle – cannot be linked to a single definition of any of these key concepts.

Indeed, it is hard to think of a specific decision or question for which a WGI would or should be the crucial piece of evidence. The inference is that the WGIs add little value for either the academic or the practitioner. Indeed, they may create more disbenefits than benefits, by encouraging decision makers to think they need not spend much time probing the detail of particular cases, because a reliable general yardstick is ready to hand. Partly because of this seductiveness, the one purpose they *could* serve quite effectively (bottom row in table 2) would be to influence agendas by pointing up apparent "extreme" values and low positions. The governments or ministries seen as responsible for those scores would then have to explain themselves, not only to the World Bank but to the mass media and to any other potential or actual partners who took notice of those media.

Table 4.2
Usefulness of WGIs for Answering Practitioners' Key Questions

Purpose	Usefulness of WGIs	Comment
To identify problems with a government that needs attention	Marginal	Gives only a very broad signal of problems that would normally already be clearly apparent
Directing aid to well-governed states	Not useful	Too aggregated and opaque to support specific programmatic decisions.
Allocating general budget support programs	Not useful	Ditto
Choosing development projects	Not useful	Far too aggregated to assist in detailed selections of this kind
Enabling governments to manage better ("steering")	Not useful	As above. These indicators tell nothing about specific management tools or techniques
Agenda-setting for other governmental and inter-governmental organizations and the media	Potentially rather useful	Useful in terms of bureau and media politics, but this usefulness is not based on effectiveness in any of the purposes listed in the rest of this table

If we ask what the World Bank itself thinks the WGIs could be used for, we encounter a curious reticence. As we saw earlier, the official website carefully states that "the WGI are not used by the World Bank Group to allocate resources or for any other official purpose" (http://info.worldbank.org/governance/wgi2007/, accessed 20 November 2007). Since the direct authors of the WGIs have shown a praiseworthy willingness to discuss and explain their work, there is also a fair amount of supporting technical literature, but most of this is rather coy about precisely what kind of decisions could be based on these indicators (e.g., Kaufman et al. 1999, 2007). Here are two of the somewhat small number of direct claims on this point:

these aggregate governance indicators are useful because they allow countries to be sorted into broad groupings according

to levels of governance, and they can be used to study the
causes and consequences of governance in a much larger
sample of countries than previously. (Kaufmann et al. 1999,
summary findings)

The aggregate indicators we construct are useful for broad
cross-country and over time comparisons of governance, but
all such comparisons should take account of the margins of
error associated with the governance estimates ... We also
caution users that the aggregate indicators can in some circumstances be rather a blunt tool for policy advice at the country
level. We expect that the provision of the underlying data will
help users in identifying – and acting upon – more specific
aspects of governance that might be problematic in a given
country. (Kaufmann et al. 2007, 23)

As far as the first claim is concerned, we obviously have to ask, for
what purpose would countries be sorted into "broad groupings,"
and by whom? One could also ask whether WGIS added much to
the accuracy of such taxonomies: academics frequently sort countries
into broad groupings for any number of specific purposes (e.g.,
countries with strong legislatures, countries with high degrees of
corruption, countries with extremely low per capita incomes, countries with large inequalities in the distributions of incomes and
wealth). Do the aggregate measures significantly improve the accuracy of such sorting processes?

As for the second claim – that the WGIS can be used to study the
causes and consequences of governance – it should be apparent from
the earlier discussion that this is distinctly questionable. Disentangling
specific causes and consequences from such mongrel aggregations
would be a risky business indeed, and there does not seem to be
much evidence that the World Bank itself is prepared to use the WGIS
for such a purpose. It follows from this that any attempt to use the
aggregate WGIS to assess specific reforms would be deeply problematic. It is perhaps easiest to see this by applying the idea to a developed rather than a developing country. Could indicators of this kind
contribute significantly to the assessment of the big public management reforms of the Blair administrations in the United Kingdom –
public service agreements, joined-up government, best value,
foundation hospitals, city academies? Definitely not. Why then, does

anyone suppose that they could be used to make a similar assessment in any of the developing countries?

The later, 2007, citation is interesting on several counts. First, the direct claim to explain causes and consequences has disappeared. Second, the claim about "broad comparisons" is immediately hedged about with extensive qualifications and warnings (more than I show in this brief extract). For policy advice at the country level, users are advised to go to more disaggregated data. But then why did we need the aggregate indicators in the first place? Perhaps this softening of position reflects some weakening of the position of WGIs in the internal debates of the World Bank (e.g., Arndt 2008, 6–7), but, as indicated earlier, this is not the place to go into the detailed bureau-politics of the issue.

THE POWER OF NUMBERS

The preceding arguments need to be set within a more general framework, namely that of the power of numbers and their promi-nent role within late modernism. We now have a number of scholarly studies of this more general "condition" (e.g., Alonso and Starr 1986; Boyle 2004; Porter 1995; Tsoukas 1997) plus an entire library full of works on the use of performance indicators by national and local governments (e.g., Bevan and Hood 2006; Boyne et al. 2006; Bouckaert and Halligan 2008; Hood 2007a; Van Dooren and Van de Walle 2008). Porter offers numerous historical and analytical insights concerning the long march to quantification, one of which seems especially apposite to the brave new world of comparative governance indicators:

> strategies of quantification work in an economy of personal
> and public knowledge, of trust and suspicion. In recent decades,
> especially, democratic politics has been decisive in forming a
> context of overwhelming distrust, or at least distrust of personal
> judgment. But lack of trust is also characteristic of new or weak
> disciplines. It might also be taken as the defining feature of
> weak disciplines. Standard statistical methods promote confi-
> dence where personal knowledge is lacking. (Porter 1995, 200)

This is exactly right. The World Bank is certainly an object of suspicion from the developing world and from many groups in the developed world (e.g., Stiglitz 2003; Woods 2001). It is desperate to avoid any accusation that its momentous decisions are influenced by personal judgments. In its WGIS it therefore strives to clothe what are, in effect, huge judgments of merit and demerit of particular states and societies in a cloak of confidence-enhancing statistical methods.

Furthermore, indicators such as the WGIS have a strong de-contextualizing effect. Tsoukas sees this as a general problem in late modern societies:

> In the information society, the abundance of information tends to overshadow the phenomena to which the information refers: the discussion of crime easily slips to debating crime rates and spending on police; the debate about quality in education more often than not leads to arguing about league tables; the concern with the performance of hospitals leads to debating readmission rates and other indicators. In short, the more information we have about the world, the more we distance ourselves from what is going on and the less able we become in comprehending its full complexity. Information becomes a surrogate for the world – what is actually going on tends to be equated with what the relevant indicators (or images) say is going on. (1997, 833)

Thus, some people may be misled into thinking that they can "know" something about specific countries simply by reading their WGI scores. It is not only journalists who may be tempted to try this shortcut. Consider, for example, one of the World Bank's own research papers (Islam 2003). Islam claims that "this paper shows that countries with better information flows govern better" (1). It uses indices based on the presence or absence of freedom of information laws and the frequency with which certain types of economic data are published and correlates these with WGI transparency indicators and other good government indicators such as "contract repudiation risk." It is shot through with large assumptions about how and how far laws are implemented, and how and how far citizens use the information that is theoretically available to them (but see, e.g., Van de Walle and Roberts 2008). It shows no sensitivity to local factors (other than income levels) and de-contextualizes the issue of transparency (a culture-bound concept to begin with!) to a truly startling degree.

Whilst the wGIs are the main focus of this chapter, it should not be assumed that they are entirely unique. Bannister (2007) charts the rapid rise of the international benchmarking of e-government. He details a long list of conceptual and practical difficulties with these measures and says, "The main conclusion from this analysis is a simple one: benchmarks are not a reliable tool for measuring real e-government progress. Furthermore, if they are poorly designed, they risk distorting government policies as countries may chase the benchmark rather than looking at real local and national needs (185). Interestingly, he also notes the instability of one particular survey that the wGIs incorporate within their government effectiveness indicator – the global e-government survey (see West 2006). Of this survey, Bannister remarks that "Ireland jumped from 36th to 95th to 34th to 9th to 7th place in successive years. This seems implausible to say the least" (ibid.).

WHAT COULD WE DO INSTEAD?

One way of stepping back from wGI-type indicators would be to avoid composite aggregates and stick to international comparisons of specific services, such as schools or hospitals or the courts. Another would be to use panels of experts, working within strict rules of procedure, to develop nuanced, consensual judgments (as happens with "consensus conferences" in health care or when the Delphi technique is used to obtain predictions of the future or assessments of the status quo from those with relevant expertise). (However, these panels would need to be composed of experts in specified aspects of governance, rather than just the business risk experts whose views already pervade the wGIs.) A third would be not simply to siphon data from other data collection systems that were often created for other purposes but to perform direct evaluative research – comparative experiments or tests. A fourth route would be to fore-swear all international league tables and explicit comparisons of any kind. But that would be such a paradigmatic shift, with such manifold consequences, that it is both too fundamental and too unlikely be considered further here.

To take the first route, there are already many such specific indicators, in particular sectors, difficult though even these "simpler" indicators are to construct. Two of the most fruitful sectors in this regard are education and health care. In each there are many sets of indicators and a long history of international comparison (e.g., Maxwell 1981), but we may briefly refer to one widely used set that is produced by an intergovernmental organization. The World Health Organization publishes periodic studies of national health care systems that set the performance of each national system firmly within the framework of international comparative data (e.g., World Health Organization Europe 2005, 2006). These are widely respected exercises, which differ from the WGIs in some crucial respects. First, they directly measure concrete events or processes or outputs, whereas much of the WGI data consist of opinions – and often opinions about fuzzy concepts such as "voice" or "the quality of bureaucracy." Thus the WHO tables such relatively concrete events as life expectancy, infant mortality, the incidence of breast cancer, and so on. Second, they do not aggregate their findings into one or a small number of composite indicators – they keep them separate. This statement has to be qualified somewhat because of two important "summary measures" that are deployed alongside the specific measures. The first is the HALE – a measure of the number of years people in a specified country can expect to live in decent health – and the second is the DALY, a measure of disability-adjusted life years (i.e., of the burden of disease in each jurisdiction). However, the derivations and explanations of these two summary measures are arguably considerably more straightforward than those for the WGIs, and in any case they appear only after extensive consideration of the more specific measures: "The conventional indicators and the summary measures are mutually supportive, rather than alternatives" (WHO 2005, 5).

The second route is to try for a degree of consensus in expert judgments, where these are gathered through carefully structured processes that require the giving of reasons (such as the Delphi technique – see Rowe and Wright 1999, 2001). In respect of the topic of governance we might expect this to produce more finely nuanced and graded assessments than the WGIs. However, there would also be some major limitations. To begin with, we could not expect the coverage to be nearly so wide. It would be impossible to find anyone who was an "expert" in each of the 212 countries covered in the World Bank's 2006 set of figures, or indeed across all sectors even in a much smaller group of countries. How many genuine, independent experts are there who could draw on their experience to rank even, say, "quality of bureaucracy" in Afghanistan, Pakistan, and Turkey, or "policy consistency and forward planning" in Congo, Rwanda, and Tanzania? And if the number of available experts is small, the resulting central estimates are vulnerable to a few extreme judgments. Furthermore, organizing the procedure properly could easily become quite bureaucratic and time- and resource-consuming. There would need to be rules defining the required degree of expertise and of independence. And more rules governing exactly how the process (Delphi or other) would be conducted. And a central staff to administer all these rules and collate and publish the data. Thus, this second route, whilst it might partly solve the problem of the de-contextualization of the WGIS, would probably do so at the expense of both scope and extra organization. And at the end of the day one would still be relying on the assessments of a limited number of fallible experts.

The third alternative is exemplified by PISA, where the comparisons are based on a standard set of tests administered under controlled conditions. Even so, they remain controversial, and there are fierce arguments about the extent to which the tests can assess national educational systems (which may have somewhat differing goals and assessment criteria) or, more widely, can be said to be a proxy for "good education" (see, e.g., Goldstein 2004). Like WGIS, such measures are very much open to hype and dramatization by the media (*Daily Mail* 2007).

The development of specific sectoral comparisons such as the WHO measures carries another message that may be of relevance to the WGI exercise. It is that allowing for contextual factors is crucial and that designing ever-more sophisticated ways of modeling contexts is a central dynamic in the measurement system. Thus, hospital performances need to be read in the light of their "case mix," and school performances in the light of the socio-demographic characteristics of their catchment populations. De-contextualized indicators are dangerous and likely to be misleading (Tsoukas 1997). Yet even quite advanced systems for incorporating contextual factors may turn out to be unsatisfactory, as appears, for example, to be the case for the "Contextual Value Added" (CVA) measures of English schools introduced in 2006. School rankings based on this measure are said to be "largely meaningless" because when confidence limits are taken into account "almost half of English secondary schools are indistinguishable from the national average" (Wilson and Piebalga 2007, 1). Compare all this to the WGIS. Here there is no coherent "story" about contexts, no allowances for huge variations in wealth, educational level, political and administrative culture and history or anything else. Instead we have wholly de-contextualized, composite indices, footnoted with the rather vague advice that "we also encourage using these aggregate and individual indicators in conjunction with a wealth of possible more detailed and nuanced sources of country-level data on governance in formulating policy advice" (Kaufmann et al. 1997, 23).

To summarize, the first route – international comparisons that are more sectoral or single-aspect – has some strong attractions but certainly does not lead to universally agreed, uncontroversial indicators. On the contrary, the story of these more specific comparisons is that while, positively, hard work over many years may produce reasonably transparent and context-adjusted measures, there is also, negatively, the fact that even such carefully crafted indicators remain bones of contention, with a good portion of the expert community being highly critical of their actual or possible effects. The second route – expert consensus – carries with it some formidable practical problems and cannot get beyond its essential nature as a set of "in-group" expert or elite assessments. The third – experiments and testing – gives an attractively high degree of control over data collection but is expensive and organizationally demanding. Furthermore, it is hard to see how it could be applied to such an omnibus concept as "governance."

To summarize, there are other, more modest ways of trying to make international comparisons. They are more limited in scope and coverage, but more specific, concrete, and understandable to non-expert or only partly expert audiences. In many cases they have a far more explicit and thought-out approach to contextualization than do the wGIs. Yet even these exercises attract their fair shares of controversy and media hype and misrepresentation. A recent survey of comparative public sector performance measures by the Dutch Social and Cultural Planning Office came to the following assessment: "Our main, sobering conclusion is that policymakers can draw no quick and easy lessons from our analyses of these data" (Social and Cultural Planning Office 2004, 25). All of this reminds us that, though such specific comparisons can be thought-provoking and useful, they are very difficult to do well. By comparison, the wGIs appear to be both radically de-contextualized and grandiose in scope.

CONCLUSIONS

To put it combatively, the main conclusion is that the WGIS – and similar aggregate measures of "good governance" – are almost worthless. It is hard to imagine a decision where they could safely be used as a clinching or even a main argument. On the other hand, it is easy to imagine WGIS playing a part in agenda-setting. With, or even without, media amplification, they could easily be used in a misleading way or as an excuse for discriminatory treatment for or against a particular country. (The fact that in practice this will usually be a developing country hardly improves matters.) Even if it is true that in some cases changes in scores over time are so big as to make it very likely that there is some real, underlying change (Kaufmann et al. 2007, 18–20), it is also the case that, in these same cases, it is so glaringly obvious that something has shifted that we do not need WGIS in order to notice it (e.g., "voice and accountability" apparently got worse in Nepal between 1998 and 2006 – what a surprise!). In short, the occasions on which the WGIS offer substantial value-added in terms of evidence for either practitioner decision-making or academic theorizing are very few and far between.

This is *not* a wish for a general prohibition on attempts at constructing and improving composite indicators, but it *is* an argument against important international institutions such as the World Bank or the European Central Bank lending their authority and scarce resources to the assembly and publication of such tempting oversimplifications. It is a case for self-restraint, not censorship. If academics or private organizations wish to continue to pursue the Holy Grail of an aggregate measure of good governance, let them do so, but IGOs and, indeed, national governments should refrain, at least until the day when far more meaningful, clear, and unbiased measures can be provided. That day, one suspects, is far off.

It is uncomfortable to find oneself thus in the company of the World Bank directors from China and Argentina, both of whom objected to the publication of the WGIS. The first did not like China's low score on "voice and accountability" and the second objected to his country's apparent decline in the quality of government between 1998 and 2006 (Guha and McGregor 2007). Nevertheless, however much we may suspect these governments of the desire to use their political muscle to conceal inconvenient truths about their own regimes, their general point is sound. For all the statistical huffing and puffing, these are opaque measures of wobbly concepts, and the media attention they provoke seems if anything to *distract* attention from more concrete and focused debates about specific issues on specific countries. Instead we are treated to a kind of diversionary meta-debate about league tables.

The World Bank, of course, benefits – to the extent that it receives additional publicity and appears as an Olympian actor, able to encapsulate global and cultural complexities in a few tables of figures. Arndt reports that "the popularity of the wGIs contributed to a gain in strategic importance of the World Bank Institute" (2008, 12). My suggestion is that it should forego these doubtful pleasures and focus instead on much more disaggregated levels of comparison, where the meaning of the figures is sufficiently concrete to permit a much wider range of actors effectively to participate in the debate. If "governance" means anything, then it means the inclusion of a wide range of actors in the process of public debate and decision. Yet paradoxically, the way the wGIs have been constructed and presented means that only a few "experts" can really understand and use them. As Tsoukas (1997, 834) put it in his classic article: "Transparency [of expert systems] presupposes a subject: transparent to *who*?" World Governance Indicators are transparent to hardly anyone: indeed, the more one digs into the details, they less transparent they seem to become.

ACKNOWLEDGMENTS

I am particularly grateful for some very helpful comments on an earlier draft from Christiane Arndt and Steven van de Walle. Obviously they bear no responsibility for what I made either of their advice or of their excellent and original research in this subject.

5

Cyber-bureaucracy: If Information Technology Is So Central to Public Administration, Why Is It So Ghetto-ized?

CHRISTOPHER HOOD AND HELEN MARGETTS

It has now been seventy-odd years since the first computers appeared, over forty years since digital information technology came to be widely used as an instrument for the delivery of public services (for instance, in criminal records and tax and welfare payments), and more than a decade since the internet began to revolutionize the way individuals exchange information with government. But even in an age of e-government and cyber-bureaucracy, information technology remains curiously ghetto-ized in public administration, both in theory and in practice (see Hood and Margetts 2007; Dunleavy et al. 2006).

In the world of practice, information technology spending is a giant component of public spending in every developed country, but IT budgets tend to remain a separate component of spending, and IT developments are still often separated from general management of services. In the world of theory, it has become a cliché for government reformers and prophets of millenarian change to see information technology as the key to a completely new age of government, at least since the Gore-Clinton National Performance Review of U.S. government, some sixteen years ago (NPR 1993), identified the root problem of U.S. public administration as the persistence of "industrial-era bureaucracies in an information age." Increasing use of the Internet from the late 1990s offered such prophets and reformers the potential to foresee an even more dramatic effect, since earlier information technologies were largely inward-facing whereas Internet-type technologies offered government organizations new ways to interact with

individuals and organizations. Yet its information-technology dimension remains a separate and distinct element in public administration's epistemic world. For some reason, even in recent handbooks
on the subject, the study of IT and the Internet continues to be just
another specialist area, located in PA's epistemological filing cabinet
somewhere between H for hiving-off and J for judicial review, as yet
relatively unintegrated with other spheres of teaching and research.

Of course there are a few exceptions. For example, thirty-six years
ago the Nobel laureate Herbert Simon, in a revisionist account of
his own work on "bounded rationality," argued that information
processing, securing the right information for decision making, and
the use of computers to reshape organization design were key determinants of organizational performance (Simon 1973, discussed in
Dunleavy et al. 2006, 22–3). But Simon's intervention had little
impact on subsequent PA work. This state of affairs seems strange,
even paradoxical. If information technology really is as central to
public administration as the constant drumbeat of cyber-rhetoric
would suggest, why is it so marginalized?

Many possible reasons could be given. One could simply be that
PA administration has no intellectual centre, but is just a scattered
archipelago of unrelated specialisms – "a subject-matter in search
of a discipline," as Dwight Waldo (in Charlesworth 1968, 2) once
unflatteringly put it. Another is that factors specific at least to the
Anglo-American tradition of PA might explain such marginalization.
Heavily dominated by political science (in contrast to Continental
European traditions), it tends to focus centrally on issues of political
accountability and on the interest-group politics of PA changes.
Hence, it could be claimed, some of the "service delivery" aspects
of PA tended to be more peripheral, leading to the (re)development of
the "public management" approach in the 1980s, as a reaction against
the dominant political science paradigm of PA. Long-term changes
in context and technique – such as information technology – also
tend to be pushed into separate areas.[1]

Other reasons can also be advanced for the continuing "ghetto"
status of IT in PA (Dunleavy et al. 2006). For instance, as career
paths in Weberian public administration systems have developed,
they have tended to exclude IT professions from policy levels, particularly in the Westminster system countries. Further, the growth
of professions in the modern welfare state has meant that organizations in that sector (such as hospitals, social services departments,

schools, and universities) have ascribed low salience to information technology. Third, there has been slow development of IT professionalism, with high fragmentation of IT staff across occupations ranging from computer engineering to web designers. All these influences have strengthened the tendency for PA practitioners to minimize the importance of those areas that are seen as technical operations, such as information technology, creating a similar effect in academic PA and organization studies.

If any (or all) of these explanations of the marginalization of information technology in Anglo-American PA debate are true, it means there is an uphill task ahead in (re)building the intellectual foundations of the subject and/or transforming the dominant academic culture. However, there is still another explanation that could be added to all the others for the "ghetto" phenomenon. That is that IT is marginalized because it is not closely integrated into mainstream theory of PA. Much of the research on information technology in PA over the last two decades has been mainly inductive in style; or, where it has been theoretical, the ideas have often been drawn from the epistemic world of science and technology studies – in both cases tending to mean that such research would have limited impact on mainstream paradigms of PA. If that is true, what is needed for greater centrality is a more deductive focus, looking at information technology through the lenses of major theoretical approaches to PA and paying particular attention to approaches which go beyond the orthodox political science frameworks.

That is what this chapter tentatively tries to do, in the spirit of Guy Peter's interest in the tools of government and in theories of public administration. Since it is conventionally agreed by Peters and others that there is no single intellectual paradigm for PA, but multiple competing ones, it seems necessary to look at information technology from more than one perspective. Accordingly, we select three approaches that can be claimed to offer the basis for a general theory of PA and yet go beyond the conventional political science focus on interests and political accountability. And, given that it seems implausible that IT could ever have a single and blanket effect on PA, all the interesting questions are about where and when what sorts of effects occur. Hence, we will use three kinds of theoretical lenses to explore how they help us to understand the effects of the massive injection of IT into PA from the 1950s onwards. Such an approach might also be used to explore the effect of other widespread changes in PA, such as the gradual incorporation of women across the ranks of government organizations over a similar period.

THE SEARCH FOR THE PHILOSOPHER'S STONE REVISITED: THREE CANDIDATES FOR GENERAL PA THEORY

The much-debated "paradigm" question of what is the most appropriate theoretical discipline for PA's unruly subject matter remains stubbornly unsolved. We certainly do not aim to settle this issue, preferring to take it for granted that there are several possible candidates, each of which has plenty to offer. For this purpose, we have selected theories that go outside the conventional political science perspective on PA, on the grounds (explained earlier) that such perspectives may serve to obscure the effect of IT on PA. Accordingly, we have left aside some of the more popular or familiar political science faces (such as historical institutionalism, neo-Marxist state theory, or the Chicago theory of government) and selected three different contemporary candidates as capable of offering a general theory of PA. They are as follows:

1 The cultural theory of alternative viable forms of organization, which can be traced back at least to Emile Durkheim's (1954, originally 1912) work on the elementary forms of the religious life, but was notably developed in anthropology with the work of Mary Douglas (1982), elaborated and applied by her followers, such as Michael Thompson et al. (1990), and turned into a more general "way of life theory" by Pepperday (2009). The cultural theory has been applied to some extent in public administration and public policy over the past twenty years, beginning with the late Aaron Wildavsky (1990), who used it as an organizing framework in his introduction to a major American text on trends in the discipline nearly two decades ago. And this approach is clearly a prima facie candidate for a general theory of PA, in that we can in principle analyze any aspect of the field in terms of shared values and beliefs embedded in rules and institutions, or clashes among rival worldviews.

2 The cybernetic theory of control systems in organizations, originating in work on general systems theory in the 1940s, developed by Stafford Beer (1966) and others, and most notably

applied to PA in the theoretical work of Andrew Dunsire (1978, 1986, 1990, 1992). Related to the basic engineering theory that underpins information technology, this approach also in principle meets the conditions for a general theory in that it gives us a framework for analyzing any conceivable aspect of PA in terms of its underlying control characteristics, whatever its specific institutional structure.

3 The economic theory of organization, as it has developed since the 1930s, with the work of scholars such as Ronald Coase (1937), Oliver Williamson (1975) and Harvey Leibenstein (1976), and applied to PA by writers such as William Niskanen (1971), Patrick Dunleavy (1991) and Gary Miller (2000). This approach also provides a basis for analyzing most aspects of public service organization, particularly through the lenses of transaction cost theory, principal-agent theory and property rights theory. And the development of the "contract state" for public service delivery in many developed countries over the past three or four decades (following a trend observed for the United States by Murray Weidenbaum (1969)) has made the relevance of such ideas to contemporary PA increasingly obvious.

Accordingly, in the sections that follow, we discuss the applicability of each of these three "general" theoretical approaches to understanding the effect of information technology developments on PA. For each theoretical approach, we consider three types of organizational change in PA that may result. We have labeled those three types, using a metaphor of combustion, as "igniting," "fuelling," and "dampening" kinds of change. By "igniting" changes, we mean the most dramatic kinds of shift – circumstances where IT produces major qualitative changes in social or organizational behavior, creating something that did not exist before – for example, creating markets where no markets existed hitherto, or completely new forms of interaction. By "fuelling" changes, we mean circumstances where IT reinforces trends that are already in train, for example, by making existing operations much easier, cheaper, or quicker, or by supporting changes in social relationships or behavior that are already developing. By contrast, "dampening" changes refer to cases of conservative change or dynamic conservatism – that is, to cases where IT acts as the sort of change that allows things to stay the same, operating as a counterweight to social or organizational changes that would otherwise occur. For example, IT may serve to reinforce much-discussed traditional features of bureaucracy, such as inaccessibility, facelessness, and inflexibility in handling cases, as in the frequently observable cases where organizational websites do not give personal names or usable phone numbers for the curious or distraught inquirer to use or where administrative software proves more inflexible than even the most rigid of human operators. Clearly, this typology of forms of change is crude, its elements are hard to distinguish at the margin, and opinions will obviously differ as to what precisely counts as "igniting," "fuelling," or "dampening" change. But it nevertheless offers us an opening set of categories to see what changes IT can make to PA from these three different theoretical perspectives.

A CULTURAL THEORY PERSPECTIVE: INFORMATION TECHNOLOGY AS FUELLING AND DAMPENING?

Cultural theory claims to identify alternative forms of viable organization, the typical bundle of attitudes and beliefs that go with each type, and the strengths and corresponding weaknesses of each form. The central implication of cultural theory for PA is that no form of organization can be good for all purposes or can enjoy general legitimacy from the society at large; and that some forms of organization are more challenged than others by any given circumstances (for instance, those that carry high risk or require sacrifices to be made for some putative collective benefit).

From the perspective of cultural theory, the main social effects of information technology in PA might be expected to be of a "fuelling" type, reinforcing existing cultural biases. Wildavsky (1985), in reviewing the literature on government growth, once argued that for every received explanation of why government spending should grow with economic and social development, there was an equally plausible counter-argument to the effect that such development would cause government spending to shrink. He argued that only an understanding of underlying cultural bias could explain the "sign" (positive or negative) of the relationship between social development and government size. A parallel argument could be made for the social effects of information technology on PA, and it would link with the now widely held view, originating from research from the earlier age of computer developments, that information technology tends to reinforce prevailing tendencies in organizations and will ordinarily be used in ways that strengthen existing cultural biases.[2]

Accordingly, "hierarchist" organizations or regimes will find ways of using IT or developing e-government in ways that fit with a hierarchist world view and help to ward off threats from individualists and egalitarians. For example, hierarchist organizations or regimes will be especially programmed to implement high-risk, large-scale information technology programs that offer the prospect of maintaining or enhancing high-differentiation control systems, such as the ambitious high-integrity identity systems so beloved of governments in the post 9/11 era. Hierarchist organizations will find ways of using information technology to elaborate security controls and multiple access levels, with the organization's high-grid rules "built in with the bricks" of software systems and website architecture.

Egalitarian and individualist organizations or regimes will similarly find ways of applying the same technology to underpin their chosen ways of life. Such organizations or regimes will be programmed to seek applications of information technology that "open up" organizations and reduce social differentiation, for instance in maximum access and sharing. An early example of this sort of application was CAPOW, an Australian government-financed quango set up in the late 1980s (Sawer 1990). CAPOW (Coalition of Australian Participating Organizations of Women) was established as a "peak organization" for the Australian women's movement. Its convoluted title reflected the egalitarian sensibilities of many of the organizations in the Australian women's movement at that time and the inherent difficulty of reconciling the very idea of a "peak organization" with the egalitarian world view. Accordingly, CAPOW's first major government-financed project was to construct an electronic database to link the participating organizations together – a classic early instance of the "egalitarian" application of information technology that developed much further with the advent of web-based technology a few years later. In the 2000s, so-called peer production or Web 2.0 applications, relying on co-operative networks and user-generated content, not only facilitated existing egalitarian tendencies but also brought in a raft of new groups and quasi-organizations with explicitly egalitarian aims, such as the open-source movement and the producers of the co-operatively and voluntarily written online encyclopedia Wikipedia. Again, organizations and regimes with an individualist bias will be programmed to find ways of applying information technology for creating or mimicking markets or other competitive forums, as in the case of the web-based bidding systems for railroad and airline tickets that have developed over the last decade or so. Another example to be discussed further later is the use of information technology to create a market among rival suppliers on a single electricity grid under a utility regime designed by "econocrats."

From this perspective, IT technology developments pose very different challenges and threats to different types of organization, given their inherent strengths and weaknesses as elucidated by the cultural theory. Drawing on cultural-theory ideas, originally applied to eco-systems, about the "myths" that underpin institutional responses to certain environments (Thompson et al. 1990), Margetts and Dunleavy (2003) explored the specific cultural barriers that different organizations were likely to encounter when embarking on "e-government" initiatives. The "Technology Benign" myth, which underpins the individualist response, will encourage the view that the technological world is forgiving, encouraging and justifying trial and error (Thompson et al. 1990, 27). By contrast, the "Technology Ephemeral" myth underpinning egalitarianism holds that the technological world is an unforgiving place and that the least jolt may trigger complete collapse, so the managing institution must treat technology with great care. This myth is justification for those who would resist technological innovations (particularly large-scale projects) and use technology only in modest, decentralized ways. Hierarchism is underpinned by the "Technology Perverse/Tolerant" myth, a view that technology is forgiving of most events but must be controlled; organizations must regulate against unusual occurrences, and technological experts will be vital to negotiate a somewhat unfamiliar world. In contrast to the other three, the "Technology Capricious" myth, which underpins fatalism, leads to a view of technology as random, uncontrollable, and impossible to manage or learn, even in modest ways. This myth leads to a view that technological development is something to be coped with rather than actively managed.

Given such divergent views of the technological world, IT developments could be expected to play out differently according to cultural bias. Such developments have in some cases posed a threat to hierarchist organizations because of their capacity to inject a new organizational army of technocrats who did not readily fit into established well-defined authority systems, and open up information systems to all comers, like the nineteenth-century railways, with their threat to established caste and class distinctions. Similarly, IT developments can threaten individualist organizations through the problems such organizations face in accepting the planning requirements, distribution of shared overhead costs, collective choice, and potential inflexibility of application. The equivalent threat to egalitarian organizations lies in the capacity of IT to increase social differentiation (for instance, by increasing the potential for more sophisticated differential charging systems and access codes or by opening up a new divide between literates and illiterates in the organization) and by the difficulty such organizations will experience in accepting the scale and risks involved in major information technology projects.

Different phases in IT development may have changed the opportunities and handicaps faced by each basic type of organization in the cultural-theory framework in using that technology to maintain and develop its preferred way of life. For example, it seems likely that the mainframe, large-scale batch-processing computer systems of the 1950s offered the greatest opportunities to hierarchist organizations like tax and social security departments (see Avgerou 1989), because they were well adapted to take risks, undertake central planning, and reinforce social distinctions. The subsequent advent of personal computers, with their own storage capacity and multiple software applications, was a development that seemed more suited to the individualist way of life, since collective choices can to a greater extent be replaced by competition and rivalry. The later move into web-based information systems in the 1990s, with their networked structure of websites and hyperlinks, has lent itself to an egalitarian world view, as noted above, particularly the social networking technologies (such as Facebook and MySpace) and "peer production" applications of the 2000s. But it has also lent itself to further individualist applications, notably in the "weightless" e-commerce economy based on information products in the form of downloads. And it has also provoked a hierarchist response to deal with some of the predictable problems that arise for the Internet when a system whose basic architecture reflects the elite egalitarian world view of those who originally designed it (for instance in domain names and open systems) meets other cultural world views, such as runaway cyber-crime and cyber-terrorism, for which that architecture was never designed. That response, of course, takes the form of security systems and content monitoring.

A CYBERNETIC PERSPECTIVE: INFORMATION
TECHNOLOGY AS FUELLING HOMEOSTASIS?

Cybernetic control theory in PA is much less fashionable and less thickly populated than the cultural theory or the economics of organization. It was much in evidence in political science and management in the 1960s, when general systems theory and cybernetics-based ideas were important intellectual themes, and is perhaps making a certain comeback in the guise of complexity theory, spawned from the same general perspective (see, for instance, Perrow 1999, 2007).

Cybernetic theory focuses from an engineering perspective on the process of control, formally defined as the ability to keep the state of any system within some desired subset of all its possible states. The theory claims to specify the underlying conditions for "viability" in control systems, to distinguish the fundamental components of any system of control, and to identify alternative styles of control. To be viable, any control system must meet the requirement of requisite variety, because something can be said to be "under control" as defined above only if the information capacity of the controller matches that of the controlee (Ashby 1956). Consequently, most social control systems can be viable in this sense only if they incorporate large elements of self-control in their "director," "detector," and "effector" components.

Applying this perspective to PA, Andrew Dunsire (1990) has distinguished three basic types of control systems:

1 the "simple steering" mode, in which the same individual combines the function of director (the goal-setting element of any control system), detector (the element that compares actual states to desired ones), and effector (the element that changes the state of the system to bring it more closely in line with the desired state);

2 the "homeostatic" mode, in which target-setting (the director function) is separated from detection and/or effecting, and in which the control system operates like a thermostat, with pre-set goals, monitoring arrangements and negative feedback mechanisms;

3 the "collibration" mode, in which no pre-set target or datum line is defined in advance, but in which there is a continuous tug-of-war between opposed forces, each of which can be

selectively inhibited by outside pressure. The metaphor here
is with the continuous "struggle" between orthosympathetic
and parasympathetic impulses in the nervous system (with
no stable "target" analogous to that commonly thought to
be involved in the human body's temperature-control system),
or with the type of desk lamp that can be continuously
adjusted by selectively inhibiting the pressure of springs in
opposed tension. "Collibration" is distinguished from the
simple steering mode by the use of pent-up opposed forces
to augment the power of external intervention, and it is
distinguished from the homeostatic mode by the lack of
any clear pre-established set of goals and priorities.

On the face of it, information technology developments seem to offer
the prospect of radically strengthening the possibilities of the target-
setting "homeostatic" mode of control in PA and taking it to new
levels of sophistication. In that sense, it could be seen as fuelling the
dramatic shift towards a government-by-numbers "managerial" style
of control in PA organization in which clear-cut targets are laid out
in advance for each operational unit of organization and negative
feedback mechanisms (such as performance-related pay) are set up
to bring behavior in line with the target. And indeed the dramatic
growth of performance indicators for public services over the past
generation (with those indicators being used for targets and rankings,
as well as background intelligence) has coincided with the development of modern information technology. That technology might fuel
the development of this style of control – central to the reforming
thrust of the "new public management" – by increasing the "detection" capacity of the system and making a target-setting, managerial
control style more viable in requisite-variety terms than in the days
before cyber-bureaucracy. Specifically, IT could be expected to fuel
the so-called "accountingization" of PA (a term coined by Power
and Laughrin 1992) by facilitating a huge increase in performance
indication that allows more areas of PA organization to be under
datum-line forms of control.

If IT developments do indeed fuel the target-setting "homeostatic"
control style in that way, they raise the question whether Dunsire's
elegant analysis of PA control systems may be obsolescent. In *Control
in a Bureaucracy* (1978), Dunsire argued that orthodox bureaucracies could be controlled only by the "collibration" style. That is,

incompatible managerial desiderata are institutionalized in a permanent tug-of-war that acts as a sort of servomechanism. The built-in antagonism allows relatively feeble "outside" pressures – from the political process, public opinion, or the political directorate acting as the "detector" element of the control system – to effect large changes in bureaucratic behavior by disturbing the balance of pent-up opposed forces within the structure. The example Dunsire gives is the well-known conflict between pressures for speed in processing cases and pressures for quality and accuracy in decision making: pressures that are incompatible, at least at the margin. If there are strong and permanently institutionalized forces pushing bureaucracies in both directions, "finger-tip" pressures from outside (for instance, in response to political scandals over excessive delay or excessive inaccuracy) can swing the balance between those forces and so set the organization onto a different course until a further disturbance takes place. Dunsire argued that there were no other effective ways of keeping large-scale bureaucracies under control and claimed that this account of how underlying PA control systems work filled major gaps in the classic Weberian account of bureaucratic functioning.

The idea that IT could be the key element in rendering obsolete Dunsire's analysis of control systems in PA and in pushing PA from a "collibration" to a "homeostatic" control style in line with managerialism, deserves closer investigation. If it is true, it does indeed locate that technology at the heart of a behavior change that could not be more central to PA theory. But there is an alternative view under which the centrality of IT might be argued to underpin rather than undermine Dunsire's analysis. That is, the development of IT has itself posed very problematic issues of control in PA. Indeed, it might be claimed that information-technology developments in PA have frequently been "out of control" in the sense defined earlier, with dramatic cost blowouts and operational and quality failures unanticipated by technology evaluation – precisely because there has been a lack of counter-balancing, "collibratory" mechanisms to check and challenge the easy promises of major cost savings, quality improvements or organizational transformations to be obtained from large-scale ambitious investments. Whereas in the private sector, arguments of competitive advantage will figure large in the evaluation of such technology, public sector information-technology projects have tended to constitute a special form of "client politics" pattern, in J.Q. Wilson's (1980) well-known terminology. That is, they involve a concentrated grouping of easy-to-organize contractors, project workers, and consultants, with high stakes in promoting large-scale, indivisible, long-term, state-of-the-art developments and resisting cutbacks (features that display the properties of "inflexible technologies" as defined by Collingridge (1992) and Collingridge and Margetts (1994)). By contrast, there is no balancing force to apply the brake, because costs from excessive scale, lack of determined budgetary restraint, and the failure of "great leap forward" ambitions tend to be diffused among a larger hard-to-organize grouping of actors, each of whom has low stakes in the issue.

Accordingly, it could be argued that any effective control system for this aspect of PA would need to be *more* rather than less "collibratory" if the condition of requisite variety is to be met. To have effective machinery to prevent information-technology projects running out of control, there would need to be an *equally* concentrated set of *equally* technologically expert actors with *equally* high stakes (through promotion or winning new contracts) in paring down costs, challenging "great leap forward" assumptions and pressing for simplicity, staging, and robustness. The institutional requirements of such a system are very demanding (see Hood 1996) and were never fully spelt out by Dunsire. At a minimum it would seem to require strong incentives for "poacher to gamekeeper" movements within government and an institutional base for project overseers with substantial veto powers – features that have been conspicuous by their absence in most governments' IT regimes.

AN ECONOMICS OF ORGANIZATION PERSPECTIVE: TOWARDS CYBER-ECONOCRACY?

Modern economics of organization theory begins by analyzing the costs of transactions in alternative organizational forms against varying levels and distributions of information. Such theory has implications for the design of efficient organization, in terms of the boundaries and size of organizations, the relative advantage of commanding the services of organizations by contract (or other arm's-length relationships) as against direct ownership, and the design of incentive systems in circumstances where there is asymmetry of information between principals and agents. Within this general approach, three streams of ideas seem to have particular relevance to PA:

1 Principal-Agent Theory. Taking its basic metaphor from the law of agency, principal-agent theory aims to analyze and understand how incentive systems work in circumstances where there is asymmetry of information between subordinate and superordinate, as in the case of the classic "Yes Minister" problem in PA, and the framework used by Niskanen (1971), Dunleavy (1991), Dowding (1995), and many others to analyze bureaucratic behavior. Principal-agent theory led to the development of a more sophisticated justification of performance-related pay systems for managers as optimal incentive structures (see Holstrom and Tirole 1990, 89), and the language of principal and agent became widespread in PA from the 1980s, though more recently it has been challenged or at least modified by labour market sorting theory (for instance by Besley 2006).

2 Property Rights Theory. Property rights theory is concerned with analyzing the differences between direct ownership and contract relationships, typically in conditions where information is imperfect (such that complete contingent contracting is impossible) and relationship-specific investments are involved (see Hart 1989). Important to this analysis is the proposition that where contracts cannot be fully specified (because of uncertainty) and control over residual uses of assets is important, ownership may bring benefits that cannot be achieved by contracting, for example in allowing owners to selectively dismiss the top management of an organization.

3 Transaction Cost Theory. Transaction cost theory aims to understand why the boundaries of organization are drawn where they are: for example, why firms develop instead of using spot contracts in a market, why multinational corporations develop, why low-trust and high-trust contracting patterns are successfully adopted in different circumstances, and why organizations structure themselves as they do. From this perspective, information technology is mainly of interest in terms of what it does to transaction costs in PA, with transaction costs defined as the costs of reaching agreements, monitoring observance, and resolving disputes, through markets or organization. If transactions (either in markets or organization) are not regarded as costless, the most efficient institutional forms are those that minimize transaction costs.

From the perspective of principal-agent theory, we would not expect technology *as such* to change the fundamental characteristics of PA, unless it changed the basic incentive structures of bureaucrats, managers, and workers. After all, a cyber-bureaucracy is still a bureaucracy in terms of its basic incentive structure if it involves the classic bureaucratic features of block budgeting, information asymmetry, and non-transferable ownership rights, and therefore can be expected to continue to behave like a bureaucracy. Aspects of bureaucratic behavior that are conventionally attributed to principal-agent "distortions" (such as over-production, bureau-shaping, management avoidance, predilections for prestige projects with low investment returns) would not be fundamentally affected by the development of information technology, though they might take new forms.

That conclusion might, however, be qualified in cases where that technology shifts the balance between principals and agents in terms of the information asymmetry that is basic to all principal-agent models. For example, if that technology substantially lowers the cost to superordinates of monitoring their subordinates' behavior (by means such as monitoring employees through their computers and keystrokes or making it easier for top office-holders to obtain anonymous information about misbehavior on the part of lower-level officials) and of operating complex employment contracts and variable payment systems, it may have helped to fuel a broad trend to "managerialization" in PA. One issue at stake here is that of how far developments in information technology have begun to create the conditions for the sort of centralized control systems linked to individualized variable payment systems that Frederick Winslow Taylor envisaged for engineering shops in 1895 (and that in 1911 he termed "scientific management") or that Jeremy Bentham contemplated even earlier in his famous 1825 essay on reward. If that is the case, principal-agent theory can also show us how IT developments could lead to a more managerial, target-based approach to control in PA, reaching a similar conclusion to that which could be drawn from the cybernetic perspective.

However, principal-agent theory also alerts us to IT-linked issues in PA that go beyond the conventional subordinate-superordinate relationship in the implementation chain. As already noted in the previous section, IT developments have created new principal-agent problems because of the degree of information asymmetry between those who supply or operate the technology (IT professionals either inside government or within firms providing computer services to government) and those for whom the services are provided. At the least, that adds another substantial level of complexity to politicians' understanding of administrative problems. And in another part of the forest, Internet developments have in some cases substantially altered the relationship between public service professionals and the individuals with whom they deal, in the much discussed phenomenon of "cyber-chondria" in medical care and its analogues in other fields.

The Internet, as opposed to IT developments more generally, may play a particular role in reducing information asymmetries between citizens and government, and e-government initiatives are often promoted (at least ostensibly) for that reason. It is far easier than in the pre-Internet era for the significant proportion of the population in developed countries who use the Internet to find government-related information quickly and efficiently, and these Internet-using individuals are exposed to a far greater range of information sources, including the online presence of non-governmental organizations and private firms. New developments in web-based technologies – the so-called Web 2.0 applications based on user-generated content and peer-to-peer interactions noted above – provide further possibilities for an enhanced role for citizens as "principals" in the government-citizen relationship, increasing their ability to make informed choices across services and potentially facilitating user engagement in public administration. Many government organizations have been slow to realize the potential of such applications (see for instance NAO 2007), which include the possibility for service users to provide testimonials on service provision and even to rate individual practitioners, for instance in education and health care.

From a property rights perspective, the key issue is what information technology does to relationship-specific investments in PA. So this approach puts the spotlight on areas where information technology has destroyed the incidence or logic of such investments, with effects that might be argued to be at least "fuelling" and possibly to be "igniting" in character. Specifically, the shift towards an information-based services economy in the developed countries can be argued to have had the effect of destroying what was once distinctive about much of government's operations (its role in collecting, storing, and retrieving information on paper) as against those of the private sector, just as the development of electronics destroyed the distinctive electromagnetic technology of telephone exchange equipment and made computer manufacturers potential entrants into the telecommunications market.

This replacement of what were once government-specific information-handling styles by automated systems spanning the public and private sectors indicates the role of information technology developments in the post-World War II PA trend of movement from direct ownership to contract relationships, particularly in countries like the United States and the United Kingdom. That trend certainly predates modern information technology (see Weidenbaum 1969), but from a property rights perspective information technology greatly weakens the logic of drawing the lines of public ownership in the traditional way, and thus lends itself to the development of liberalization and market testing in areas once clearly marked by relationship-specific investments.

However, a property-rights perspective also points to some of the new relationship-specific investments bound up in information-technology developments. PA information technology involves many investments that are just as relationship-specific as the paradigm case in property rights theory of a power station located beside a coal mine. There are well-known difficulties of contract specification in large IT projects, owing to the specialized knowledge required and the speed of social and technological change making the future hard to predict. Given the importance of controlling "residual uses" of assets in such circumstances, property rights theory suggests a logic of government ownership of accumulated technological expertise that sharply conflicts with the stress that has been placed in practice on contracting out IT projects to massive corporations in many countries.

Most recently, web-based technologies have put new pressures on property rights to information itself. The phenomenon of volunteer-produced and freely disseminated information on the Internet, such as Wikipedia, alters the property-like regulatory structure of patents, copyrights, and similar exclusion mechanisms applicable to information, knowledge, and culture (Benkler 2006, 143). Some commentators have argued that contrary to the normal predictions of property rights theory, "a flourishing commons exists in respect of information that is communicated via the Internet" (Cahir 2004). On this view, the Internet has brought a dramatic rise in common (as opposed to public or private) property as an alternative form of institutional space, with implications for the capacity of both public and private organizations to provide information or control access to it. But this view is contestable and whether any such trend will prove to be substantial or lasting remains to be seen.

"IGNITING" CHANGES FROM ALTERED
TRANSACTION COSTS

Of all the theoretical perspectives explored here, it is the transactions cost variant of the economics of organization that most lends itself to understanding IT as an "igniting" factor in PA change. Those igniting changes could be understood both as IT-driven transaction cost changes causing the boundaries of PA organization to be dramatically redrawn and changes as lowering the transaction costs of operating market or quasi-market systems as against direct government organization.

Much has been written about the way that IT developments have altered the shape of PA organizations as a result of their impact on transaction costs, most notably in undermining the logic of common siting of back office and front office functions in the same building. And sixteen years ago Patrick Dunleavy (1993) used a similar logic to predict a trend towards internationalized or globalized private corporations specializing in public service functions such as tax collection or benefit payment – producing a new era of IT-based international tax-farming analogous to the spread of the East India Company as a specialized tax collector across the Indian states in the eighteenth century. Such trends raise challenging issues for government counter-strategies to the bargaining power of those new tax-farmers, for instance in the formation of international public buyer cartels or the taking of strategic stockholdings in the relevant corporations, in the style of the nineteenth-century Anglo-French Suez Canal Company.

That does not, of course, mean that changes such as split-siting and multi-agencification of PA organization is necessarily transaction-cost-free. Indeed, the hidden transaction costs of providing services that way have often been revealed only after the fact, for example, when limited interoperability (before the web-based information era, at least) has limited the ability of different units to share information, when the arrangements turn out to introduce inflexibilities that involve substantial extra costs to at least some actors in the system or when the inaccuracies or unreliability of the information cannot be readily worked around by the ability to pool intelligence as a result of operating on a single site.

In addition to its role in helping to reshape PA organization, IT's most dramatic capacity for "igniting" change may lie in creating markets where they did not previously exist. A case in point is that of network utilities, which up to the 1990s were mainly the province of public enterprise or regulated monopolies. Christopher Foster (1992, 73) argues that when the United Kingdom's national electricity grid was set up in the 1920s, there was no alternative to monopoly provision, because only complex computer systems could have provided the basis for a market in electricity on a common grid. As he put it: "the building of a publicly owned electricity grid after 1926 to be used competitively by both private and municipal distributors was then beyond the competence of the regulators to coordinate, and this was a fundamental reason for the eventual nationalization of the whole industry ... Public ownership seemed the only way of managing such a system – the computers and computer-based mathematics did not exist which would have made it possible for there to be a truly commercial electricity market buying and selling through the grid." And since that time the market-creating capacity of IT developments has extended to domestic retail markets for electricity and gas by the development of "smart" metering systems allowing consumers to switch their electricity purchases among suppliers.

IT has also created other market mechanisms that had not previously existed within PA, for example in creating networks of information about prices and vendors, in the form of electronic marketplaces for government procurement, both of the dedicated kind (in the form of specialized forums in which prospective vendors can see other vendors' prices and details of recent transactions, enabling them to make their price decisions accordingly) and even of the general kind, in the use of auction sites such as eBay. The "virtual call centre company" LiveOps, which allows twenty thousand individuals scattered across the United States to perform call centre operations for over two hundred private firms, could be another pointer to the future. In such cases, information technology has provided the possibility to replace older contracting systems with something closer to a "spot market" for some kinds of products and services.

That sort of transformation seems more likely to apply to relatively standard products than to relationship-specific developments. Nevertheless, it seems plausible to understand the role of information technology as igniting significant aspects of commodification – the trend of bringing more aspects of PA into the realm of marketized or quasi-marketized services – as a result of shifting transaction costs. According to Internet gurus such as Yochai Benkler (2006), the rise in "social production systems" noted above works against this trend, by avoiding transaction costs owing to less need for precise specification. He argues that peer production of information, knowledge, culture, and sharing of material resources can outperform market-based systems in motivating human creativity and also in allocating computation, storage, and communications capacity in networked information economies. But at the time of writing these systems are relatively scarce within government organizations. And government finds itself pitted in competition against such systems too, for example, when trying to disseminate online messages to society at large.

SUMMARY AND CONCLUSION: PUTTING PA IT IN ITS PLACE?

Any "theory-driven" examination of information technology in PA is limited by the absence of any single, generally accepted theoretical basis for PA, as noted earlier. But the alternative inductive approach that has been widely used in the study of such technology has its limits too, in that the results of the inductive method are sensitive to selection in the cases chosen and in contestable interpretation of data. And the advantage of looking at information technology in PA through different theoretical lenses is that each brings different aspects of IT-linked change into focus and shows their relationship to central theoretical concerns in PA.

For the cultural theory, there can be no single expectation about changes brought about by IT in PA, because the social effects of such technology – and even the selection of applications – will vary according to cultural bias. From this perspective, any universal "globalized" vision of IT-linked change in the vein of Osborne and Gaebler's (1992) hubristic early-NPM-era proclamation of the advent of a "global" and "inevitable" new paradigm in PA, is fundamentally implausible. From this perspective, the social effects of IT in PA will be mainly of the "fuelling" or even "dampening" kind, as different viable forms of organization find ways of applying the new technology to reinforce their hierarchist, egalitarian, or individualist character and to ward off threats coming from their cultural competitors. The key research questions from the cultural theory viewpoint are whether IT developments are equally capable of being adapted to different cultural biases, whether IT projects could be improved by a so-called "clumsy approach" combining different cultural world views in policy-making (Verweij and Thompson 2006), or whether the technology inherently loads the scales among those biases in some way. Different technologies emerging at various points through the last fifty years may have suited different cultural biases, as suggested earlier, but any technological advantage of this kind seems to be constantly shifting.

For cybernetic theory, the key questions about IT developments are whether they increase the underlying "variety" available to PA control systems and how that technology can itself be controlled. "Igniting" changes could occur only if basic problems of requisite variety in control systems would be decisively and permanently changed. Again, "fuelling" and "dampening" changes linked to IT developments in PA seem much more likely than "igniting" ones from this theoretical perspective. IT developments in PA can fuel the managerialist dream of target-setting control and monitoring in a homeostatic control style, facilitating a latter-day realization of Bentham's dream of elaborate league-table controls over public sector providers and the fourteen different kinds of accounting that he prescribed for all public agencies in his 1820 Constitutional Code (Bentham 1983). The key research questions from the cybernetic theory viewpoint concern the extent to which IT developments in fact make traditional collibration mechanisms in PA obsolete by increasing the variety of homeostatic modes of control and the extent to which IT development itself presents a control problem in PA that can be handled only by collibration.

For the economics of organization theory, it might be supposed that IT development as such would make few fundamental changes in PA organization, because though it affects production possibilities, it does not itself change the basic incentive structure of bureaucracies. So the basic problems of PA are unlikely to change, unless IT developments were to be linked with fundamental redesign of incentive structures, and in that sense too we might expect IT-linked changes to be mainly "fuelling" or "dampening" in character. However, IT developments from this perspective are also capable of producing dramatic "igniting" changes by radically lowering the transaction costs of operating markets and quasi-markets in place of administered allocation systems, by altering the information asymmetry between various kinds of principals and agents in PA, and by undermining the logic of conventional ownership structures where relationship-specific investments are concerned. Perhaps the key research questions from the economics of organization viewpoint concern the issue of what "transaction costs" in PA actually amount to, how they can be measured, and how they change.

But such theories can perhaps tell us more in combination than each can do individually. Both the cybernetic theory and the principal-agent element of the economics of organization theory can help us to understand ways in which IT developments may have underpinned the "managerialization" of PA in the recent past. But ultimately, all such theories can do is alert us to changing production possibilities: only when it is linked to preferences in cultural theory are we likely to be able to explain the "sign" or direction of change as between igniting, fuelling, and dampening. For example, the link between IT developments and the development of greater "economicization" in PA (substituting markets or quasi-markets for directive allocation systems) can be understood only when new transaction-cost configurations combine with "individualist" cultural preferences. Equally, the cultural theory is relatively sterile on its own, because all it can do is alert us to competing cultural biases and the "timeless" strengths and weaknesses of different forms of organization; only when linked to changing production possibilities can concrete social changes be understood. Accordingly, promising possibilities for future theoretical development relating to IT development and PA may well be found precisely in the areas where the theories overlap. If both mainstream PA studies and mainstream IT studies are subject matters in search of a discipline, a combination of three disciplines in search of a subject matter may help us to ask questions that put IT development in its proper place – as a central concern of contemporary PA.

NOTES

1 We owe this insight to a comment made to us by Klaus Goetz in the early 1990s.
2 Especially in relation to centralizing and decentralizing tendencies (see for instance Kraemer and King 1986; Margetts 1991).

PART FOUR

The Design of Reform: The Evolution of Policy Tools

6

Reforming Management and Management Systems: Impacts and Issues

JOHN HALLIGAN

The reform era elevated "management" as a core concept of public sectors, a centrality reflected in the reform slogans of managerialism and new public management (NPM). After two or so decades of reform the question of the long-term impact of management is of interest and the question of how it has been accommodated within the more recent focus on public governance.

In this chapter, these questions are addressed first by examining the standing of management and management systems and how they have evolved during the reform era. Specialized management systems can be examined separately, and management generically, but management is not an end itself: it is embedded in a particular public sector and government context that it is designed to support. That management cannot be understood in isolation from context has been a theme in Guy Peters' work, in particular, the interaction with the political environment, the governance framework, and specific processes such as coordination. His early judgments on these questions have been confirmed by international experience during the reform era, where the neglect of context and relationships impacted on the results. Reform agenda to decouple, to devolve, to disaggregate, to privatise, and to marketise have revealed both the potential and the limitations of management.

A second inquiry addresses several interpretations of management reform. Management has formed the basis of distinctive paradigms and models (i.e., managerialism and new public management). Recent studies have offered representations of how management reform has been worked through, and several models have interacted, an approach that reflects Guy Peters' explorations of typologies of reform and governance. In examining the standard reform models, we might ask, is the pattern over time one of succession (one model replacing another) or layers (one or more models superimposed upon another) or contending models (e.g., devolved NPM versus central capacity and control)? Alternatively, the role and impact of management systems can be approached through examining the executive branch in terms of complementary (and competing) systems – administrative, management, and political – that combine in different ways depending on the approach to design.

There continue to be issues around management that derive from contradictions in the agenda and the approaches underlying the handling of management and from the effectiveness of the alignment between management processes and other features of governing. This chapter examines these questions on a comparative basis, including examining different levels of management incorporation, but a focus on countries with a strong management emphasis inevitably means an emphasis on Anglo-American systems.

MANAGEMENT AND CONTEXT

Evolving Conceptions of Management and Management Systems

One traditional conception of management saw it as the "doing" side of government, which was appropriately located underneath and was subsumable within administration and the preoccupation with policy-making (Wettenhall 1997). A subordinate conception was not universal, however, management having a much longer tradition in the United States (Lynn 2006). For the purposes here, however, it is simply necessary to indicate the general ascendancy of management to a more prominent position. An emerging orthodoxy of public administration in the 1970s and 1980s was that the management skills of civil and public servants were deficient and undervalued relative to administrative and policy skills (Halligan and Power 1992). As management moved beyond being a matter of skill augmentation to a full-fledged framework for activity, it replaced administration as the core concept in the reform era.[1]

Managerialism emerged as the term that encapsulated this new emphasis and was grounded in management (Pollitt 1990), with new public management becoming identified more directly with markets, and developing variations on both became a popular preoccupation in the 1990s, reflecting both derivative adaptations and academic speculation (e.g., Ferlie et al. 1996).

The early debates about management that centred on whether it was best viewed in generic terms or as a variant of private sector/business administration (e.g., Gunn 1987) were worked through long ago, as a more fully fledged understanding of public management emerged. The claims under new public management about the private sector's significance, even superiority, were digested. The techniques and methods of management needed to be combined with the public sector values that had hitherto been most closely identified with administration. Many of the normative elements of traditional public administration and the instrumental emphasis of management had to be reconciled in public management.

Several of the continuing debates reflected the shifting boundaries between public and private and politicians and public service, and the eventual reclaiming of colonised realms (at least at the level of ideas if not always in practice).[2] Several of these debates are examined later in this chapter.

The vagaries of political agenda and interests worked against the fulfilment of managerial agendas and the dominance of management. Cut-back management soon ran up against the expansion of staff and expenditure in new policy areas, a recurrent experience internationally, as governments were unable to simultaneously reconcile decrement and resourcing new policy agenda. Even one of the neo-liberal governments of the 1990s was accused of big government less than a decade later (Halligan 2008a). Risk management ran up against risk adversity as security issues took precedence in a phase of international terrorism and securing borders against unwanted entrants.

The architecture of the public service has evolved from the traditional multi-purpose departments that often monopolised public policy and operated within the distinct boundaries of a public service. Apart from sprawling third-party roles, particularly in the United States, there now existed alongside the public service in several Anglo-American countries a concentration of private sector expertise producing the semblance of a diarchic structure consisting of public agencies and para-public private firms specialising in management consultancy (on the latter see Saint-Martin 2004), as well as internal auditing and advice on technical matters. The move to permeable boundaries for public sectors meant more regular exchanges, collaboration, and hybrid public-private arrangements, in short, shared management for many purposes.

Management Systems and Integrated Management

The expansion of management fields followed the early ascendancy of financial management, and the emergence of new functional needs (e.g., managing contracts and third parties). In the past, countries such as the United States have adopted management systems "singly and incrementally, resulting in a set of insular systems, each with its own rules, regulations, and perceptions of effective performance" (Poocharoen and Ingraham 2007, 178). While practice varies substantially, this insularity continues to be evident in many governments with regard to core management systems such as financial systems, human resources, capital and information technology, and managing for results. Integration has become regarded as a hallmark of well-developed management systems. The differences between high- and low-performing systems for u.s. state and local government can be defined by integrative facilitators – including vertical and horizontal integration, comprehensiveness, and linkages with central agencies and the political executive (Moynihan 2007; Ingraham 2007).

Similarly, types of managing performance have been differentiated based in part on the extent to which different management systems are integrated. "Performance management" is defined as one of several types by the presence of coherence, comprehensiveness, consistency, and of course integration. The integration of performance information goes beyond ad hoc connectedness for the purpose of using it in a coherent management improvement strategy. Performance management is conceived as a framework that comprises several systems, but they must be hierarchically connected to satisfy the criteria of "performance management" as an ideal type (Bouckaert and Halligan 2008).

Politics and Management: A Constant Dynamic

Where management became prominent it had to take into account the political environment, and attempts to isolate management from politics came to be seen as dysfunctional. This operated at two levels: that of ministerial interaction and of central direction (discussed later). The relationship between politicians and public managers is subject to many variations (Peters 1987). One interesting dynamic of the reform era has been how the political and the managerial have been worked through in different contexts, three interesting possibilities being the ascendancy of politicians at the expense of public managers, the assertion of management systems in relation to politicians, and the operation of parallel operations that do not intersect effectively.

The overall trend has been towards the assertion of the political executive over the public service (Peter and Pierre 2004. In anglophone countries a new form of instrumentalism emerged that was defined in terms of management. This change was not uniform: Canada was an exception insofar as the politicians did not consistently take up the options available under the Westminster-derived system to lead on reform, leaving it to the public service leadership (Halligan 2008b) (but compare the expanded role in central steering discussed below).

Where managerialism was in the ascendancy, the relationship could unravel. It was observed that "NPM enthusiasts ... prescribe a set of roles for ministers that few minsters seem able or willing to fit" (Pollitt 1998, 71). A clear case of a managerialist reformulation of the ministers' role occurred in New Zealand, where the relationship between ministers and department heads was redefined by separating political and managerial roles through the association of outcomes with ministers and outputs with chief executives. The minister selected the outcomes and purchased the outputs from the chief executive, who selected the necessary inputs. The contractually based relationship was designed to allow the chief executive to be held accountable by the minister for departmental results. The shift in the focus of chief executives' accountability from inputs to outputs was linked to greater managerial autonomy (Halligan 2001). Reforms in effect "depoliticised" government activity (see Gregory 1998 on "fencing off" the political and technocracy) and detached ministers from being held responsible for public actions. Managerial accountability was developed while the political responsibility of ministers became more tenuous.

A comparison with Australia highlights New Zealand's approach. Both started from a similar base, grounded in the Westminster model, but pulled in different directions. Both combined management and political changes, but one element was dominant in each case, the two pathways offering different solutions. Australian departments declined in importance with the expansion of ministerial authority and resources. New Zealand chief executives became more important relative to ministers; managerial accountability was enhanced, while political responsibility remained unclear. Australia became more "politicised," while New Zealand experienced the managerialisation of politics. New Zealand has since sought to strengthen outcomes and the political executive through using ministerial advisers.

Performance Management as an Achilles' Heel?

The question of performance in the public sector has attracted extensive debate in an unprecedented era of public sector reform. Performance is invariably "for someone" or "to someone" (Bouckaert and Peters 2002, 361), underlying the relationships involved in management.

Positions on performance management have been polarised, with advocates contending against the opponents, who argued that the fundamental premises were wrong and produced dysfunctional behaviour. However, the long-term trends have supported the ascendancy and durability of performance ideas as a dominant force in public management internationally. A new generation of studies has been addressing the impact of the age of performance and its pervasive influence on governments. This growing middle ground of analysts sees the limitations of performance management but believes there is something worthy of careful investigation through examining assumptions and exposing faulty thinking, in order to narrow the gap between rhetoric and practice (Radin 2006; Moynihan 2008). Early exponents (Bouckaert and Peters 2002, 362) examined possible adverse consequences of performance management, and observed that most of these problems could be resolved "by careful design and implementation of the performance management system."

The Anglo-American countries have been highly committed to performance management over two decades, during which they have refined their measurement and performance framework and increased their capacity to monitor performance. The countries have followed different pathways within a performance management framework, with implementation styles differing in terms of conceptions of the relationship between outputs and outcomes, the responsibilities given to chief executives, and the roles of central personnel agencies in handling performance oversight. The exigencies of reform agendas have produced considerable convergence in managing performance during the twenty-first century.

Despite common elements among these countries, there continue to be differences in approach, levels of implementation (reflecting reform cycles), and key aspects of a performance management framework, including the technical treatment of outcomes and outputs. These variations reflect institutional contexts, as well as different approaches (see Bouckaert and Halligan 2008).

More importantly, however, practice falls short of aspirations, and significant questions remain about the quality and use of performance information in the budget process, about internal decision making and external reporting, and about the variable engagement of agencies. There continue to be issues about implementation, significant challenges to accomplishing sophisticated performance management, and limits to a heavy reliance on this approach (Bouckaert and Halligan 2008).

The limitations of country approaches include questions about how well the framework is working (Australia), the level and quality of implementation (Canada and New Zealand), and the issues arising from top-down complexities in a unitary system and dysfunctionalities (the United Kingdom). The use of performance measures against targets in the United Kingdom shows performance improvements, but they are modest (and possibly insufficient when other factors such as declining productivity are taken into account) (Flynn 2007). The structural features of u.s. government, which are not reflected in the parliamentary systems of the other Anglo-American systems, have a major impact on the handling of performance management. Radin's (2006) sustained critique of the performance movement in the United States reveals the limitations of an approach that is insensitive to the complexities and requirements of public management in diverse jurisdictions.

Performance management is arguably at a turning point with the intensification of questioning by external observers, as well as insiders struggling with its limitations in practice (Bouckaert and Halligan 2008; Flynn 2007; Moynihan 2008). Performance management systems have been modified to improve operability but can expect their viability to be undermined unless they better serve internal and external needs, particularly those of politicians. Performance management remains vulnerable, indicating the need for a new generation of more effective frameworks that can be adapted selectively and implemented.

INTERPRETING MANAGEMENT'S PLACE

A number of distinctive frameworks have been developed to interpret reform and, directly or indirectly, the role and location of management.

Management under Different Models?

The level of engagement with management varies. Reform models have provided a basis for exploring and clarifying clusters of change that renovate management and reconstitute relationships. The standard models of reform cover managerialism in which management is the central concept. The theoretical underpinnings of new public management combined elements of institutional economics, as well as managerialism (Christensen al. 2007), and the market element is prominent, as well as features such as disaggregation and privatisation.

In turn, the recent focus on public governance has spawned a range of models with different impacts on management. Take, for example, one set of models – market, participation, flexibility, and deregulation (Peters 1996b) – each of which has different implications for management, which shows up as one component with variable roles and significance. Under this type of conception, management is submerged within public governance. It can also be depicted as nestling within governance and playing distinctive and complementary roles (Bovaird 2003).[3] Under public-private partnerships, management roles are shared across boundaries. Government management has increasingly entailed third parties.

Integrating Governance

While once, reinventing government was seen as the pathway, a subsequent trend points to reintegrating governance becoming more prominent. This model is an amalgam of new elements and design features from previous models. This mix can be represented as moving away from a previous model (hence the "beyond NPM" perspective) or as moving towards some form of amalgam based on the co-existence of features derived from different models. There has been a reconfirmation of the organisational components of the traditional machinery of government such as cabinet, ministerial department, and central agency. There have also been indications of the revival of features associated with traditional bureaucracy – such as risk aversion – suggesting the emergence of neo-Weberianism.

There are, however, several features that are different from those of the earlier hierarchical model of integration. The public service operates under a political executive with a brace of instruments in the twenty-first century for securing and sustaining control and direction and driving the system strategically at several levels. Empowered departments may have greater responsibilities than traditional arrangements, and performance is conceived differently and receives priority. Management processes are well institutionalised. The options of going to some form of market and the private sector continue as elements of flexible management.

Integrated governance serves the dual purpose of renewing the public sector to improve capacity and resetting and refocusing the core public service to increase performance. The term reflects the strong impulse to integrate, recognition of its attendant features that cover the whole of government and coordination, the roles of central agencies and line departments, the autonomy and governance of public bodies, delivery and implementation, and the performance focus. The roles of and relationships between public and private sectors and capability and capacity questions have also been revisited.

This type of approach has been prevalent in countries such as Australia and New Zealand, based on the focus on different modes of coordinating and control that confer greater coherence and capacity on the public sector. Even New Zealand's "contract governance" has been replaced by a variation on "joined-up governance" (Boston and Eichbaum 2007).

The main themes resonate across Westminster countries: horizontal collaboration through some form of joined-up government, the reassertion of the centre giving central agencies greater capacity for leadership and direction, re-aggregation and rationalising of public sector bodies, and new instruments for securing and facilitating delivery and implementation. Under this conception, elements of new public management persist, which is especially the case with performance management, which continues to provide a cornerstone of the public management framework, as indicated by the growth in and continuing high commitment to performance, despite the overall fate of the NPM model.

Layering

A distinguishing feature of reform in some systems is that it has been comprehensive and may involve different generations, stages, and programs over time. Fundamental to comprehensive reforms has been that different approaches may be implemented and applied in a serial process over time or in tandem. One may invoke another as seemingly complementary strategies, but just as likely is that they may be contradictory themes.

New conceptions of public governance address a different mix of features from those once prevalent (Lynn 2008). The reaction against new public management features has produced similar trends in a range of countries. Recent analysis of patterns of change indicates that successive phases of reform have added new frameworks, rather than replacing old ones (see Christensen and Laegreid 2006). The characterisation of past practice as "uniform and clear-cut" has been challenged (Hood and Lodge 2006, 5). The long-term condition of these systems suggests the need for a multi-dimensional and dynamic view of change. While once it may have been appropriate to articulate a single administrative tradition, that has become increasingly difficult as new layers of process and values are added and the operational features of a tradition become more ambiguous and complex. This indicates several interpretative frameworks and the need to recognise multiple layers and also that countries may adopt different styles as the need arises.

Some interpretations have recognised the complexities by distinguishing tiers of NPM or contending models, and it is clear that coordination and integration have co-existed with disaggregation. British observers have sought to unpack the case of a large and complex unitary system of government by distinguishing levels and co-existing models (Richards and Smith 2006; Dunleavy et al. 2005). The United Kingdom has displayed several tendencies concurrently as it has wrestled with different demands to deregulate and regulate, devolve and control. Ultimately, "the reason that governments have pursued contradictory actions is that there are real contradictions that cannot be reconciled" (Flynn 2007, 283).

This conclusion also applies to the neo-Weberian state model (Pollitt and Bouckaert 2004), which provides a descriptive representation that combines features of the traditional model with the addition of a stronger external focus on citizens' needs and engaging their views and on aspects of management. The balance remains one between results and correct procedures and between being a professional manager in addition to being a specialised legal expert. Take, for example, the Norwegian case where "traditional Weberian features, NPM features, and post-NPM features are blended in a complex combination" (Christensen and Laegreid 2008, 20).

Resurrecting Central Steering

A strategic issue about government effectiveness was discerned at an early stage in the reform era: "As government loses control over functions considered to be public, it may lose the ability to effectively direct the society; it may lose the steering ability that constitutes the root of the word government" (Peters 1984). This was revisited in the context of the 1990s. The dictum of "steering rather than rowing" offered few insights about central policy coordination. "Most of the examples of 'steering organizations' are pitched at a much lower level than central departments of state such as cabinet offices, prime ministers' departments, or ministries of finance." Central policy coordination was a significant issue that managerialism lacked and did not offer a theoretical or practical answer for (Pollitt 1998, 71).

The Westminster framework is still regarded as conditioning how civil servants and ministers operate, particularly in Britain, where civil service reform has been contained by the constitutional framework, which has limited the options for reforming institutional arrangements that influence the bureaucracy (Richards 2003). The working through of the tensions between political control (or variants of the Westminster model) and administrative autonomy (variants of new public management) has demonstrated the dynamic interplay between contra-directional reforms. One schema sees a tendency for "governments in the Anglo-Saxon world to move from the Westminster Model 1 to a New Public Management Model 2." The more recent development of what is termed Westminster Model 2, "is an attempt to re-impose WM1 mechanisms of control onto NPM2 systems of delivery and, in doing so, reconstitute many of the key features of the original Westminster model" (Richards and Smith 2006, 298). These features cover, in particular, political authority in the centre and re-imposition of central control using direct political control, as well as regulation and targets (Richards 2008).

Management under the Rule of Law

Beyond the Anglo-American systems, the place of management varies widely. In contrast to the more comprehensive and integrated management models of the Anglo-Americans, there are administrative systems that incorporate management elements and management-oriented systems that use management in specific fields.

This can be clarified by considering administrative traditions and, in particular, the "stark dichotomy" between law and management in the choice involved in defining fundamental administrative tasks (Peters 2003, 2008). The managerial conception recognises law as a starting point, whereas the legalistic position is concerned with administering public law. Management ideas have been absorbed in continental Europe, yet it is clear that management is either subservient to the rule of law or at best that they co-exist. The pattern varies between different traditions, the northern European (the Scandinavian and a hybrid like that of the Netherlands) being more susceptible to management, the Napoleonic and Germanic systems less so. For example, Norway has incorporated some management elements through a performance assessment system focused on results (Christensen and Laegreid 2008). For many of the others, the monopoly of legalism has prevailed (Kickert 2007, 2008).

The notion of the neo-Weberian state has been advanced as an alternative model prevalent in Europe. The "neo" aspect contains two management elements: a greater concern with managing resources to focus more on results, and not simply on procedural correctness, and the conception of the public servant as a professional manager, in addition to being an expert in law (Pollitt 2007a).

While differences between administrative traditions remain important, there are common management elements. The reform process may take longer in Europe, but for specific management reforms the results may be similar (Yesilkagit and de Vries 2004).

Management and Administration Again in Contention

One framework for interpreting reform defines three policy systems in the executive branch: the administrative system specialises in the maintenance of structures, rules, and principles that constrain the way resources are disposed; the management system focuses on directing and processing resources; and the political system's functions address the patterning of authority within the executive and determine the appropriate balance between the administrative and the management systems. The framework has been used to examine early reform through the interactions among the three systems and to generate models and scenarios (Halligan and Power 1992).

This approach has the advantage of exposing the role of the political executive in transferring its focus to a combination of political and management systems (the latter at the expense of administration). The executive branches studied by Halligan and Power (1992) were moving towards "political management," but the extent to which it was embraced and the forms it assumed varied. The Australian federal government was well advanced down this path, but was unlikely to become as managerialist or political as some state governments, for it was not so preoccupied with the direct delivery of services.

Just how reform would shape executive branches in the longer term was far from clear in the 1980s, but viewing the long term through the changing interactions among political, administrative, and management systems suggested scenarios that still have relevance. One scenario saw the future in terms of management's continuing dominance of the executive branches, as it moved from an immature form of the managerialist to becoming institutionalised. There was also an argument that the symbiosis of the political and the management systems would prove a fragile one if the viability of the administrative system was seriously impaired. A second scenario envisaged the re-emergence of a stronger administrative system. As Savoie observes (Savoie 2006, 600; Peters and Pierre 2003), "administration matters too." There have been indications that, following experiments with new-public-management type reforms, the administrative system has again been favoured. Of particular significance have been the mixed results of attempts in European countries to implement management systems in the face of the entrenched administrative law tradition. The third scenario is a synthesis of the claims of the administrative and management systems. One could be tempered by the other, with different results in different contexts: the management system will remain stronger in Anglophone countries and the administrative system dominant in European countries.

The value of this framework in tracking elements of the management function over time and its position relative to the other systems is again apparent. The aftermath of the last two environmental shocks – the international security crisis from 2001 and the financial crisis of 2008 – have confirmed a different direction from the heights of NPM. Markets and risk-taking have been discredited, and government intervention has been revived. The implications for the public sector are clear: "risk" in management is no longer a primary precept for action, market options appear less attractive, and the private sector is less valued for solutions and practices.

IMPACTS OF AND LIMITS TO MANAGEMENT REFORM

Impacts: Meaning and Significance of Reform

There are well-known difficulties in evaluating impacts, and the use of exacting criteria often challenges the significance of impacts. Reform has been about improving the public service and governments' capacity to govern, but these results need to be differentiated from broader outcomes, which are more difficult to determine. Effects may be unintended as well as intended. At specific times it is possible to point to clear results, but over the long term the effects appear more ephemeral and difficult to determine with precision. Particular types of impact are more challenging as you move from the more concrete, operational, and micro-activities to the effects on system capacity. There are problems with units of analysis and meaning, appropriate data and criteria, and determining change at several levels (Pollitt and Bouckaert 2001; Boyne et al. 2003; Pollitt and Bouckaert 2004; Christensen et al. 2007).

The arguments for managerial autonomy, importing ideas and concepts from the private sector, and measuring performance have for long been said to make resource use more effective, but any clear evidence is not always apparent. Countries may employ measures to control resource use through built-in reductions (e.g., Australia and Sweden exacting an efficiency dividend annually from departments), but questions remain about public sector productivity and effectiveness at the agency level. Basic savings and reductions in public servants have been achieved (but have often been countered by staff expansions due to new government initiatives). There is evidence in the United Kingdom of improvements in impacts on the public as measured by performance indicators (Flynn 2007), even if the evidence remains unappreciated by the public.

The elements of a management approach have been incorporated in the operational approaches of civil services internationally. They are reflected in the early formulation of Keeling (1972) as covering a focus on strategic objectives, resource use, results, and risk. There is a strong association between organisations' management capacity and quality and being effective in defining purpose, prioritizing, aligning resources and priorities, and measuring progress. Being able to sustain management reform over time is important because it involves the "long-term building of the competencies and components necessary to effect change" (Ingraham et al. 2003, 118, 119).

Limits to Management Reform

At times during the reform era little appeared to be immune from management reform as corporate services, defence functions, and enterprises regarded as public institutions (e.g., the post office) were outsourced or partly or wholly privatised. Even policy advice, the traditional staple of the senior civil service, was colonised by political appointments to policy positions (the precedent being set much earlier by the United States) and the greater reliance on external consultants and ministerial advisers. The implications for the management of politicisation (Peters and Pierre 2004) went further where political operatives claimed management functions or subjected public management to stronger political influences.

The realm of the *public* sector has changed as the traditional boundaries contracted and its role was conceived as more about steering and enabling than direct production and management (Haque 2001). It is also apparent that where the line is drawn depends on context, with countries having different institutional limits (the United States and the United Kingdom demonstrate a significant propensity to go beyond the public sector). The hybridisation of the margins of the state worked against boundary clarity as the range and extensiveness of hybrids expanded greatly through cross-boundary relationships and organisational forms in various fields of management.

The debates about the limits to management reform and of core functions have partly been resolved by time (Pollitt 2007b) with decisions that do not have a strong sustainable basis (because of ideology, contingencies, fashion) being the most vulnerable. The limits of markets are challenged by questions about controls, transaction costs, and the limitations of contractualism. The in-house capacity of line departments and central agencies can be stripped down only so much: outsourcing departmental corporate services takes hollowing too far. Government tolerance for run-down capacity leads to reversals,[4] and central agencies have their roles augmented so that they can manage strategically. Path dependency in the sense of "the range of policy choices available" has become more cogent for reformers (Peters and Pierre 1998, 224).

The "public" aspects have been reaffirmed as irreducible in several respects, even if they mattered less at the technical end of different modes of management. With the emergence of a more supportive climate – in part reflecting the demise of NPM – there has been a strengthening of public values and management. Clear positions, however, continue to be articulated (Christensen and Laegrid et al. 2007), and the question of publicness is being examined more: "the issue of what must remain public in order to uphold public ethos and other core administrative values has come to the forefront" (Pierre 2008, 26). This renewed emphasis on public sector-centred conceptions and the "public" in public management, ensure that the debates continue.

CONCLUSION

Management systems are pervasive internationally and serve several purposes, in particular that of managing the use of resources and results and providing a flexible vehicle for the transfer of ideas, techniques, and solutions between public and private sectors. At the same time, levels of integration and the alignment of management systems are subject to significant variations in practice. Management prevails in many countries but must co-exist with public law in others. While management's place is relatively secure – despite the stronger claims of administration and the broader framework of public governance – it is not as clearly differentiated as doctrine suggests, either from traditional administration or from private management, and is embedded in a hybrid system that draws on several models and the public/private nexus. This provides a continuing source of issues.

NOTES

1 There have been intriguing variations and hybrids such as "administrative management" in the United States in the 1930s (Hood 2005), a term reproduced forty years later with the establishment of the Japanese Institute of Administrative Management. On the transition from "administration" to "management" in Britain, and the normative implications, see Learmouth (2005).

2 The competition among professions for agenda control (e.g., accountants and economists) is important but cannot be taken up here.

3 Another variation is to regard NPM as has having evolved from a narrower conception to a more governance- and externally focused model (Richards 2008).

4 An example is the outsourcing of departmental briefing documents for a new government, a concern of the incoming prime minister of New Zealand, Helen Clark. A government U-turn on reforms was the discontinuation of mandatory outsourcing of IT and corporate services in Australia.

PART FIVE

The Design of Reform: Western Ideas and Models in Non-Western Settings

7

Implementing Developed Countries' Administrative Reforms in Developing Countries: The Case of Mexico

JOSÉ LUIS MÉNDEZ

INTRODUCTION

The year 2003 saw the approval in Mexico of a merit civil service, introducing elements contained in the traditional approach to civil service (merit entry, for instance), as well as elements closer to the so-called new public management (such as performance assessment). In that context, there are at least two questions of interest, given this book's approach. The first one asks, how did the administrative ideas or reforms in developed countries influence the reforms in a developing country like Mexico? To answer this question, the first section of this chapter will discuss the administrative trends in those countries, and the following sections will examine the Mexican reform's approval process, the characteristics of the new civil service, and its subsequent development.

The second question asks, which factors could explain the introduction of a merit civil service in Mexico, on the one hand, and its evolution, on the other? To answer it, the last section will present, in the form of general hypotheses, some possible explanations.

ADMINISTRATIVE REFORMS IN DEVELOPED COUNTRIES

If we wish to see the impact that administrative ideas or reforms in developed countries have had on developing ones, we must first identify those reforms. In the next pages, I will try to briefly do that, even though the recent agenda of administrative reforms in most developed countries has been quite diverse, complex, and sometimes even contradictory.

Pollitt and Bouckaert's recent study (2004) is quite useful in this regard, as it seeks to offer a general view of reforms using four basic models: maintaining, minimizing, marketizing, and modernizing. For the purposes of this chapter, reference to the last two will be especially useful.

The marketizing strategy (frequently combined with minimizing) was defined – and popularized – mainly on the basis of the British reforms of the 1980s and 1990s. The background to the strategy was formed by the exhaustion and distortions of the welfare state in the United Kingdom in the 1970s, along with a decline in productivity and overall economic competitiveness, all of which led to the introduction of deregulation, market liberalization, and government efficiency reforms. The latter came to be known as new public management (NPM). Initially understood as the reduction of the state apparatus and the improvement of its efficiency, it originated in the Efficiency Strategy adopted during Prime Minister Thatcher's government.

In turn, the Next Steps program would expand the decentralizing theses developed for purposes of economic efficiency into the larger level of government organization. Some of its main proposals distinguished between types of government units; for example, between the units designing policies and those implementing them. The practical corollary of this distinction was the creation of executive agencies, with managerial autonomy predefined and specified through contracts, agreements, or "performance bases."

As these initiatives were introduced, the traditional civil service system was criticized for being too expensive and rigid to adapt to complex and changing realities, too bureaucratic and complex, too prone to favor bureaucrats instead of citizens, and too resilient to change. Thus, the NPM promoted a more enterprise-like administration, supposedly more flexible, decentralized, "performance-oriented," and concentrated on achieving the results demanded by individuals seen as "customers," while it was less concerned with the general interests of individuals as citizens (many of those interests were related to the administrative process: for example, equal treatment and honesty).

More or less at the same time, problems similar to those of the United Kingdom also started to be highlighted in the United States.

Reforms in the United States started to develop with the revival of "neo-conservatism," resulting from Ronald Reagan's election as president in 1980. For electoral and fiscal reasons, the welfare state that had been developed during the previous decades in that country was also severely criticized, and free market theses were vigorously reaffirmed. In this context, proposals were made to reduce the bureaucratic apparatus and its "heavy" regulatory interference.

The neo-conservative approach, however, sought to reduce the state's functions, rather than to renew the way in which these functions were fulfilled. Moreover, to a certain extent this approach was a rhetorical instrument rather than a real policy. Thus, the more significant changes actually began with President Clinton. The trigger for reform was the National Government Performance Review Act, voted in 1993. The bases for this reform were taken to a great extent from Osborne and Gaebler's 1992 book, *Reinventing Government*, which established goals such as "steering" rather than "rowing," empowering rather than serving, encouraging competition among service suppliers, and developing an enterprising, anticipating, decentralized, results-oriented government that focused on costumers and markets (Osborne and Gaebler 1992). Although this creed had multiple goals and developed unevenly owing to the politically fragmented u.s. system, by and large it specified, ordered, completed, and encouraged the NPM agenda internationally.

The following administration (of George W. Bush) would continue this tendency to transform the career service and make it more flexible. The new Department of Homeland Security, for instance, was exempted from civil service regulations and adopted more flexible hiring practices. Some u.s. states have also sought to relax or even abandon the civil service system.

Although the NPM soon became known throughout the world, it is important not to overstate its scope. To begin with, the implementation of the reforms, both in England and in the United States, did not entail the disappearance of career civil services. Even though agencies relaxed their hiring methods and opened competition to candidates external to the civil service, this did not mean that such countries abandoned merit entry in most public administration offices, especially in the central government. Moreover, post-Thatcher governments in England would gradually attenuate the intensity of these reforms and actually reorient their efforts towards rather modernizing-type strategies (involving rather incremental changes).

On the other hand, although a number of authors, institutions, and governments saw the NPM as the next frontier in administrative reform, some analysts and civil servants – either from the same countries that started the reforms or from other ones – voiced their doubts about its real contribution to government efficiency. They even talked about possible negative effects on the public sector's motivation, governance, professionalism, legality, coordination, and even efficiency (Hood 1991; Peters 2004). NPM was also criticized for viewing people as "customers" instead of as "citizens."

The aforementioned problems, together with the weight of their own administrative traditions and cultures, led certain countries, such as Germany and France, to receive NPM rather unfavorably. In these cases, the stability, legality, and centralization principles of the career service remained largely unchanged, and the creation of autonomous executive agencies made little progress (Pollitt and Bouckaert 2004), for the most part, because of the government philosophy and culture of those countries. In France and Germany, says Konig (1997), the idea of NPM collided with a number of cultural premises specific to the European "continental" countries, where the state and the law have traditionally carried a much larger weight.

Thus, France has continued with its own concept and rhetoric of administrative reform, while focusing on modernization and decentralization. Several reform attempts have caused large strikes (Konig 1997), like those in 1995 and 2002, and, more recently, in 2007. Even though more attention has been given to newer, NPM-type issues, such as performance assessment, most of the machinery of a centralized civil service has remained unchanged (Uvalle 2000).

In relation to Germany, Pollitt and Bouckaert (2004) mention that constitutional and federal structures, as well as tradition, make any radical institutional reform difficult. A change will hardly be uniform, since German management is extremely diverse and complex. The central government has only a modest role in the direct management of public services. Most public policy areas, such as education and the police, are managed by the states (which possess considerable power and autonomy) and local authorities. The federal administration's role is limited to designing laws, and it bears little relation to the direct provision of services, which makes administrative reforms difficult.

On the other hand, the German public administration is characterized by a classical bureaucratic model, largely emphasizing legality and regulation, that belongs to a cultural tradition dating back to the early eighteenth century. The constitutional status of public servants will hardly change in a substantial way (partly because many members of Parliament are also public servants). Thus, the impact of NPM in Germany has been minor and quite differentiated (Uvalle 2000). This more cautious model, which values the essential principles of the civil service but gradually improves it with elements such as performance assessment, is what Pollitt and Bouckaert (2004) call modernizing (although according to them there can be two versions of it: the neo-Weberian and the participative).

It could be said that the existence of the modernizing model, along with the criticism of the marketizing model, has led in the first years of the twenty-first century to a revaluation, maybe even an assertion, of the civil service model, even though one relatively transformed or supplemented by principles such as performance assessment, job "certainty" rather than "permanence," and an increased accountability.

ADMINISTRATIVE REFORM IN MEXICO

Background to the Reform

Until 2003, Mexico did not have a merit civil service. Although the idea had been latent since the early twentieth century, it had never been implemented either at the federal, state, or local levels of government. After serious scandals of corruption and government inefficiency, leading to the 1982 economic crisis, President Miguel de la Madrid (1982–88) assessed the possibility of establishing a civil service system, but he discarded the idea on the grounds that it could strengthen the power of unions (Pardo 1991; Guerrero 2001). The next president (Carlos Salinas 1988–94) had a sort of patron-client view of the public service and therefore did not even consider such reform. However, his government ended again with corruption and inefficiency scandals and a severe economic crisis.

Thus his successor, Ernesto Zedillo (1994–2000), considered the idea once again, this time more seriously. During the mid–1990s, some articles specifically proposing a civil service were published (especially significant were two at that time: Pardo 1995 and Méndez 1995), and the idea gradually gained public recognition. In the end, however, it was discarded again by the president, this time owing to disagreements between the Ministry of the Treasury, which proposed a centralizing and rather "old-fashioned" project, and the Ministry of the Comptroller, whose project was more flexible, performance-oriented, and decentralized. The economic crisis of 1994–95 also presented an obstacle (Guerrero 2001; Heredia 2002; Arellano 2003).

It is important to note that all these presidents belonged to the Partido Revolucionario Institucional, or PRI (Institutional Revolutionary Party), which had been in power since 1929, usually with large majorities in Congress. Therefore, the Mexican system was usually thought of as authoritarian, and a merit civil service did not fit with it very well (Guerrero 2001).

Still, as I said, in the mid–1990s the proposal gained recognition on the public agenda, and it reappeared among the reform offers of the three main candidates during the 2000 presidential campaign. Although Zedillos' government had not been marked by corruption scandals and did not end in economic crisis, by then the PRI's lengthy political background had perpetuated the government's image as a rather inefficient and clientistic institution.

Partly because of the discredit the governing PRI had accumulated through the last decades of the twentieth century, victory in the 2000 presidential elections went, for the first time in Mexican history, to a candidate from a different party: Vicente Fox, of the Partido Acción Nacional, or PAN (National Action Party). This victory was seen as a confirmation that democracy had finally reached the country. At the beginning, as part of a government with a business background (Fox himself had for many years been a high-level Coca-Cola manager), the civil service seemed to have some disadvantages. Some members of the presidential office were originally ignorant of the recent efforts at civil service reform. They had in mind the orthodox nineteenth-century civil service, which, owing to the civil servant's safe tenure, was considered as an obstacle, rather than an aid, to the president's ruling capacity (one member of the presidential office even feared that reform would "nail" civil servants to their positions). Furthermore, during the first years of Fox's government, the public agenda was overloaded with other issues.

However, in those initial years of the administration the proposals of several legislators in favor of a civil service initiative multiplied. First, a PRI senator, Carlos Rojas, put forth a professional service law initiative in October 2000. Another senator, PAN's César Jáuregui, followed in April 2002, and in October of the same year the PRD's

(Democratic Revolution Party) representative Magdalena Núñez did likewise. In this context, around the middle of 2002, after several discussions between various presidential staff members, the Presidential Office for Governmental Innovation (part of the presidential house staff), led by Ramón Muñoz, decided to support the reform and started to lobby for it among legislators. At first, having the proposal approved by the end of 2002 seemed feasible. However, once again reform efforts failed, partly because of the typically overloaded end-of-the-year legislative agenda and partly because there were still differences among some of the actors involved in the process.

To deal with this situation, the Presidential Office decided to expand the reform's supporting coalition by bringing together a group of civil servants and academics who backed the proposal. In early 2003, this group established a civil association called the Professional Service Mexican Network.

With USAID's support and in cooperation with various national and international organizations, this network put together an international forum on civil service. Many civil servants, former civil servants, and academics from throughout the world took part in the forum, which was attended by some seven hundred people. More importantly, the closing ceremony was presided over by representatives and senators from different political parties who were then able to witness the significant acceptance of and support for the establishment in Mexico of a modern professional civil service (Red Mexicana de Servicio Professional 2003).

The forum was able to show a consensus among experts and international organizations about the positive effects of the merit civil service on state institutional capacity and, more generally, on democracy. This conclusion was added to the findings of various academic and institutional studies showing that the civil service had worked well in some Mexican institutions, such as the Federal Electoral Institute (Heredia 2002; Uvalle 2000; Auditoria Superior de la Federación 2000; Martínez Puón 2005, 242).

However, for the reform to be approved it was still necessary to overcome two challenges. First, rather than being a "presidential" initiative, the reform had to "be and look like" a congressional initiative, more particularly one presented by several political parties and supported by the executive, if you will, but all in all a parliamentary initiative. Three factors contributed for this reason to the approval of the reform: the existence of initiatives presented by three legislators; the (intentional) absence of presidential initiatives on the issue; and the inclusion in presidential speeches of the right remarks at the right times. The reform's low profile had to be maintained at all costs and Congress had to know that the president agreed with it but would not take (immediate) political advantage of it.

The second challenge was to write a law based on the legislator's three initiatives, which were similar in some ways but different in others. The key to consolidating the three initiatives into one a couple of months later was the work done by the Presidential Office for Governmental Innovation, partially supported by the Ministry of the Public Function, together with some legislators and their parties.

The reform was finally approved on April 2003, with 374 votes for and none against in the House of Representatives and 93 votes for and none against in the Senate. In an overall analysis of the reform, Pardo (2005, 615) mentions three key factors leading to its endorsement: the most important parties supported it, it was discussed at the beginning of the administration, and, perhaps most importantly, it was supported by the Professional Service Mexican Network (for the importance of the latter, see also Martínez Puón 2005, 284).

THE LAW AND MEXICAN CIVIL SERVICE REGULATIONS

The civil service law established public competition for filling government job openings, the possibility of a merit-based "horizontal" career in the same position, and compulsory training and performance assessment, as well as job tenure and incentives dependent on the last two.

Six civil service positions within the central federal government were involved in the reform: analyst, department chief, under-director, area director, deputy general director, and general director (the latter is the position just below deputy secretary). Only freely appointed employees within the deputy secretaries' and secretaries' closer teams were exempted from the civil service.

The law applies to civil servants in the so-called central public administration, i.e., in federal departments or ministries. It does not apply to a number of ministries or groups that already had a civil service – such as the Ministry of Foreign Affairs or teachers or physicians – or to the decentralized public administration (consisting mainly of state-owned companies and social security institutes). Nor does it apply to "operative" state workers, such as messengers, secretaries, drivers, and so forth, who are unionized (they are subject to an orthodox regime in which they cannot be fired, but they have very low salaries and no possibility of promotion). Thus, as of now the reform includes around 37,000 federal government positions out of a total of about 1,500,000 (of which more than 600,000 are in the central government). However, this group represents the core of central public administration, as its members have comparatively very high salaries (actually equal to or even higher than those in several developed countries) (Carrillo and Guerrero 2002), and they are the ones who establish and/or guide most of the country's public policies.

The organization and operation of the civil service was entrusted to the Ministry of the Public Function, together with ad hoc committees in the other ministries. The civil service law provided that these committees would choose and operate the specific instruments of the service, while the Ministry of the Public Function was given the task of developing general regulations and promoting the service through strategies of cultural change – rather than through a usually inefficient centralism – besides, of course, supervising and rectifying its operation in case of deviations. An expert unit was created within the ministry, the Federal Human Resources and Professional Service Unit, to be directly responsible for the implementation of the service.

The designers of the Mexican civil service knew quite well that a merit civil service offers advantages such as equality of opportunity and greater efficiency than the former spoils system, less extensive politicization of government programs, and a more extensive institutional memory. As was mentioned before, they also had in mind civil service studies of Mexican organizations showing that it was possible to successfully implement the service in Mexico. However, they were also aware of the NPM's criticism leveled against the traditional (i.e., nineteenth-century) civil service.

Because of this, they sought to establish a "second-generation" merit system that would promote "democratic governance" by balancing the Weberian values of professional service and some NPM elements (Méndez 2004). To give just some examples, regulation and supervision of a central regulatory unit was balanced with the decentralization of operations towards ministries; medium- and long-term planning was balanced with periodic revision of plans; competency- and merit-based entry and the opening of all positions to external candidates was balanced with a career civil service; and merit based-entry (i.e., merit evaluation) was balanced through the introduction of a (limited) veto capacity on the part of the immediate boss when selecting a winner among the competition finalists (although this may seem an odd measure, and it has caused some debate, in the Mexican context it had the purpose of avoiding lesser accountability of bosses who might claim that their collaborators were "imposed" on them). Moreover, position profiles included specific technical abilities but also some managerial and more general abilities; career and training plans were established vertically (towards higher positions), but also horizontally (towards higher grades within the same position), to encourage motivation across public administration.

Regarding performance assessment, a strict and effective evaluation system (with only two opportunities to pass the assessment, as well as group and individual goals) was introduced, but there were also provisions to make it functional and just (assessed individuals had to know their goals beforehand; rights and responsibilities were clarified; the possibility of appealing the evaluation or entry results was guaranteed).

The reform designers tried to establish a sanction system that would be strict and timely, on the one hand, but also fair, on the other (also a certain separation was sought between authorities "revising" cases and those deciding on them in legal or sanction procedures). Finally, the law clearly specified that the implementation of the civil service should be gradual, although it established that all its parts should be operative by the end of 2006. It must also be said, however, that the civil service law resulted from a negotiation between political parties and government branches. Some issues were therefore not solved adequately. For instance, although some wanted the implementation of the system to be monitored by a plural body, open to society and even political parties, only an advisory council was approved, one with no real influence and mainly composed of officers of the ministries.

In order to implement the law, the Federal Human Resources and Professional Service Unit was established during the second semester of 2003, along with the Service Advisory Council and the technical committees of the different ministries. After studying various professional services from throughout the world and reaching a compromise among the different ministries, the professional service unit developed the law's operative statute, which was signed by the president on

31 March 2004. This statute followed and strengthened the above-mentioned "balanced" design.

After the law's approval, government positions started to be filled through public and open competitions. From that moment to late 2006, when Vicente Fox's administration ended, the various parts of the civil service system were gradually implemented. The next section will describe some of the achievements and problems of the reform's implementation.

ASSESSMENT OF THE REFORM'S IMPLEMENTATION

In spite of the balanced design and all the political support the reform had achieved, during the following years the law was implemented in a rather centralized, inefficient, and incomplete way. Unfortunately, some of the risks predicted by a number of academics occurred (e.g., Arellano 2003; Arellano et al. 2003). First, the Ministry of the Public Function turned into a centralizing, an over-regulating, and, even worse, an operating unit (even though the law and the statute had clearly established a decentralized operative frame). This was in turn the result of two mistakes: the secretary and deputy secretary tried, first, to take part in the implementation and operation of every civil service process, instead of giving a minimal managerial autonomy to the Professional Service Unit, and, second, they pushed to implement all parts of the service in a very rigid, quick, and almost simultaneous way, instead of in a more gradual and decentralized fashion.

This too short-term, centralist, and exhaustive view led to several wrong decisions. To begin with, it led to a faulty selection of instruments for the operation of the civil service. For example, the first stage of entry competitions – the résumé examination – was done through a software system (Trabajaen) that did not work properly and generated distrust and discontent, since it was controlled as a "black box" by the Ministry of the Public Function. Moreover, the job competence assessment systems that were centrally imposed on all ministries for entry exams (AMITAI, PPP, and CDG) did not measure competencies adequately, so that in many cases the selected candidates were not suitable for their positions.

Another consequence of such an approach was that the implementation strategy – which provided for a division of functions between the Public Function Ministry (to regulate, evaluate, and sanction) and the rest of the ministries (to implement)- was broken. By concentrating on too many tasks, the ministry was not able to fulfill any of them well (it could not regulate and implement because it lacked the capacity to do both; it could not initiate sanctions against practices not based on merit, because obviously it would not sanction itself). One clear indication of this problem was the important delay during the first years (2004–5) in the issuing of several key regulations.

Besides, practically since the competitive entry system was established, competition has frequently been avoided, mainly by two mechanisms: one, surreptitiously by giving the exams to the favored candidate and, two, by resorting to article 34 of the law, which establishes that competitive entry can be avoided, exceptionally, in cases of extreme need, e.g., during earthquakes and other natural disasters. (In addition, 263 positions were taken out of the merit civil service between June 2004 and October 2006, although in these cases the change was justified by their special features (Secretaría de la Función Pública 2006c, 76)).

Use of the first mechanism obviously is not reported, and there is no way to know its magnitude. As to the second, in the last three years of the Fox administration there were, in total, 2,290 article 34 appointments (2004:1,435; 2005:422; 2006:433) (Secretaría de la Función Pública 2005, 21; 2006a, 159; and 2006b, 90). In the subsequent Calderón administration (2006–12), that number increased significantly: between January 2007 and July 2008 there were almost 7,000 such appointments (1,979 in January–June 2007; 4,879 in September 2007–July 2008; plus an unknown number in July–August 2007)(Secretaría de la Función Pública 2007, 100, and 2008a, 64).

Thus, contrary to what is stipulated in the law, non-merit appointments have not been "exceptional" at all: the number of non-merit Fox appointments (2,290) was almost the same as the number of merit ones (2,904 appointments were made through an open competition from April 2004 to September 2006) (Secretaría de la Función Pública 2006b, 90). In turn, the almost 7,000 non-merit Calderón appointments made in the first year and a half of that administration (January 2007–July 2008) amounted to more than twice those made during the last three years of the previous administration; also, they amounted to more than twice as many merit-based appointments reported for the same initial period of Calderón administration (a total of 2,486: 472 for January–July 2007 plus 2,014 for August 2007–July 2008) (Secretaría de la Función Pública 2007, 100 and 2008a, 64). These 7,000 non-merit appointments represent about one-fifth of the 37,000 government positions subject to the 2003 law, and about the same number (7,000) of civil servants who so far have become "career civil servants" (either by winning a competition or fulfilling certain legal requirements). Although article 34 appointments are temporary – lasting up to ten months – appointees have the opportunity to learn enough of the job to more easily win the competition when it comes, thus violating the principles of merit and equal opportunity.

All these problems reveal the difficulties inherent in passing from a culture of favoritism to a merit-based culture in three or four years, but they also testify to the Ministry of the Public Function's lack of will and/or capacity to supervise and correct non-merit entry procedures.

Eduardo Romero, the secretary of the ministry of the public function from 2003 to 2005, acknowledged that "the hiring process was not as prompt as we wanted it to be … so that … we are proposing for December of this year to fill the openings in no more than two months" (Romero 2005, 26). The secretary points out that inefficiencies in the hiring process are the result of departmental problems in defining staff profiles and structures, but it must be added that the excessive regulation applied by the Public Function Ministry to this task is partly to blame for the inefficiencies.

At least in the beginning, the combination of all these factors led to an incredibly high number of competitions being declared void. According to figures published by the secretary of the public function (Romero 2005, 25), of a total of 1,973 competitions held between April 2004 and April 2005, 584, or 30 percent, were declared void. In other words, practically one in three competitions was declared void. This situation had a number of effects on the adequate provision of services and the waste of public resources, since often, declaring a competition void was a way of appointing by article 34 an unsuccessful but favored candidate.

Besides, applying the performance assessment system has been difficult, and the resulting marks have predominantly been high (usually around 80 percent of candidates have received "excellent" marks). At the end of Vicente Fox's administration in September 2006 – three years after the approval of the Career Professional Service Law – no civil servant had been fired because of a poor performance assessment (Secretaría de la Función Pública 2006b, 94). This problem of rather high marks in performance assessment systems has been very common in other Latin American countries (Echebarría 2006), although at the same time the overall difficulty of designing and implementing such systems in any country must be acknowledged (Bouckaert and Halligan 2008).

As for the training, it has been based on electronic courses (Mexico does not have a national training school for the public sector), it has had little or no orientation toward promoting the development of skills (Dussauge 2007), and it has operated through some poorly recognized training centres. Furthermore, at least at the beginning, the training system was not connected with the certification system. Civil servants were therefore taking courses that would not give them the job competence certifications required of them by the law. Thus, because the law required civil servants hired before the reform to pass some courses to become "career civil servants," these problems prevented most of them from becoming career civil servants towards the end of the Fox administration. Later on, career civil service appointments were closed because of the upcoming change of government. Thus, by 2006 only around 3,500 public servants were career public servants. By 2007, there were only slightly more than 7,000 career public servants – out of nearly 37,000 positions governed by the civil service law (Secretaría de la Función Pública 2008b, 18–19).

In addition, software systems were used to integrate all staff management systems, which caused further problems because the Ministry of the Public Function was not able to operate all systems at once, and the software that was supposed to help was instead more of a hindrance (for example, it constantly crashed and mixed up the contents of the different systems).

It must be added that besides wanting to implement every part of the career civil service agenda at once, the Ministry of the Public Function was in charge of an even larger administrative modernization agenda, which included other goals such as transparency and deregulation, as well as cost-saving programs, e-government, and government quality programs (Dussauge 2007). All the aforementioned factors led to a marked dissatisfaction among government departments and citizens regarding the implementation of the civil service reform, and generally to its delegitimation.

This may have been one of the reasons why several departments chose to withdraw from the career civil service. Thousands of civil servants in the Ministries of Foreign Affairs, Public Security, the Navy, and some decentralized bodies of other ministries were withdrawn from the system, so that by 2007, as already noted, only around 37,000 positions were included within the merit civil service. This figure is close to half the one previously published by the Ministry of the Public Function itself (62,000 public servants) (Romero 2005, 23).

In 2005, the Federal Auditing Agency considered that the Program for the Career Professional Service did not include goals and indicators that would have allowed for an adequate assessment of the application of the regulating principles for the civil service, i.e., the principles of legality, efficiency, objectivity, quality, impartiality, equality, and competence. The agency made thirty-five recommendations, many of them pertaining to the lack of application of such principles, a lack of awareness of existing civil service positions, and thus a lack of supervision on merit procedures for entry. It also detected some cases of civil servants who had entered without passing the entry exams (Auditoria Superior 2005).

In 2004, the Inter American Development Bank (IDB) carried out an assessment of personnel management practices in Mexico. The results involved low and intermediate marks in the evaluation scale used, mainly because the implementation of the service was in its initial stage, positions were not aligned to objectives, there was no system to identify low performance, there were problems in the operation of some of its parts, and the personnel system of operative (unionized) public employees had not yet been improved (Iacoviello and Rodriguez 2006).

In late 2007 the Ministry of the Public Function, already under the new president Felipe Calderon, published a new statute decentralizing responsibilities to the ministries. The new authorities argued that the new statute was necessary because its predecessor had been too centralizing. Changing some aspects of the old statute was probably necessary, since it could be argued that the merit system needed to enter a new stage. However, it is worth noticing that the excessive centralization had not been caused by the first statute – which involved, following the law, a decentralized framework (Martínez Puón 2005, 308)- but by the operative guidelines developed by the Public Function Ministry, as well as by the overall way in which the system had been implemented. For this reason, it is believed that the real purpose of the new authorities was not to decentralize the operation of the system but to reduce its scope and then to "decentralize" the responsibility of a "lighter" implementation to the ministries.

This assumption is confirmed by two facts. First, the second statute removed several mechanisms aimed at promoting merit principles: it removed career civil servants from the ministries' civil service committees, allowed for more closed-entry competitions, reduced even more the role of the Advisory Council, reduced the requirements to be satisfied by public servants who had already been hired and wished to become career civil servants, reduced the number of performance evaluations, and so on. It is also confirmed by the above-mentioned large number of article 34 appointments made in the months following the publication of the new statute and the still large number of void competitions (1,366 out of 3,380 by July 2008) (Secretaría de la Función Pública 2008a, 64). Along the same lines, it is also worth mentioning the large number of civil servants subject to the civil service law who, in the first thirteen months of the new administration, were removed from their positions (close to 1,000: 295 in December 2006, and 670 in 2007) (Secretaría de la Función Pública 2008b, 18) apparently for reasons unrelated to merit (reports acknowledge that there were almost no cases of officers fired as a result of evaluations).

In 2008, the Public Function Ministry presented the Management Improvement Program, one of whose main objectives is to improve the performance measurement systems of the federal government agencies, in order to facilitate the improvement of services but also to better allocate budgetary expenditures. Perhaps it is significant that this program does not speak of improving the merit service but of "implementing successful human resources management policies, models and practices" (Secretaría de la Función Pública 2008c, 32).

SOME POSSIBLE EXPLANATIONS FOR THE REFORM AND ITS IMPLEMENTATION

As I have already mentioned, the first question this chapter tries to answer is, how can we explain the introduction of a merit civil service in Mexico? Kingdon's (2003) "streams" approach is especially useful in providing some possible answers. Thus, we could say that in the Mexican case, the inclusion in the government agenda of the civil service reform and its approval was the result of the concurrence of three streams. The first was the problem stream. Problems such as corruption, inefficiency, and patron-client practices had been present in

Mexican public administration for a long time. They were highlighted by the PAN government that reached power in 2000 (it wanted to distinguish itself from the previous era of PRI governments). Thus, they were very much present in the public mind by the time the civil service law began to be discussed.

The second stream was the solution stream. Although several experts and legislators had already been encouraging the reform, it did not advance until a proposal combining traditional and new principles (i.e., merit entry and performance assessment) was accepted as a good solution to the corruption and inefficiency problems, as well as to the related problem of lack of institutional memory (which was present during the PRI years but was expected to increase with the more frequent government changes associated with the democratization of the country). Finally, the third stream mentioned by Kingdon is the political one. In this regard, it is important to stress that by 2003 the representatives elected in 2000 were reaching their last year without having made any worthy reforms (representatives in Mexico have a three-year term). Thus, internal and external pressures to approve reforms increased, opening an opportunity for initiating "intermediate-type" reforms such as a merit civil service.

I have argued that the difficulties involved in getting approval for major reforms in Mexico largely result from the combination of a presidential regime with a multi-party system. In my view, this combination hinders the predominance of one party in Congress and helps to level the distribution of seats among the main political parties, producing a "divided government" with a clear division of power between the executive and the legislative branches (Méndez 2007a). The possibility of change also tends to be reduced by the greater number of actors (and often the greater ideological differentiation) of multi-party systems. However, if in this context opposition parties do not wish to support major reforms that go against their particular ideologies or might be used by the party in the presidency to win the next election, often they do not want to be seen either as "boycotting" or as "inefficient" parties, a situation that – I argue – tends to result in "soft" or "intermediate-type" reforms. The civil service reform was brought forth precisely as a reform of intermediate importance, as opposed to the so-called structural reforms (such as the energy, the fiscal, or the labor reforms, which were actually not approved during Fox's administration – nor have they been approved during the current government).

Furthermore, Geddes (1994) has pointed out that power equality among political forces in Congress favors the introduction of a merit civil service, since in this case the cost of such a reform in terms of patronage loss is distributed equally among all parties. She presents some cases – including that of the United States in the late nineteenth century – as evidence supporting the relation between "political equality" and civil service reforms.

It is worth mentioning that in addition to the three streams, Kingdon underlines the importance of a policy entrepreneur joining them all. However, in the case of the Mexican civil service reform, there were, three of them (i.e., the above-mentioned Muñoz, Rojas, and Jáuregui). So, perhaps we should instead talk of a sort of advocacy coalition (Sabatier and Jenkins-Smith 1993), which began to be developed in 2002 within the Office of the Presidency and ended up including legislators of different parties, as well as university professors.

Following Geddes (1994, 154), we could say that the president's incentive to approve the reform came from the fact that he did not have a very deep relation with his own party and thus that he probably favored initiatives that benefited the public servants he had already appointed (many of whom did not belong to any party) and that therefore would strengthen his personal support base. In turn, opposition parties saw in the reform a means to restrict the ruling president's power to appoint more civil servants from his own party or group.

Although at the beginning some members of the coalition feared that the civil service would turn out to be too rigid, they afterwards resolved their doubts with a solution that balanced two different views of public administration (that of a career civil service and that of NPM) and that tried to retain the advantages and avoid the disadvantages of each of them. The coalition included actors who were familiarized both with the civil service traditions of developed countries and with the strong criticisms directed towards such traditions by the NPM (as well as with the problems and limitations of the NPM itself).

It must be stressed that an important factor was the strategic view adopted by the Presidential Office and the president himself. On the one hand, as I have already said, rather than being a "presidential" initiative, the reform had to "be and look like" a congressional initiative, more particularly one presented by several political parties: an initiative supported by the executive if you will, but all in all a parliamentary one. The fact that the president did not present a related initiative of his own was therefore important (he could have done so, since in the Mexican presidential regime the executive has that capacity).

Finally, as I have also said, it was crucial that the president made the right remarks at the right times in his speeches: the reform's low profile had to be maintained at all costs if its perception by political actors as an intermediate-type reform was to be maintained, and the Congress had to know that the president agreed with it, but that it was not part of his main political agenda and that he would not use it for his own (immediate) political advantage. In short, the coalition was of fundamental importance in the development of an agreed-upon solution and in the strategic management of the timing and methods of the reform. I believe that from these (hypothetical) explanations it can be seen that factors related both to institutional arrangements (mainly within the third stream) and to the nature, capacities, and positions of specific actors (mainly in the first and second streams) were at play.

The second question this chapter tries to answer is, how can we explain the fact that, in spite of a balanced design and the good intentions of political leaders, the implementation of the civil service reform actually turned out to be so centralized, incomplete, and inefficient? This question is probably harder to answer than the first one, but I would suggest at least three possible, preliminary explanatory factors.

The first factor is related to the characteristics of some of the political actors involved, such as the secretary and deputy secretary of the public function, whose "micro-administrative" centralizing and overreaching managerial style led to the incomplete, distorted, and inefficient implementation of the law, since it did not allow for the delegation of tasks to the professional service unit and the civil service committees of the ministries. A vicious circle emerged in which the inefficient implementation of the civil service law strengthened the tendency among many civil servants to avoid its application. In fact, in 2006 it even generated initiatives in Congress to reduce its scope (*El Universal*, 19 April 2006), initiatives that so far have not passed. As we saw, the current administration of Felipe Calderon decentralized the implementation of the law, but, as the record shows, the purpose was in fact to avoid implementation.

A second factor is the strong politicized or personalized culture still prevailing among many Mexican civil servants and politicians.

This personalism, in turn, can be related to various factors, such as the strong interpersonal distrust characteristic of Mexican culture (a recent survey revealed that 80 percent of Mexicans do not trust their fellow citizens (Butcher 2007)) and the client culture still prevalent in Mexican political parties, as well as to the tendency to interpret rules flexibly (paradoxically augmented by the overregulated administrative environment that was established to avoid such flexibility).

The third, institutional factor is related to the kind of organization that was responsible for the implementation of the reform – i.e., a classic bureaucratic organization that was part of the executive (the Ministry of the Public Function) and that blocked the adoption of a merit-based and transparent approach. This problem might have been avoided if the Civil Service Council had been put together in a more plural and open way, or perhaps this reform should have been undertaken by a more autonomous agency, an agency external to the central government structure.

For example, there have been other civil service frameworks in Mexico where merit procedures for entry have been followed to a greater degree, thanks to the presence of more powerful citizen-involving or autonomous supervising councils (for example, in the Mexican Federal Electoral Institute). Also, when agencies have been given greater autonomy, institutional reforms have been implemented more effectively, as was the case with the Access to Information Law and the Mexican Federal Institute for Transparency and Information Access (a reform passed around the same time as the civil service reform). Thus, a further step for the Mexican civil service could be the establishment of an independent agency to manage the merit exam for entry into the public sector (Martínez Puón 2005, 309)(as is, for instance, the case to some extent in the less client-oriented – although also less "performance-oriented" – Spanish civil service).

Thus, although the centralizing positions of some actors and the prevailing client culture no doubt affected the implementation of the reform, I would still argue that institutional design matters and that the reform might have advanced to a greater extent had there been a different institutional design.

CONCLUSION

In this chapter I have tried mainly to answer two questions. First, how have the administrative ideas or reforms in developed countries influenced reforms in a developing country like Mexico? To answer this question, I discussed the administrative changes in the developed countries, concluding that there have been two prevailing trends: a modernizing approach and a marketizing/minimizing approach. It would seem that the Mexican reform that began in 2003 has been closer to the modernizing approach, at least to the extent that it involved a "modernized" civil service that introduced some NPM elements (such as performance assessment) without introducing all of them (for example, it did not introduce executive agencies or subcontracting, as was the case in other Latin American countries such as Brazil or Chile).

The second question was, what factors could explain the introduction of the reform, on the one hand, and its evolution, on the other? To explain its introduction, I turned to Kingdon's streams approach, within which I highlighted several institutional and agent-related factors. To explain why the reform failed to evolve very successfully, I also mentioned both institutional factors (the bureaucratic organization in charge) and actor-related factors (the overly ambitious and centralizing mind-set of its higher authorities). Although perhaps related, the two factors did not necessarily cause each other.

It must be recognized that the approval of a merit civil service law in Mexico was a great step forward. First, clientelistic practices, which were seen as natural before, can now be identified and (at least) criticized. Second, it must be recognized that by 2008 many of the close to ten thousand competitions have led to merit-based appointments and that in general civil servants in key positions in Mexico now have more access to training and are to a greater extent subject to performance evaluations. Furthermore, as Ingraham (1995, 141) once said of the United States, it is necessary to separate the pitfalls of a merit system from the sound principles and the importance for good government of the concept of merit itself.

However, although the Mexican reform was originally conceived of as a starting point for the further professionalization of the remaining areas of public administration, its inefficient implementation has led observers to question not only its progress but even whether anything has been achieved. There is no doubt that the consolidation of a true merit civil service in Mexico will still take several years. Different comparative analyses (Ramió and Salvador i Serna 2007; Echebarría 2006; Grindle 2003) show that civil service reforms are complex and hard to implement. On the practical side, at least two lessons can be learned from the Mexican case. First, because clientelistic practices are usually strong when a merit system is initiated, the presence within it of true citizen bodies that are really able to monitor the implementation process is crucial. As Grindle (2003, 105) warns, "reforms need interested publics to support them." At the same time, as Ingraham and Getha-Taylor underline (2005, 656), getting the support of the people for the reforms may be the greatest challenge of all.

Second, when a country does not yet have a developed civil service, it would be advisable to first build the foundations, working mainly on some parts of the civil service (merit entry, training, and basic sanctions) and allowing these to consolidate before developing the remaining pieces (planning, performance assessment, and performance-based incentive systems, perhaps in that order). Although the Mexican merit system was devised more or less in this way, for the above-mentioned personal and institutional reasons it was unfortunately not how it was implemented. (And, since that means that the merit system has not yet been consolidated in Mexico, the Management Improvement Program of 2008, which attempts to relate performance to the budget, is no doubt worrisome.) Thus, we could say that for a country introducing a civil service, it would be better to focus first on the goals of legality, honesty, merit (as opposed to patronage), and procedural standardization for equal treatment of citizens (Peters 2004; Ramió and Salvador i Serna 2007; Bouckaert and Halligan 2008, 177). Once these goals have been achieved, the aspects that are more closely related to NPM could be put in place.

In a similar vein, we could refer to "contingency approaches" that may allow a better match between different kinds of organizational structures (such as the civil service) and different public situations or functions. In a particular version of a contingency approach that I have developed, I have argued that a merit civil service may work better for functions whose policy goals and means are comparatively clear (functions like health policy) or for certain general state functions (like justice) than for others (Méndez 2007b). Needless to say, contingency approaches such as this offer no panacea, and reformers around the world will always face a difficult task when dealing with institutional change.

NOTE

Research-Professor and Coordinator of the Political Science Program at El Colegio de Mexico. As chief of the Unit of Analysis of the Presidency (2000–2003) and chief of the Federal Human Resources and Professional Service Unit (2003–2004), the author participated in the design, lobbying, and implementation of the civil service reform described in this chapter. Thus, some of the statements in this chapter are based on his "direct observation" as a participant.

8

Western Models and Administrative Reform in China: Pragmatism and the Search for Modernity

JOHN P. BURNS

INTRODUCTION

Political leaders play a key role in the initiation and implementation of public management reform (Pollitt and Boukhaert 2000). In various contexts they perceive the need for reform, draft reform proposals, assess their feasibility, and sell them to the bureaucracy and the public. Which reforms get on a public management reform agenda depends largely on the convergence of problems, policies, and politics (Kingdon 1995). In the process leaders look around for reform ideas and in an increasingly globalized world, their search can be global. This paper examines the incentives political leaders have to investigate and adopt "Western" models of public administration in their public management reform programs, taking a developing country, China, as a case study.

Western models of public administration such as new public management (NPM) and "good governance" have had great currency. Thousands of books and articles have been written about them as part of the globalization of reform ideas. Multilateral organizations and consultants push these models, and leaders of developing countries for various reasons are encouraged to accept them. Aid of various kinds is sometimes linked to implementing these models. Thus, for example, the leaders of dependent nearly bankrupt post-communist Mongolia apparently believed that they had little choice but to accept New Zealand-style NPM pushed by the Asian Development

Bank and other donors, although the conditions for implementing
the model hardly existed. Many leaders also apparently believe that
at least symbolic acceptance of Western models is an indication
of modernity.

To a large extent reformist China has resisted these developments,
and China's communist leaders have looked with suspicion on
Western models, especially of the political system. Insofar as administrative models are tied to politics (such as the link between incre-
mentalism and political pluralism in Lindbloom) Western models of
public management are also suspect. China's very successful economic reforms have left the country in a position of economic strength,
not dependency. The Chinese Communist Party's relatively strong
organizational capacity means that the leadership has been able to
clearly articulate its own goals and policies, and to multilateral
organizations offering aid the leadership has said: "You can either
help us implement *our* goals and policies or get out of the way."

This has not always been the case in China, however. Historically,
in weak and divided China leaders borrowed heavily from the West.
In the 1920s liberal intellectuals looked to the United States and
John Dewey, while both communist and nationalist revolutionaries
looked to Marx, Lenin, and the Soviet Union. Both the CCP and the
Guomindang (Nationalist Party, Kuomintang) borrowed heavily
from Leninist principles of organization. On achieving victory in
1949, the CCP organized the state in China along Soviet lines, complete with the collectivization of agriculture, industry, commerce,
and so forth, all managed by government departments nominally
under a national five-year plan. To this day Marxism and Leninism
are enshrined in the Chinese Constitution as part of the country's
official ideology.

Given this mixed heritage, it may come as somewhat of a surprise
that leaders in contemporary China have looked to non-Marxist/
Leninist Western models of public administration. I argue that which
organizations adopt Western models depends on the incentive structure for leaders. In contemporary China, which has adopted market
mechanisms to a large extent, those institutions closest to the market,
such as state-owned enterprises (SOEs), are more likely to adopt
Western models of public administration insofar as they are adopted
internationally at all. Thus, for example, to be listed on a foreign
stock exchange, SOEs may be required to adopt some corporate
"good" governance principles.

We need other explanations for those institutions further from the market and closer to the political executive, organizations such as government bureaus. Whether or not bureaus adopt Western models of public administration depends overwhelmingly on the leadership incentive system. I argue that the incentives for leaders vary according to a leader's position and that for those in the promotion "zone" the desire for promotion fuels a search for models that can enhance their performance credentials. These models sometimes come from the West.

In this paper I examine briefly three cases in which Western models were at least considered by the Chinese leadership for the reform of bureaus. In the first case, mixed-motive top leaders motivated by a drive for modernity and economic development adopted what they perceived to be a Western civil service system, characterized by competitive selection. In the process they also considered and then discarded other features that might be considered Western, such as separate roles for politicians and bureaucrats. In the second case multilateral aid organizations pressed leaders to embrace "good" governance as a principle of governance. Chinese leaders, motivated by a mixture of altruism and self-interest, reacted cautiously at first but after considerable hesitation adapted the principle (symbols are important) and then endorsed and popularized it ("good governance with Chinese characteristics"). In the third case, Chinese leaders identified performance measurement and management techniques, part of NPM imported from the West, and adapted and then popularized them in pursuit of improved performance and accelerated promotions.

THEORETICAL CONSIDERATIONS

Given that public management reform is usually a top-down exercise, the perceptions of elites play an important role not only in defining what reforms are desirable and feasible but in shaping official value systems that determine what is possible (Pollitt and Bouckhaert 2000). Historically, the role of elites has been especially important in authoritarian China where the titular or paramount leader has played an exaggerated role. After decades of ideologically driven policy, when Deng Xiaoping came to power in 1978, he insisted on pragmatism in economic policy. "Deng earned the label [pragmatist] largely because of his Two Cat theory which suggested that he was unencumbered with ideological constraints and thus would be able to focus on efficiency as his guiding principle" (Pye 1995, 32). This is a fair evaluation of his economic policy, which relied less on markets and entrepreneurs and more on technocrats and technology. Deng's pragmatism extended to public management, but less to reform of the political system. Given his control of the centralized official personnel system, Deng's pragmatism in economic development came to be widely shared among officialdom. The Chinese elite's focus on pragmatism in economic development allowed some imports from the West so long as they "caught the mouse."[1]

Because I am interested in the incentives for officials to adopt Western models of administrative reform, we need to have some understanding of the motives of officials generally. Following Downs, I assume that officials seek to maximize their utility, where utility is defined broadly to include a variety of motives such as power, both within the bureaucracy and/or outside it, money, prestige, convenience, security, personal loyalty, pride in a job well done, a desire to serve the public interest, and a commitment to a specific program or policy (Downs 1967, 84). The first five goals may be considered manifestations of pure self-interest, while the others may be partially or even wholly altruistic (such as the desire to serve the public interest). Based on these motives, Downs derives five types of officials, two of which are purely self-interested and three others that are mixed-motive.[2] I examine each of these types.

Climbers are motivated almost exclusively by power, income, and status. For them promotion is everything, and conforming to or manipulating the promotion rules is all-important. Given the rules and the leaders' pragmatic approach to economic development, climbers are the most likely among the five types to adopt Western models of administrative reform under certain conditions (for example, if the rules promote officials based on "performance" and Western models are perceived to improve performance).

Conservers are motivated by convenience and security. They seek to maintain their current power, income, and prestige, rather than to maximize them. They resist reform if it has implications for their power position. Although relatively unlikely, they could be involved in pushing Western models of administrative reform if keeping their current position depended on it. For this reason many officials have paid lip service to the performance management movement once officials in Beijing made it clear that performance of a kind mattered.

Mixed-motive officials combine self-interest and altruism. They include *zealots*, *advocates*, and *statesmen*. *Zealots* are motivated by loyalty to relatively narrow policies or concepts. They seek power for its own sake and to affect the policies to which they are loyal, which become sacred policies. Examples in China might include Cao Siyuan, "father of China's bankruptcy law." Cao spent decades lobbying the party for a bankruptcy law for state-owned enterprises and eventually succeeded. Zealots do not push general public management reform but narrow reforms to which they are loyal.

Advocates are motivated by loyalty to a broader set of functions or to a broader organization than zealots. They seek power because they want a significant influence on policies. Some Chinese officials, such as Gu Jiaqi, former deputy head of the General Office of the State Public Sector Reform Commission (*zhongyang jigou bianzhi weiyuanhui bangongshi*) as he became more powerful arguably sought to influence "administrative reform work." As officials are promoted to the most senior positions, such as that of vice premier or state councillor or to membership in the party's Politburo, they become responsible for broad policy areas (*xitong*), which could encourage them to become advocates (Lieberthal 2004).

Statesmen are motivated by loyalty to society and seek power so that they can have a significant influence on national policies. "They are altruistic to an important degree because their loyalty is to the 'general welfare' as they see it," and as such, they resemble the theoretical bureaucrat of public administration textbooks (Downs 1967, 88–9). Arguably Deng Xiaoping in our narrative was a statesman in this sense. His interest in economic development and his pragmatic orientation made him open to solutions from various sources, including the West.

Downs's typology of officials serves our purposes relatively well. I argue that promotion is a strong incentive for most Chinese officials, and therefore especially climbers among these types have had the incentive to adopt Western models of public administration. They are constrained, however, by promotion rules.

Efficient organizations are those that provide incentives for employees to work hard. Incentives are distributed based on performance, as with performance-based pay, or where that is not possible, as is often the case in the public sector, incentives are distributed in the form of performance-based promotion (Milgrom and Roberts 1992). Given reform China's efficiency and economic development orientation, we could reasonably expect that official promotion rules would stress performance.

In 1980 paramount leader Deng Xiaoping laid down the reform direction for the civil service. The cadre corps was to be made younger, better-educated, and better-qualified professionally. To this end, retirement rules since 1982 have required men to retire at age sixty and women at age fifty-five for all but the most senior positions. Thus, for those approaching retirement, a "climber" strategy is no longer rational. If climbers among our purely self-interested official types are the most likely to adopt Western administrative reforms under certain conditions, then we should look for officials who are still in the promotion game. These officials are found in large numbers in local government.

Officially, promotion is based on performance (merit). According to the Civil Servants Law officials should be promoted based on the principles of "both moral integrity and ability, and appointment of those on merits, paying special attention to work accomplishments" (Civil Servants Law). Officials should also have served for a certain number of years in two positions at a lower grade (an experience, or seniority-type, of criterion). Although officials should normally be promoted one grade at a time, high flyers, defined mainly in terms of performance, may skip a grade.

In practice the assessment of performance of Chinese officials may depend on annual performance appraisal results and on performance in various tests and interviews. In the 1990s officials established elaborate lists of performance targets that local leaders, especially, were assessed against, the most important of which was growth of GDP. The performance criteria, while heavily weighted toward economic indicators, also included measures such as the extent to which officials achieved the one-child-per-couple target and the extent to which all children received nine years of compulsory education (see box 8.1).

Studies have shown that local leaders whose counties, districts, or provinces do well on the economic indicators, especially indicators of economic growth and remittances of taxes, tend to have a greater chance of promotion.[3] The emphasis on economic criteria has had some perverse consequences, however, with officials using whatever means, including violating labor and environmental protection laws or illegally accumulating huge public debt, to achieve their goals. In 2006 some local governments began experimenting

---

BOX 8.1

National Guidelines for Performance Criteria of Local Party
and Government Leaders, 1991

- Gross national product
- Gross value of industrial output
- Gross value of agricultural output
- Gross value of output of township- and village-run enterprises
- National income per capita
- Rural income per capita
- Taxes and profits remitted
- Fiscal income
- Labor productivity of state and collective enterprises
- Procurement of agricultural and subsidiary products
- Retail sales
- Infrastructure investment realized
- National population growth rate
- Grain output
- Local budgetary income
- Local budgetary expenditures
- Forested area
- Nine-year compulsory education completion rate

Source: Whiting (2001, 103).

---

with new performance criteria that reduced the weight given to economic growth and broadened the criteria to include such things as the extent to which young people had received fifteen years of education and the extent to which local government had guaranteed the basic livelihood of farmers who had lost their farmland to development (Lin 2008).

Promotion rules in practice also include seniority, bribery (the purchase of offices), and the influence of personal relations (*guanxi*) with more senior leaders. Because these strategies do not involve adopting Western models of administrative reform, I do not discuss them here. In this paper I assume that promotion is mostly performance-based and that this provides the key incentive for leaders to scan for methods and styles that can boost their performance credentials. Western models of administrative reform may be among the techniques they consider. In the more pragmatic atmosphere of Deng's China, mixed-motive officials may also adopt Western models of administrative reform.

CASE STUDIES

I turn now to a discussion of three cases in which Western models were adapted for China's administrative reforms. In the first case leaders of the central government, having determined that their system for managing officials was inefficient, introduced a competitive selection mechanism, which they perceived to be Western. They also considered a new public management-like reform – separate roles for politicians and bureaucrats – but ultimately rejected it. Statesmen were involved in these policy decisions. Conservers resisted the change and climbers scrambled onto the bandwagon of the Western model after central policy leaders endorsed it. In the second case multilateral organizations introduced the notion of "good governance" to the Chinese leadership, which was initially skeptical. Advocates among the central leadership then picked it up, adapted it, and popularized it. Climbers scrambled on board. In the third case, given promotion rules that emphasized performance, climbers in local government picked up the Western notion of performance management (for example, performance pledges) to enhance their performance credentials. Climbers in the central government then pushed the reforms there as well.

Civil Service Reform

If we take a long view, civil service reform in China has come full circle. A competitive, meritocratic civil service was first introduced in China during the Song dynasty (960–1279 AD) (Ebrey 1999). By the mid-Qing dynasty (and especially from 1850 to the end of the dynasty in 1910) the system had become utterly corrupt. From 1927 the Republican government, which overthrew the Qing, introduced a modern civil service system that included competitive selection through civil service exams (Strauss 1998). How extensively these reforms were implemented, however, is unclear. With the Japanese invasion and post–World War II civil war, they may have been implemented in the capital and in major urban areas. With the 1949 revolution, officials nationalized the economy and introduced central planning. Under these conditions the CCP managed officials ("cadres") according to centrally drafted manpower plans that in practice encouraged leaders to select civil servants based on personal relations (*guanxi*). Indeed official policy encouraged them to choose officials personally known to them as loyal and reliable (Burns 1999, 200–4; Burns 1989; Bian 1994).

By the mid–1980s, however, the inefficiencies of the centralized system had become increasingly obvious, and civil service reformers in China began looking around for solutions, including to the West. Reformers did not look to China's imperial past, which they saw as having kept the country poor and undeveloped. In the words of one official, the imperial system, while initially innovative, had in the end contributed to the "protracted continuity of our feudal society" (Dai 1990–91, 68).[4] Reformers observed approvingly that the civil service system in the West had "created an environment in which people feel that they are able to compete on the basis of equality and this has helped to draw talented people into government, thereby facilitating the stability of capitalist society" (Dai 1990–91, 68). How did Chinese officials come to see that the competitive element of the Western civil service system might be appropriately adapted for China?

In August 1980 after winning a bruising leadership battle with Mao's heirs in the wake of the Cultural Revolution, paramount leader Deng Xiaoping put reform of the official leadership system on the CCP Politburo's agenda (Deng 1984).[5] The opening for this policy initiative, which culminated in reform of the civil service, came with the party's change of leadership and policy direction in 1978. On the one hand, party leaders wanted to institutionalize a state personnel system to prevent one-person rule, which had been very destructive during the Cultural Revolution, while, on the other hand, they took rapid economic development to modernize China as their primary policy goal. Officials perceived that a more open market economy that entailed competition was an appropriate way forward. This orientation encouraged officials to replace the uniform and all-inclusive "cadre" system in which the party managed virtually all white-collar occupation groups in the economy according to uniform rules (see Barnett 1967) with more market-oriented systems, including a system designed specifically for state functionaries. Thus was born the hunt for models of state personnel systems that emphasized competition.

As officials considered what form the new civil service system should take, they studied the question "of whether a civil service system that originated in the West can be adopted in a socialist country" (Dai 1990–91, 67). For a country that had just come through the Cultural Revolution, when things foreign were condemned and those who were perceived to have knowledge of or to be interested in things foreign could be arrested, tortured, and killed (See Brady 2003; Robinson 1971), this was a significant question. How could the party now justify examining foreign, especially Western, civil service systems, let alone adopting some foreign practices?

While acknowledging that "between countries with different social systems, there are fundamental differences in the foundation of the personnel system," a small high-level party group set up to make policy recommendations on the reforms acknowledged that "in certain areas of scientific and reasonable management methods, each [country] can learn from the other" (Dai 1990–91, 68). The small group then set about studying the civil service systems of various foreign countries. As part of the study, which actually commenced in 1984, detailed accounts of foreign civil service systems were published. In one influential three-volume work officials examined the civil service systems of the United States, the United Kingdom, France, Germany, Australia, Japan, the Soviet Union, and various Eastern European countries (Cao 1985). Officials concluded that

in general, there are certain characteristics, or shall we call them principles, in western civil service systems that should not be seen as related to the contradictions between our social system and theirs, and can be adopted by us. These include, for example, recruitment of personnel through open, equal competition and examination; rigorous evaluations, reviews, and promotion on the basis of achievement and merit; protection of civil servants' rights – [the idea that] except for legal cause and through legal procedures, personnel cannot be dismissed or penalized; strengthening the training of civil servants; managing affairs according to law, and so on.
(Dai 1990–91, 68–9)

Leaving aside the question of the extent to which these characteristics are Western (clearly, strengthened training is not peculiar to Western civil service systems) Chinese officials apparently were willing to adopt certain techniques they perceived to be Western, such as open, equal competition and selection based on examinations.

But reformers also apparently favored the adoption of more fundamental reforms, such as the rule of law to govern the system. As we
will see, many of these Western techniques found their way into
China's civil service regulations and law.

While reformers were willing to look to and adopt certain management techniques used in the West, not surprisingly they excluded
from consideration principles that challenged the CCP's monopoly
of power, such as introducing multi-party competition or the concept
of political neutrality. Officials were clear that "there are certain
principles such as that of 'political neutrality' that cannot be adopted"
(Dai 1990–91, 69). In the one-party Chinese system civil servants
are expected to "contentiously be in political step" with the CCP.
Chinese officials may be CCP members and may vote and stand for
election and participate in all sorts of party activities. Moreover, the
small group concluded, civil servants in China did not constitute a
special "interest group" in society, nor would China's new civil service system be the product of any kind of multi-party competition.

With these caveats officials concluded: "In short, a civil service
system, as a personnel management method, can be adopted by a
capitalist country and equally by a socialist country. Moreover, we
are learning from and absorbing its scientific methodology while
integrating it with China's actual conditions. Therefore, no one can
say that we are simplistically transplanting something from the West"
(Dai 1990–91, 69).

Our extended discussion of the origin of China's civil service
reforms indicates that China's leaders perceived that they had borrowed from the West. The period up to 4 June 1989, when Party
General Secretary Zhao Ziyang, arguably the key leader backing
the reforms, lost power, was one of remarkable openness about
the borrowing.

Although reformers were clear that the concept of political neutrality was inappropriate for one-party China, early versions of the
reforms called for separating the roles of the party and the government (*dangzheng fenkai*). Officials anticipated then that such a separation would result in a "relatively major shift" in the functions of
party organization departments, the CCP's key personnel agency,
which previously had directly managed the selection, training, and
discipline of all white-collar employees in public institutions of all
sorts in China. Reformers anticipated that party organization departments would focus more narrowly on research, policy-making, and

manpower forecasting ("comprehensive researching of the cadre and personnel system, on cadre and personnel policy, and on the fore-casting of personnel conditions and needs for cadres") and not on the day-to-day management of the cadre corps (Dai 1990–91, 66). That is, party organization departments would select and manage directly only the most senior officials, and most other civil servants would be managed by government agencies, staffed of course by party members.

In keeping with this policy direction, early versions of the civil service reforms distinguished between two types of civil servants: "political affairs" civil servants, senior officials who would be elected by people's congresses and directly managed by party organization departments; and "professional" civil servants, who would be selected through the new Western-inspired competitive means that emphasized expertise and who would be managed by government agencies.[6]

Arguably, introducing separate roles for politicians and bureau-crats was a more significant borrowing from the West than the civil service management techniques discussed above. In Confucian China the model of government was bureaucratic and unitary, a character-istic of the state that fit well with China's post–1949 official ideology, Leninism. "In this model [Confucianism] political order [was] remarkably monolithic, with all political power and actions centered in a single bureaucracy headed by the Emperor" (Dao 1996, 51). In Confucian states the division between civil servants and politicians was blurred and the bureaucracy tended to be more powerful and autonomous than in Western states (Dao 1996, 58). China's modern political system made no distinction between the roles of politicians and bureaucrats. Under the Nationalist and Communist regimes on the mainland, China was ruled by cadre-officials that continued to combine both political and administrative roles. Had China's reform-ers carved out separate roles for politicians and civil servants, this would indeed have been remarkable for it could have indicated a significant retreat for the ubiquitous role of party organization departments and could have been seen as significant borrowing from the West.

After several false starts officials introduced China's "new" civil service system in 1993, and it did contain many elements that reform-ers had previously identified as Western. In table 8.1 I have indicated where in the Provisional Regulations on Civil Servants (1993) and the subsequent Civil Servants Law (2005) the Western elements,

Table 8.1
Comparison of Perceived Western Characteristics of Civil Service Systems
with Formal Rules Adopted

Perceived Western principles officially identified as adoptable	*Inclusion in "Provisional Regulations on Civil Servants" (PRCS), or "Civil Servants Law" (CSL)*
Recruitment through open, equal competition and examination	PRCS, chap. 4, art. 13, 16 CSL, chap. 4, art. 21, 26
Rigorous evaluations	PRCS, chap. 5 CSL, chap. 5
Promotions based on achievement and merit	PRCS, chap. 8, art. 38 CSL, chap. 7, art. 43
Protection of civil servants rights (dismissal or penalty only with legal cause)	PRCS, chap. 2, art. 7 CSL, chap. 2, art. 13
Strengthened training	PRCS, chap. 10, art. 51 CSL, chap., 10
Managing affairs according to law	PRCS, chap. 2, art. 7 CSL, chap. 2, art. 13

Sources: Dai 1990–91, 68; Ministry of Personnel (1993); National People's Congress (2005).

mostly techniques such as open competition, rigorous evaluations, promotion based on merit, and so forth, may be found.

Surprisingly, given the build-up in the 1980s, the new system omitted any reference to separate roles for politicians and bureaucrats. This policy was a casualty of elite-level in-fighting within the CCP that publicly manifested itself with the violent crackdown on pro-democracy demonstrators in Tiananmen Square on 4 June 1989 and the sacking of Party General Secretary Zhao Ziyang. A party investigation group subsequently condemned aspects of Zhao's civil service reform plans. The group complained that his policies had weakened the party's role in personnel management and especially its authority to make personnel appointments. The post-June 4 victors also accused Zhao of condoning excessive decentralization, neglecting the quality of cadres, encouraging irregular (non-collectivist) personnel procedures, and failing to curb wage inflation (Burns 1994, 464). In this kind of atmosphere, adopting arguably the most Western of the reforms was simply not on.

Table 8.2
Number of Vacancies and Applicants for Centrally Managed Civil Service Positions,
1994–2005

Year	No. of Applicants (A)	No. of Vacancies (B)	Ratio of A to B
1994	4,306	440	9.8
1995	6,726	490	13.7
1996	7,160	737	9.7
1997	8,850	NA	NA
2001	32,904	4,500	7.2
2002	62,268	4,800	13.0
2003	87,772	5,400	16.3
2004	140,184	8,000	17.5
2005	406,000	8,662	2.1

Source: Interviews, Ministry of Personnel 22 July 1996, 12 August 1999, and 19 March 2004;
Posts advertised in 2005 for 2006 recruitment at http://www.china.com.cn/ chinese/MATERIAL/
1014867.htm (accessed 31 October 2005).

Note: The number of vacancies and of applicants grew as more and more posts were covered by
the civil service system. Centrally managed posts include posts in the central government and posts
managed by central institutions (e.g., Customs, People's Bank of China).

The political crisis delayed the introduction of the more technical
reforms until 1993. One indication of the changes they brought has
been the selection of many new civil servants based on the results
of competitive examinations (see table 8.2). Official data indicate
that hundreds of thousands of people are now applying for many
thousands of civil service posts.

The incentives for China's political leaders to adopt these reforms
varied with their positions. The introduction of civil service reform
was clearly a top-down initiative. Initiated by China's elder "statesman," paramount leader Deng Xiaoping, they were designed to
facilitate China's economic development and modernization, which
required selecting competent officials who could get the job done.
Once the reforms became official policy, local political leaders supported them for various reasons. Because the reforms were introduced with salary increases (a new salary system for civil servants),
the reforms appealed to some income-maximizing officials. Officials

seeking promotion (climbers) were motivated by the need to improve their performance, which hiring competent public servants could accomplish. They were also motivated by the need to demonstrate that they were actually implementing official policy, another criterion used for promotion. There seems to have been very little resistance to the policy, probably because throughout the country virtually all "cadres" who worked for government agencies were, after some formalities including exams, transferred into the new civil service (See Burns and Wang, forthcoming). The real impact, if any, would be on the newcomers.

Public Management Techniques

Many public management ideas currently adopted by Chinese officials have come from the West ("Everything modern is a western idea").7 China's adoption of a modern market economy was accompanied by an interest in management techniques to improve the efficiency of public service delivery. Repeated campaigns to downsize the public sector also encouraged reformers to search for alternative public service delivery modes (see Burns 2003). Local government authorities, charged with implementing public policy and evaluated based on their performance, adopted NPM techniques such as *contracting-out* for some services (separating the provider and purchaser of the services), for example, for the provision of agricultural technical services at the township level in many provinces, such as Hubei (Zhang 2007). In 2006 Wuxi City government contracted out TB prevention to private hospitals; previously it had been carried out by the public health bureau. Reportedly, the results have been good (*People's Daily*, 17 August 2006). Some local governments also introduced voucher systems to give citizens more choice. In Chongqing, for example, pregnant women, who previously could obtain subsidized checkups only from their own township hospital, were given *vouchers* to obtain the services from a list of hospitals in the county. Hospitals then competed for business and reportedly improved their service (*People's Daily*, 17 August 2006). These public management ideas have come from the West through various channels, including academic channels, aid agencies, and overseas training tours for officials. Working with key government agencies such as the Organization Department's Training Center and the National School of Administration, donor agencies such as the

UNDP and the European Union have introduced ideas such as the balanced score card and "comprehensive performance assessment" (CPA) in pilots at township and county level in various provinces of China. The Ford Foundation has also established a government innovation award, offered once every two years, to local governments with outstanding public administration innovations. Governments compete for the award, which brings fame to local government officials, thereby bringing them to the attention of more senior officials (Zhou 2007).

Reformers have also used various institutional forms to manage the public sector, including bureaus, hybrids of various kinds, and state-owned enterprises (see Horn 1995). In the 1990s, for example, officials hived off the production functions of government bureaus and turned them into state-owned corporations. Trade promotion functions were turned over to state-sponsored councils or associations. China's interest in raising capital on foreign capital markets and the country's accession to the World Trade Organization (WTO) has forced the country's SOEs to adopt modern practices of corporate governance, including the use of international accounting practices. Arguably, all these changes have originated in Western market economies. Unlike the civil service reform, which was a top-down exercise (see above), other reforms have been initiated by local political leaders, undoubtedly to improve their chances of promotion. The introduction of China's performance pledge system, inspired by practice in the United Kingdom and Hong Kong, is a case in point.

A key part of performance management is being able to measure performance, and China's post–1949 central planning regime has been concerned with this issue for a long time. Undoubtedly, considerable borrowing from the Soviet Union accompanied the introduction of central planning in the 1950s. Although modern performance measurement in China has taken several forms, reformers have clearly borrowed some ideas from the West (see Zhou 2006). Western ideas on modern performance management entered China through various channels, both official and unofficial. According to an expert in this area, Chinese cadres were first introduced to the experience of Western local government in performance management through the translation of David Burningham's and John Brown's chapters in Pollitt and Harrison (1993) provided by a scholar-official, Zuo Ran (1994), who then worked in the CCP's Central Public Administration Reform Commission (*zhonggong zhongyang jigou bianzhi weiyuanhui bangongshi*) (Zhou 2007) [8]. These articles, circulated among officials in the government, introduced the experience primarily of the United Kingdom. In 1995 Peking University's Zhou Zhiren wrote an article evaluating that country's experience of performance measurement and suggesting how it could be applied in China (Zhou 1995). Local officials picked up these ideas. They also travelled abroad on study tours and attended in-country seminars and training sessions led by consultants and organized by multi-lateral aid agencies such as the United Nations Development Programme.

In a clear case of borrowing from the United Kingdom through Hong Kong, in June 1994 officials of the Construction Commission of Yantai City (Shandong Province) introduced a "service pledge system," acknowledging its foreign origins (Hu 1998, 1091; Zhou 2006). In the reform nine agencies of the Construction Commission (some were state-owned enterprises and others were bureaus) produced performance pledges. When these agencies reported high levels of performance, officials decided that all twenty-eight agencies of the commission should use the system beginning in 1995. Six months after the pledges were announced (in a "Social Services Pledge Bulletin" published for this purpose), the commission reported that it had handled 95 percent of the complaints from the public during the period. By 1996, the city had produced 82 pledge programs that contained 117 different service standards for a variety of services. According to government statistics, the various agencies operating under the performance pledge system have achieved their pledges by rates of from 90 to 100 percent (this result is similar to the experience of government departments in many other parts of the world, including Hong Kong). In 1996, the central government instructed eight central ministries to experiment with the performance pledge system (Hu 1998, 1092–3). Scholars have reported widespread use of performance pledges by local governments (Zhou 1996).

Unlike the experience of Hong Kong, where the introduction of performance pledges was a top-down exercise, local leaders in China took the initiative to introduce the service pledge system in order to demonstrate their performance credentials. The Chinese political system gives local leaders sufficient discretion to introduce programs such as this, which, if handled well, can present citizens with data indicating performance improvements. Local officials could use the innovation as evidence of their commitment to high performance in their scramble for promotion. In this case the borrowing from the

United Kingdom through Hong Kong is clear, and the initiative came from local leaders. Central government officials picked up the practice after observing it in operation in Shandong province.

Our discussion indicates that officials in China have borrowed Western public management techniques quite liberally. Undoubtedly, however, they have adapted them to China's circumstances.

"Good" Governance

In the last case, officials were introduced to notions of "good" governance through the efforts of international aid agencies to attach conditionalities to lending and through the writings of mainland academics, especially those who had studied overseas. Initially government officials resisted the idea, which did not even have an agreed translation into Chinese, but they came to see that it could be adapted to suit their purposes. Indeed, elements of various "good" governance paradigms coincided with central government policy designed to impose greater levels of bureaucratic accountability on local government and on state-owned enterprises. After some hesitation and reflection the central government accepted a version of "good" governance "with Chinese characteristics" that has emphasized bureaucratic accountability, more stakeholder participation, and increased, but still very limited, transparency, especially at grassroots levels.

Notions of "good" governance emerged in the post – Cold War era in the documents of multilateral aid agencies, such as the World Bank, which eventually sought to impose them as conditionalities on their lending (see Chowdhury 2005). Although the notion of "good" governance is not well defined (see Doornbos 2003; Nanda 2006), various versions of the concept do have a common core of characteristics that includes accountability, participation, transparency, and integrity (see Asian Development Bank 1995). These ideas imply a strong civil society and the rule of law (see World Bank 1994).

In the mid-1990s Chinese academics also began discussing notions of "good" governance then circulating in the West. Among the most influential was Yu Keping of Peking University, a homegrown PHD who has become an advisor of senior party leaders (he was deputy head of the CCP's Central Translation Bureau in 2008). Yu published *Governance and Good Governance* in 2000, in which he discussed such ideas as accountability, transparency, participation, and performance management.

When approached by international aid agencies about China's position on "good" governance, central government officials reacted with caution.[9] While the Chinese academic community had by 2000 agreed that governance should be translated as *zhili*, official China queried the translation (Why not use *guanli* (management) or *xingzheng* (administration), concepts traditionally associated with *government,* they asked). With the passage of time, official China came to embrace the term, adapted to suit its own purposes. As touched on briefly above, officials have made elaborate performance measurement regimes, which are a key ingredient especially of bureaucratic accountability, an important part of performance assessments and promotions. Officials have also emphasized improving stakeholder participation, increased transparency, and improving the integrity of officials (reducing corruption). In the paragraphs that follow I focus on one of these characteristics, increased transparency, offering an explanation of the incentive structure for officials to move in this direction.[10]

Public administration in China has been among the most secretive in the world, a characteristic that is reflected in China's comprehensive secrecy laws, which, after listing items that are secret, end with a statement that includes "anything else that ought to be secret" (Burns 1994, 80).[11] Beginning in the 1990s, however, central leaders began to demand that local governments become more open about the process of governance. In 2000 the central CCP required that town and township authorities make public information on a long list of government budgetary, social policy, and personnel matters (see box 2). Items included how government funds were spent and the results of bidding for contracts for public works projects. Information on these items was supposed to be made public throughout China's nearly forty thousand towns and townships, the lowest administrative level in the countryside.

Central authorities imposed these requirements on town and township leaders to improve the effectiveness of their control over them. If these matters were made public, citizens could also more effectively monitor local leaders as they implemented centrally determined policies. Central authorities hoped that greater transparency would reduce corruption and increase the likelihood that official candidates

---

BOX 8.2

Items To Be Made Public (Town/Township Level)

- Annual work targets of government departments and their implementation
- Government budgets and their implementation
- Amount and disposition of special funds allocated to the government
- Claims made against the government and its liabilities
- Government enterprise contracts, leases, and auctions
- Bidding and award of tenders for government engineering projects
- Government development projects
- Amounts and types of all taxes and fees collected
- Family planning situation
- Land resumption (the state taking privately held land to use for public purposes) particulars and re-settlement arrangements
- Policies and practices for approving house construction
- Policies and practices for providing disaster relief and welfare
- Situation of collection of water and electricity bills
- Nature of the duties of government officials, their remuneration, and any disciplinary measures taken against them
- Situation surrounding any penalties to be levied in towns or townships, including the amount of the penalty and how and when it will be collected
- Matters related to officials' behavior
- Matters related to officials' use of entertainment allowances and travelling expenses
- Matters related to the transfer, appraisal, reward, and punishment of local officials, and
- Other important matters

Source: *New China News Agency* (2000), 25 December.

---

would be supported in town and township elections. Improved transparency, then, would help leaders maintain their positions of power.

From 2002, in response to the central government's policy of "opening up government affairs" (*zhengwu gongkai*) many provinces and municipalities in China adopted their own "open government" legislation (see Horsley 2007). Among the first was Guangzhou City in southern China whose "Provisions on Open Government Information" became effective on 1 January 1 2003.[12] Unusually for

China (the Chinese Constitution includes no right to information among citizen's rights), these regulations established a presumption that government-held information should be made public (see Horsley 2003). They were drafted with the assistance of academics from Guangzhou's Zhongshan University, "taking into account international experience" (Horsley 2003). The Guangzhou government's resolve to implement the new provisions was sorely tested a few months later, however, with the spread of SARS. The government initially suppressed all information about the disease, declaring its existence in Guangdong to be a "state secret." Its ability to make such declarations easily indicated a major loophole in the regulations. Other local governments followed with their own provisions. Then in April 2007 the central government announced its "Regulations on Open Government Information" (*zhengfu xinyi gongkai tiaoli*), which came into force on 1 May 2008.[13] These regulations were drafted based on the experience of local regulations, on the one hand, and on foreign examples and expertise (including "Western" freedom of information laws), on the other (Horsley 2007).

China's open government regulations follow the basic structure of and many of the mechanisms found in information access systems in the West (Horsley 2007). For example, they acknowledge the types of information that government agencies should voluntarily provide to citizens on their websites, in press releases, and in other open communications. They also provide for a mechanism for citizens to request information and for institutions to oversee compliance (the State Council's General Office and local government General Offices in this case); they lay down a requirement that governments at all levels produce annual reports on how they have complied with the regulations; and they provide for a system of adjudicating disputes between citizens and the government over information requests (through the courts in China's case).

In significant respects, however, the central government's regulations depart from international ("Western") regimes. First, unlike many Western freedom of information laws, the central government regulations provide no clear statement favoring disclosure over non-disclosure. Rather, they hedge the open-information regime with all sorts of restrictions (see articles 5, 6, 7, and 8), ending with the statement that disclosure may not harm "state security, public security, economic security, or social stability" (Horsley 2007). Specific exemptions from disclosure involve state security, commercial secrets, and privacy and refer specifically to the vaguely drafted State Secrets Law (1988), which defines state secrets broadly. In general, the regulations in no way weaken the presumption of secrecy that exists in contemporary Chinese public administration. Although the regulations exempt disclosure of commercial secrets and private information, as do "Western" systems, these areas are very vaguely defined in China. There is, for example, no law in China establishing and defining the right to privacy. An analysis of the central government's regulations indicates that they favor non-disclosure as the default principle. Second, they narrowly describe the scope of information that may be requested from government. Third, they provide for no independent decision-making body to resolve disputes between citizens and government agencies (the Shanghai government's regulations do, however, provide for such an independent body.) Fourth, the regulations leave adjudicating disputes between citizens and government agencies over what may be disclosed to China's highly politically dependent courts. That is, the regulations, while following the structure and mechanisms of "Western" freedom of information laws, lay down a regime "with Chinese characteristics." The regulations provide relatively little room to challenge state authority.

By 2007 eleven provinces and more than forty city-level jurisdictions had issued their own local open-government regulations. Many central government ministries also have transparency regimes, spurred on by China's drive for e-government and appearing to be modern. Among the most successful has been Shanghai's experience. From 2004 to 2006, according to Shanghai's annual reports on compliance,[14] government agencies had made public more than two hundred thousand documents, 80 percent of the some thirty thousand information requests received had been fulfilled completely or in part, and 95 percent of the public were aware of the open government rules (Horsley 2007; Chang 2007). In Shanghai, which probably operates the most liberal open-government regime, by 2007 none of the lawsuits filed by citizens to gain access to government information had been successful. The government simply classifies the information as secret, and the courts never question the classification (Chang 2007).

Shanghai's experience reveals the motives of officials in offering to be more open about government. China's accession to the WTO, which imposes certain requirements about transparency (for example, that regulations governing foreign trade should be made public),

has provided some impetus. Increased transparency has other benefits, widely cited by Chinese officials themselves, such as helping to
counter corruption, improving efficiency, and supporting economic
development. Most important, however, is that through the judicious
use of open-government regimes, officials can maintain tighter control
(their power) over subordinates. As we have seen, China's transparency regimes are carefully and narrowly drafted. While adopting
Western forms, they maintain a Chinese essence, which perpetuates
a culture of secrecy.

CONCLUSION

In this chapter I have examined three cases in which Chinese officials considered and then adapted some "Western" models of public
administration. In the first case, central leaders were determined
to reform the leadership system, which had performed badly for
them during the Cultural Revolution. They sparked a search for
foreign, primarily Western, experience that could provide referents
for how to reform China's own "cadre" system. This top-down
exercise resulted in the CCP adopting some civil service management techniques that were perceived to be Western (such as competition), but rejecting potentially more radical structural changes
that could have identified separate roles for politicians and bureaucrats in the political system. The reforms left China's civil service
system bereft of many NPM-type innovations found in the West.
For example, China's civil service continues to be highly centralized, operates nationwide uniform rank and grade structures, and
pays pensions. Paramount leader Deng Xiaoping led the civil service
reform initiative, hoping that it would better serve China (he acted
as a statesman). Once the reforms became official policy, other
leaders, eager for promotion implemented it with alacrity. Not
surprisingly, they were most enthusiastic about the reform provisions that increased civil service salaries.

The initiative for adopting various public management technologies discussed in the second case, such as contracting-out and vouchers to deliver public services or performance pledges to demonstrate
to the public that performance mattered, came almost exclusively
from the bottom, undoubtedly in response to central policy that
mandated performance-based promotions. Local leaders, eager for
fame and eager to improve their careers, cast around for whichever

technique would "work." Some techniques came from the "West" and, suitably adapted, were implemented.

China's experience of "good governance" and improved transparency came from both the top and the bottom. On the one hand, the central government could see the benefits of increased transparency for controlling local agents. The central government's decision to join the WTO undoubtedly took this consideration into account. Local leaders, too, benefited because they also could better control their subordinates. The transparency regime as adopted, we have seen, narrowly circumscribes what information citizens may be given, and leaves the state in a strong position to protect whatever it wishes to remain confidential.

"Western" ideas have found their way into China through multiple pathways. Scholars trained abroad have introduced some Western ideas to local officials in local journals and through training sessions or MPA programs. Scholar-officials, through their translations of Western public administration literature, have introduced new ideas as well. And donor organizations have provided consultants and study tours for officials to facilitate technology transfer. Thus, there has been no shortage of opportunities to be exposed to "Western" ideas. The incentive to adopt these ideas, however, has varied. The strongest incentives, I have argued, are associated with the promotion system. Where local officials can see their careers furthered by the adoption of a Western technique, and where that technique is allowed within the system, they have pursued it. Where donor agencies have pushed techniques that have few implications for Chinese official careers, the "Western" ideas have probably been less influential.

NOTES

1 Deng's Two Cat theory was that it did not matter whether the cat was black or white so long as it caught the mouse.
2 The following discussion of five types of officials is drawn largely from Downs (1967, 88).
3 These studies are reviewed in Lin (2008). They include Bo Zhiyue (2002) and Li Cheng and Lynn White, (1990).
4 Dai Guangqian was a senior official of the Ministry of Personnel and directly involved in policy discussions leading to the introduction of the

civil service reforms. Dai (1990–91) is the English language translation of a speech he gave on 25 July 1988 in which he outlined the process of drafting the reform plan and the principal considerations of the CCP leadership.

5 Deng Xiaoping (1984).

6 See the 1988 draft Provisional Regulations on State Civil Servants, arts 3, 4, and 9, available in English translation in Burns and Cabestan 1990–91.

7 Zhang Chunlin (2007), World Bank, personal communication, October 23.

8 The Central Public Administration Reform Commission, chaired by the premier, makes policy on structural reform of public agencies. See Burns (2003).

9 For example, when one international aid agency requested that it be allowed to do a "governance assessment" of China (the agency had made it a policy of carrying out such an assessment as part of approving further aid) Chinese officials agreed to the assessment so long as the word "governance" (and several other troublesome words such as "democracy" and "human rights") did not appear in the document.

10 See Hood and Heald (2006) for a critical account of the impact of transparency regimes in the West.

11 China has no monopoly on draconian secrecy provisions. The UK's Official Secrets Act (1989) is also draconian.

12 For an English-language translation see the China Law Center of Yale University Law School's website http://www.law.yale.edu/documents/provisions/pdf , accessed August 18, 2008.

13 For an English-language translation of the Central Government's Regulations on Open Government Information see http://www.law.yale.edu/documents/pdf/Intellectual_Life/Ch_OGIRegulations_Eng_Final_051607.pdf , accessed on August 18, 2008.

14 By 2007 only two governments (Shanghai and Wuhan) had issued annual reports on their compliance (Chang 2007).

9

Bureaucrats, Politicians, and the Transfer of Administrative Reform into Thailand

BIDHYA BOWORNWATHANA

This chapter investigates the transfer of ideas about administrative reform from developed countries into the Thai polity from the perspectives of bureaucrats and politicians. They play key roles in shaping the diffusion of reform into the Thai polity. Since administrative reform involves changing their attitudes, the powerful bureaucrats and politicians tend to block attempts to introduce administrative reform that may jeopardize their power and authority in the public sector. After a reform is introduced, it meets with stiff resistance, and the intended results do not occur. Instead, reform hybrids are created that prolong or augment the traditional power of bureaucrats and politicians. This problem is widespread throughout the history of administrative reform in Thailand. As a result, governance reform in the Thai polity is marked by failure and uncertainty.

This chapter is divided into three parts. First, I describe the various roles that bureaucrats and politicians play in the transfer of administrative reform. Second, I explain the transfer of three major reform ideas: the guiding paradigm for reform, the institutions of accountability, and the management tools. Third, I discuss the consequences of importing reform ideas from developed countries into Thailand from the perspective of bureaucrats and politicians.

THE ROLES OF BUREAUCRATS AND POLITICIANS

Since the overthrow of the absolute monarchy in Thailand in 1932, military bureaucrats and politicians from the business community have been the power-holders in Thai politics and the bureaucracy. The non-government sector and civil society in Thailand are weak and growing only slowly. As has been argued by several scholars, a bureaucrat-politician perspective provides a strong explanatory framework for the study of administrative reform (Aberbach et al. 1981; Peters and Pierre 2001). For Thailand, I have over the years argued that such a perspective provides a powerful conceptual framework toward understanding administrative reform in Thailand (Bowornwathana, 1996a,b, 1999, 2001b, 2002a, 2005a).

What Do Bureaucrats and Politicians Gain from the Transfer of Administrative Reform?

Bureaucrats want to retain and perpetuate their strong traditional power in the bureaucracy. They search for opportunities to expand their domain and bureaucratic empires by, for example, increasing the number of ministries, departments, and offices and upgrading organizations and positions. The political game is to allow themselves to climb up higher and higher in the bureaucratic ladder. A lot of time and effort is spent by bureaucrats at moving higher in the position classification system and therefore the salary scale. Political bosses wield power over bureaucrats because of their power to promote bureaucrats to higher position classification levels (PCS)and their authority to approve measures expanding the bureaucracy. Not surprisingly, therefore, the Thai bureaucracy is characterized by networks of patron-client relationships among bureaucrats and politicians. Internal conflicts among bureaucrats and politicians involve competing patron-client factions (Bowornwathana 2001a). They compete for transfers and promotions, the bidding for government projects, and powerful positions. Corruption, conflict of interests, nepotism, and double standards are common among bureaucrats and politicians, but, ironically, they go hand in hand with calls from the same bureaucrats and politicians to reform the bureaucracy and combat corruption.

From 1932 to 1973, the Thai polity was under the rule of military bureaucrats. The late Fred Riggs coined the term "bureaucratic polity" to describe this phenomenon. The bureaucrats' monopoly of power ended with the People's Uprising on 14 October 1973, which overthrew a corrupt military regime. Since then, the number of elected politicians with business backgrounds assuming the premiership and cabinet positions has increased rapidly, and career bureaucrats seem to have taken the back seat. Elected politicians introduce administrative reform measures that allow politicians to exert more control over the bureaucrats who administer a large and lucrative national budget and who are responsible for the enforcement of important public laws. Effective control over powerful bureaucrats enables politicians to practice corruption on a large scale and to get away with conflicts of interest and to act in accordance with double standards. To hold the patronage system together, politicians need firm control of the bureaucrats.

Generally speaking, both bureaucrats and politicians can play several different roles in the transfer of administrative reform. They can act as reform architects, reform importers, reform drivers, reform owners ("focal actors,") and reform implementers. At the end, they become reform gainers and losers.

REFORM ARCHITECTS

The role of reform architect is assumed by foreigners who invent reform ideas that are imported into developing countries. All reform ideas implemented in the Thai polity are imported. It should be said, however, that reform drivers of Thailand's International Public Sector Standards Management Systems and Outcomes (the PSO) claim that they invented this international public sector standards management system.

REFORM IMPORTERS

Bureaucrats and politicians are importers of reform ideas from abroad. On field trips to developed countries such as the United Kingdom, New Zealand, and the United States they learn and borrow from reform ideas. This "shopping around" requires a big budget unless it is funded by the host country, which is rarely the case. When there is a change in government and a new parliament, the new executive politicians and parliamentary MPs usually start this shopping ritual again. However, sometimes reform ideas are introduced directly by foreign experts from developed countries and international organizations such as the United Nations, the World Bank, and the Asian Development Bank (ADB) to Thai bureaucrats and politicians. However, field trips may subsequently be included in the reform package adopted.

REFORM DRIVERS

Bureaucrats and politicians can be "drivers" of reform. Once some bureaucrats and politicians are convinced that a reform innovation is promising, they may become "reform drivers" and instigate an agenda-setting process involving activities such as organizing conferences for brain-storming, hiring foreign experts or soliciting assistance from international agencies and developed countries, paying large sums of money to foreign architects of a management tool to give lectures, building blueprints, and convincing decision-makers of the importance of a particular reform idea. The reform drivers will quickly claim to be the specialists in the particular reform innovation. Reform drivers are bureaucrats, mainly from central agencies close to the prime minister, such as high-level bureaucrats from the civil service commission, the budget bureau, the office of the juridical council, and the national counter-corruption commission. They convince their political bosses of the benefits of supporting the reform plan.

REFORM OWNERS, OR THE FOCAL ACTORS

Once a reform innovation has been embraced by key policy-makers, bureaucrats will try to claim ownership of it. They would like to be the "focal actor," or owner of the "reform niche," for that particular idea so that they can control the reform process (Painter 2004). They do so by obtaining an official mandate such as a cabinet resolution or a law passed by Parliament that provides a legal mandate to their respective organizations to manage a particular innovation. National committees may be set up to instal a reform policy, with the drivers forming the secretariat. In other words, they successfully carve out their domains in order to become the official reform implementers with the authority to make demands on other government agencies and officials to follow the rules and regulations they issue for implementation of the reform. These rules and regulations are enforced throughout the government bureaucracy, requiring compliance from relevant bureaucrats. However, because politicians come and go, they are not permanent owners of the reform niche, and they may become only temporary focal actors if the bureaucrats in charge of the new reform are under their command.

REFORM IMPLEMENTERS

As the official representatives of a reform policy, focal actors will start implementing the reform ideas by issuing new rules and regulations for the reform idea: they will perform the role of reform implementers. Bureaucrats will be more involved than politicians at this stage of reform. They will evaluate and monitor other government agencies that have to follow the guidelines worked out by the focal actor. The "victims" of reform will be ordered to attend training sessions that will educate them about the "new vocabulary" and "rules of the game" worked out by the focal organization. It is at this stage that the original good intentions of a reform idea from abroad can be extensively altered to serve the interests of the bureaucrats and politicians in control of the focal organization. In this clash of ideas between the reform ideas that have proven to be successful in developed countries and the interests of Thai bureaucrats and politicians, the latter usually prevail. The non-government sector, citizens, civil society, communities, the mass media, and the academia will be too weak and uninterested in the subject of reform to overrule the intentions of bureaucrats and politicians. The result may be "ugly reform hybrids" that look different from the original innovation from abroad. The hybrids may serve the personal interests of bureaucrats and politicians, instead of improving the effectiveness of the government.

REFORM GAINERS AND LOSERS

When a reform innovation has been introduced for a while, reform gainers and losers will appear. In general, the bureaucrats from the focal organization gain from increased control and prestige, the structural expansion of their organization, position upgrades, and higher pay. The imported reform plan becomes a self-serving tool for focal bureaucrats to reassert control over others (Pierre and Peters 2000, 94–113). Some bureaucrats, especially from line ministries, can be losers, because more monitoring control is exercised on them by the focal actors from central agencies. Executive politicians that control the focal organization also gain from increased power over bureaucrats. Some reform innovations have tendencies to centralize power at the center, and in this case, therefore, executive politicians gain. In Thailand, reform importers, drivers, owners, and implementers are not accountable for the damaging unintended consequences that may be produced later on. There is no law that punishes them if they make fatal reform mistakes, and after a while things are forgotten, and new reform ideas are poured into the pipeline again. This is especially evident when new management tools invented abroad are brought into the developing countries' vicious cycle of borrowing reform ideas from developed countries.

THE TRANSFER OF REFORM IDEAS

The literature on the transfer of administrative reform is growing (Pollitt 2002, 2004; Pollitt and Bouckaert 2004; Christensen and Laegried 2001). Two observations have been made about the transfer of reform ideas into the Thai polity. First, Thais are unusually open and receptive to reform ideas flowing from increased globalization and democratization: reform importers are eager to bring in all the new reform ideas from developed countries. There is a rush, or "greediness," for new reform ideas, a quest to claim credit as the first reform importer, the reform owner, and the key reform implementer. Prospective importers shop around intensively for the latest "menu of reform fashions" (Pollitt 2004) and are quick to claim ownership and expertise. In this competitive rush, the importers are not concerned with whether a foreign innovation is transferable. Nor do they care whether a reform idea from the management world will be appropriate for the world of government. Being at the head of the rush for reform ideas will enable importers to project themselves as "trendy," and in the vanguard. The rush is also stimulated by the lucrative business of consultancies, foreign loans, grants, trips, and prospects of financial support from government.

Second, the original version of the reform idea loses its identity once it enters the Thai polity. The foreign blueprint is damaged through the manipulation and sometimes the ignorance of the bureaucrats and politicians involved in the reform. Thus, if Thailand adopts the New Zealand model, for example, the question is no longer whether it works. Rather, the question becomes, to what extent has the New Zealand model been modified during the reform diffusion process in Thailand? Are bureaucrats and politicians the beneficiaries of the reform? How useful is it for ordinary Thais?

I shall now explain the three types of reform ideas transferred from developed countries.

The First Transfer: Governance as the Guiding Reform Paradigm

At the highest general level of abstraction, the first type of reform ideas consists of the "paradigms," or selected principles, of reform that a government officially embraces at a particular moment. Being an open society, Thailand has experienced similar inflows of fashionable paradigms. For example, in the 1990s the wisdom for government reformers was to follow the business model. From re-engineering to reinventing governments, the argument was that business practices were superior to government practices and that governments must be reinvented with excellent practices from outstanding companies.

By the end of the 1990s, a paradigm shift had occurred, and the new guiding principle of good government was labelled "governance" or "good governance" for developing countries. At this paradigmatic level, suddenly influential international organizations such as the UN, the World Bank, the IMF, the ADB, the OECD, and governments from developed countries were demanding "good governance" from developing countries. Also, the revival of the movement to combat corruption by the United Nations and other key international agencies in the 1990s was instrumental in bringing good governance to Thailand's doorsteps. It was, however, the 1997 economic collapse of Thailand that helped accelerate the importation process, since the World Bank and the IMF made it a condition of providing loans that the Thai government be reformed in line with good governance principles.

In a nutshell, the Thai economy had collapsed partly because of bad corporate governance. Business practices in Thailand itself were no longer good examples for government reformers to follow. At the same time, supporters of democracy and citizen power in Thailand pushed for good governance as a means to reform the corrupt and inefficient bureaucracy and increase citizen control. Within this new context, constitution drafters came up with the completely new Constitution of 1997, which advocated governance by, for example, for the first time setting up several new institutions such as an administrative court system that would oversee the use of discretionary power by bureaucrats and politicians. At the same time, the Chuan government at that time issued a regulation on good governance that would later become one of the key guidelines for reform.

Under military rule, a new 2007 Constitution was promulgated that reinforced the principles of governance as stipulated in the previous 1997 Constitution. The new constitution was intended to close the loopholes of its predecessor, which allowed former prime minister Thaksin to violate the principles of good governance by exerting his power over the accountability institutions and manipulating the management tools to fit his authoritarian style of government.

From 1997 onwards, the word "governance" (or *tham ma pi ban*, in Thai) became the buzzword representing the good qualities that all bureaucrats and politicians must act in accordance with in the conduct of government. The problem with the diffusion of good governance into the Thai polity was the blurring of the meaning of the concept of governance. "Governance" was interpreted in several different ways by the Thais, to the extent that the concept of governance came to be meaningless, since it became anything that it was thought should be the qualities of good government and of public officials. The original idea of the governance paradigm, which assumed that citizens were the masters of bureaucrats and politicians was put aside. Bureaucrats and politicians reinterpreted the meanings of governance to justify their power supremacy. As a result, as I have recently argued, there were six interpretations of governance in Thailand: the new democracy, or democratic governance; good governance; the efficiency perspective, the Ten Guiding Principles for the King; the Thaksin system, and the ethical interpretation (Bowornwathana 2008). The upshot was that instead of empowering citizens, the transfer of the governance paradigm reinforced the monopoly of power by bureaucrats and politicians.

I contend that democratic governance covers four dimensions: smaller central government, flexible organizations, institutions of accountability, and government fairness (Bowornwathana 1997; 2006b). A preference for a minimal role for the state calls for a smaller central government that does less. Reducing the size of government means reducing the number of civil servants and reducing the number of ministries, departments, offices, and state enterprises. It also means strengthening civil society, communities, and local governments. The reform words are downsizing, streamlining, privatization, a strong civil society and strong communities, and decentralization of local governments. These principles of governance are repeatedly seen in Thailand's recent government policy statements and documents as the right ones to follow.

Behind the policy rhetoric, however, since the adoption of good governance in the 1997 Constitution, politicians and bureaucrats have done the opposite. Instead of creating a smaller government that does less, they have introduced reforms that have created a larger government that does more. For example, the number of ministries has increased from thirteen to twenty (Bowornwathana 2002b), and the number of bureaucrats has also increased accordingly. The privatization of profit-making state enterprises has provided corrupt politicians and their relatives with the privilege of buying cheap shares of good companies such as the Petroleum Authority of Thailand before others could do so. For this reason, privatization has slowed down amidst protests from corruption watchdogs and the public. The non-government sector remains weak and more dependent on financial support and policies of the central government.

Nor was the decentralization of local governments successful in transferring power to the people. Instead, the power delegated to local governments by the central government was handed over to relatives and friends of national politicians, who were corrupt businessmen and comprised an elite class of their own. This pattern provided the central government with a pretext for slowing down decentralization, and central government bureaucrats and national politicians gained from the expansion of the central government. More ministries meant that more positions had been created to be filled by politicians and bureaucrats.

The term "flexible organizations" refers to the trend in several countries to keep their core central governments small by transforming traditional ministries and bureaus into autonomous public organizations with implementing units, as happened with executive agencies in the United Kingdom. They were created to reduce the size of the ministries by transferring government officials who worked in implementing units of the ministries into contract employees of public agencies. The consequences of borrowing the reform idea of this "agencification" in Thailand contradicted the original intentions of foreign architects, however. The Thai version of autonomous public organizations was not intended to reduce the size of ministries. Instead of substitutes, therefore, they became additions (Bowornwathana 2004b, 2006c). Senior bureaucrats and politicians became more powerful because they had more public organizations to oversee, more boards to sit on, more positions to fill, and larger budgets to draw on. Again, bureaucrats and politicians were the beneficiaries of reform.

The creation of accountability institutions is the third dimension of governance. Globalization and democratization have increased the expectations of the public that they will be able to exercise more control over bureaucrats and politicians. Politicians and the educated middle class pressured Parliament to promulgate a governance-based constitution. The new accountability institutions are mechanisms for monitoring the use of power by bureaucrats and politicians so that citizens, who, in principle, own the country, will have a better government. The development of governance in this regard has not gone very far because the powerful bureaucrats and politicians have been able to intervene in the work of the new accountability institutions. Thus, only if those institutions become stronger and truly independent will bureaucrats and politicians be reform losers.

The last dimension of democratic governance, government fairness, is even more difficult to attain under the present circumstances in Thailand. The civil society, intellectuals, and the mass media demand government fairness and impartiality, but it is almost impossible for fairness to flourish in a country that is strongly based on patron-client exchange relations, where special favors and privileges are the rules of the game. Impartial bureaucrats and politicians are unknown. The more reforms are introduced, the wider the gap between the top bureaucrats and the rest (Bowornwathana 2006a). To move ahead, a senior bureaucrat must serve the powerful politicians; a lower-level bureaucrat must serve the superior bureaucrat. Corruption, both large-scale and small, becomes widespread in a patronage society, even though the governance principles in the constitution look good, the accountability institutions are there, and the management tools can be found everywhere in government.

The Second Transfer:
The Creation of Accountability Institutions

The Thai polity has embraced the efforts also seen in many developed and developing countries to build new independent democratic institutions that monitor government institutions and officials to ensure political and bureaucratic accountability. Examples of these new accountability institutions are the Constitution Court, the Ombudsmen, the National Counter Corruption Commission, the National Human Rights Commission, the Administrative Court, the State Audit

Commission, the Anti-Money Laundering Office, the Department of Special Investigation (DSI), and the Elections Commission.

Even though several classic models of accountability already existed in some developed countries, such as the Ombudsman of Sweden and the Administrative Court System of France, the past two decades have also witnessed the creation of several new accountability mechanisms in several developed countries. Not only were some of these mechanisms new to developing countries, they were also new to some developed ones. In fact, the borrowing of reform ideas also occurs among the developed countries. For example, an administrative procedure act and a freedom of information act were recent creations of several countries, such as the United States, and they are being borrowed by other countries, including Thailand. The National Performance Review (NPR) of the Clinton administration had studied the system of executive agencies in the United Kingdom and had tried, though unsuccessfully, to adapt that reform idea to the United States. As an open country highly receptive to new foreign ideas, the "reform shopping list" for Thailand became extensive. Indeed, it has embraced many accountability institutions that surpass the number of accountability institutions in several developed countries. "You named it, we have it."

Why did the powerful bureaucrats and politicians agree to support the establishment of these accountability institutions, which are intended to curb their power? The answer is that they believe they can intervene in the work and choices of the commissioners of these institutions, since the principles of independence and neutrality of such institutions do not apply to them in the Thai polity.

The creation of new accountability institutions is also welcomed by senior bureaucrats. Adding new public organizations fulfills the instinct of bureaucrats for domain expansion and empire-building. New turfs are created and occupied by the "hungry" bureaucrats. The new public organization opens the door for them to be promoted or transferred to new positions in the accountability organizations. It is heaven for high government officials who must retire at sixty. Bureaucrat and politician decision makers involved in policy formation for these institutions were keen to set the retirement age at seventy, and not surprisingly, most high-level positions in them are now held by former senior bureaucrats. Besides receiving the retirement pension and salary from their former positions, the bureaucrats who move to the new institutions also receive a handsome salary and fringe benefits, the authority to monitor others, and the social prestige and respect from being in the new positions. For example, it is now the practice for several bureaucrats from government ministries who are retiring at sixty to apply for positions as judges of the administrative court, whose retirement age is seventy.

However, the new accountability institutions do not provide the politicians with transfer opportunities. In fact, they are banned from becoming members of the commissions of those institutions. Why, then, do they support them? First, they see their creation as a way to counter the traditional power of the bureaucrats. Though they are also accountable to the new institutions, especially if they become members of the political executive, the politicians believe that their influence in the patron-client network is strong enough to enable them to avoid criticism or punishment from the new institutions. For example, during the governments of Prime Minister Thaksin (2001–6) and under the previous 1997 Constitution, Thaksin and his political allies in the former Thai Rak Thai (TRT) Party were able to dictate the choices of commissioners, who were selected by the Senate, for most of the accountability institutions, because Thaksin was able to control the majority of senators who selected the commissioners. The elections of senators did not produce a neutral Senate. Many senators were in fact relatives and friends of MPs and were connected to the government's political parties. A patronage senate and a partisan accountability institution defy the basic condition of accountability: that the members of the commissions must be neutral and apolitical. But during the Thaksin governments (2001–6), some accountability institutions became political instruments of the prime minister. Decisions made by the accountability organizations were rather supportive of the TRT Party, but damaging to the opposition party and TRT critics.

Turning now to the roles of bureaucrats and politicians in the reform diffusion process, the reform architects came from developed countries. The ombudsman concept originated in Scandinavian countries, and especially Sweden, where ombudsmen have been around for centuries. The constitutional courts of European countries such as Germany, Italy, Austria, and France provided examples for reform drivers setting up the Thai version of a constitutional court. The French administrative court system provided the model for the Thai administrative court. Examples of strong national counter-corruption agencies of several countries also provided Thai reform drivers with ideas for building a strong national counter-corruption commission. The United Kingdom model of the national audit commission was the prototype for the State Audit Commission of Thailand. The Thai Human Rights Commission and the Anti-Money Laundering office were influenced by UN models. The Department of Special Investigation is a counterpart of the United States' FBI.

It is difficult to pinpoint the reform importers and drivers of all these accountability institutions. For many years before the 1997 Constitution, there had been talks among academics, MPs, members of the mass media, bureaucratic stakeholders, and others about the need to establish these new accountability organizations. For example, a strong counter-corruption commission was seen as a solution to the serious corruption problems of the Thai bureaucrats and politicians. The old counter-corruption commission established in 1975 was known to be a paper tiger (Bowornwathana 2005c). Other accountability institutions, such as the Ombudsman, the State Audit Commission, the Anti-Money Laundering office, and the Department of Special Investigation, were all seen as ways to help solve the problems of the corruption and inefficiency of bureaucrats and politicians. The Elections Commission also provides a means to run fair elections. The Administrative Court presents a unique case where Thai public law experts trained in Continental Europe, especially France, working in the Office of the Juridical Council and in the law schools acted as an interest group of reform drivers to establish the administrative court in Thailand amidst strong opposition from judges in civil and criminal courts. The creation of the National Human Rights Commission was partly influenced by the May Bloodshed of 1992, in which many protesters were massacred by the authorities. For the Anti-Money Laundering Office and the Department of Special Investigation, the police were key reform drivers, because they were responsible for the functions of those institutions from the beginning.

Most accountability institutions were born in 1997 with the promulgation of the new Constitution, which created, for example, the Ombudsman, the Constitutional Court, the National Counter Corruption Commission, the Administrative Court, the State Audit Commission, the Human Rights Commission, and the Elections Commission. A few years later, the laws governing these accountability institutions were passed, giving them the authority to perform their functions by setting up the offices, with commissioners, staffs, and budgets, to implement the accountability mandates. All politicians and bureaucrats became part of the implementation process, since the accountability laws were enforced on them.

However, the ultimate goal of citizen control over bureaucrats and politicians through the accountability institutions has so far not been reached. Citizens have not been reform gainers: rather, the gainers so far have been the bureaucrats and the politicians. Bureaucratization has resulted from the creation of several new accountability offices, new positions, more budgets, and more personnel. Most important, the laws setting up the institutions gave the commissioners and the accountability officials the authority to exercise their discretionary power over their field of jurisdiction. The new accountability institutions wield power and are the new actors in Thai politics and administration. Another unintended consequence has been politicization. Politicians in power have been able to influence the decisions of the new institutions. During the Thaksin Governments, the powerful prime minister was able to control the Senate's selection of their members. The three institutions most affected were the Constitutional Court, the National Counter Corruption Commission, and the Elections Commission. The level of politicization was lower in the cases of the Ombudsmen and the National Human Rights Commission; the Administrative Court was the least politicized because it functions almost like an ordinary court, which is difficult for politicians to influence. On the other hand, the Anti-Money Laundering Office and the Department of Special Investigation are directly under the political executive. They were used as political instruments to harass the opposition during the Thaksin governments.

The Third Transfer: The Inflow of Management Tools

There is a constant flow of management tools or fashions from the developed West, in particular from the United States, into the Thai polity, along with claims that they will deliver higher organizational performance and productivity. Examples are branding, the balanced scorecard (BSC), strategic planning, core competencies, knowledge management, learning organizations, reengineering, total quality management (TQM), the Public Sector Management Quality Award (PMQA), Thailand's International Public Sector Standards Management System and Outcomes (PSO), ISO (International Organizations for

Standardization) 9001–2000, 5s, Six Sigma, outsourcing, e-procurement, e-learning, the medium-term expenditure framework (MTEF),
the Malcolm Baldrige National Quality Award (MBNQA), quality
control (QC), the blueprint for change, activity-based costing (ABC),
change management, customer relationship management (CRM),
economic value-added analysis (EVA), and result-based management
(RBM). It must be noted that the use of management tools in government can be found in other countries, such as Norway, as well
(Laegreid et al. 2007; Pollitt 1995).

The transfer of management tools from developed countries into
the Thai public bureaucracy has been going on for decades. I recall
that in 1978, while I was doing my doctoral fieldwork in the provinces, the provincial and district offices were filled with charts and
posters of PERT/CPM (the program evaluation and review technique,
corporate performance management)and organization development
doctrines. Today, if we go to the same offices, we will find similar
charts and posters showing visions and missions of strategic planning
and key performance indicators of the balanced scorecard. What
this means, perhaps, is that management tools are "cosmetic" instruments for building good images for government agencies. How
can a government office be inefficient if it is using the latest state-
of-the-art management tools from abroad?

Several observations may be made. First, management tools come
and go; they do not last long. They are fashions (Jackson 2001; Collins
2000; Hood 1991). First the line bureaucrats are summoned to attend
a conference in Bangkok to be told about a new, "magical" management tool that everyone must use. They listen to instructions from
officials of the central agencies who are the focal actors or owners of
reform ideas on how to work with the new tools. They are told what
they must do. The meetings to indoctrinate the line bureaucrats from
all over the country about the new management tool have a sacred
and symbolic significance. They are held in the conference room of
Thailand's equivalent of the U.S. White House, and the opening
ceremony is presided over by the prime minister or deputy prime
minister. If you are not there, you are not at the forefront.

After the grand introductory meeting, the line bureaucrats attend
other meetings to familiarize themselves with the new forms and
conditions set forth by the focal actor. They then go back to their
agencies and implement the reform idea by requiring others in their
agencies to follow the new requirements of the management tool.

They regularly report back to the focal actor, who collects performance data from each agency. Later on, they are summoned again to another grand meeting at the "Thai White House," where they are told of another new magical management tool they have to follow. It is at this point that the old management tool starts to fade away. The new tool may replace the old one if it serves the same purposes, such as achieving good planning or efficiency. If the old one is not replaced, the new one will simply add to the piles of management tools already in existence. Because of these recurring events, line bureaucrats sometimes do not take the implementation of the management tools seriously. They regard them as "toys" of central agency officials, whose purpose is to exert control over them. If the executive politicians do not show firm support for the new management tool, the line bureaucrats will probably pay little attention to it.

Second, why do some management tools last longer than others? Their lifespan depends on several factors. Some last longer because they have legal backing. The bureaucrats are forced by law to comply with the new work requirements of the new tools. For example, several new laws in Thailand stipulate that bureaucrats must follow the balanced scorecard, practise knowledge management, and use e-procurements. Management tools also last long because there are supported by central agencies who are the reform owners. The tools are vital for the survival and growth of the focal actor. Also fostering longevity are the simplicity or ease of use of each management tool and the ability of the existing IT technology to support IT-oriented management tools such as e-procurement. Also, planning tools seem to last longer than specific efficiency improvement tools.

The transfer of management tools is more an affair of bureaucrats than of politicians. Bureaucrats, not politicians, are the key actors in the reform diffusion process. They act as reform importers, drivers, owners, and implementers. Politicians are more preoccupied with politics and with building their own popularity. Some management tools can also be too technical for politicians, who have too tight a political schedule to go into details.

Fourth, the transfer of management tools from developed countries follows closely the development of the body of knowledge built by professors of management in the business schools, mainly schools in the American universities, such as the Harvard Business School. New reform ideas from the management gurus are quickly imported into Thailand by members of the Thai management community, such as the Thailand Management Association (TMA), and consultant companies in search of projects in Thailand. Several such companies are hired by the government to bring management tools into the Thai public sector. Furthermore, Thai universities offering MBAs are also keen to teach the state-of-the-art management tools. Central officials are very eager to learn about the latest tools, and they rush to claim expertise in their use in Thailand. A high official from a central agency asked me at a meeting recently whether I had a "new reform toy" for him to play with. With the increasing popularity of evaluation techniques in the management world, the new trend seems to be directed towards more evaluation tools in the near future.

Fifth, the issue of whether, and to what extent, management tools that are invented for the use in companies can be transferred to public organizations is given little attention by reform enthusiasts. Also, the problem of borrowing foreign management tools into the unique Thai socio-cultural context is taken lightly.

Sixth, after a management tool is used, improvements in the bureaucracy are difficult to detect. It is also difficult to claim that any good results one sees are the product of the tool itself. On the other hand, examples of possible unintended consequences are numerous: increased paper work, empire-building, wasted budget spending, goal displacement, tool-overload, central pull, and prime ministerialization (see Bowornwathana 2004a for explanations of these terms), and a biased perception of government reform from a managerial point of view.

Now I shall explain the transfer of selected management tools through a common framework covering reform architects, reform importers, reform drivers, focal actors, reform implementers, and reform gainers and losers.

First, the reform architects of all the imported management tools are well-known management experts, mostly from the United States. Their works are readily available in bookstores. For example, Robert S. Kaplan, from the Harvard Business School, and David P. Norton are the architects of the "balanced scorecard." Kaplan has been invited several times to lecture to the management community in Thailand. Another tool, core competencies, was developed by C.K. Prahalad and Gary Hamel in their *Harvard Business Review* article in 1990. The "learning organization" approach was proposed by Peter Senge of MIT's Sloan School of Management in his book *The Fifth Discipline: The Art and the Learning Organization*. The

TQM tool was developed by the late W. Edward Deming when he set out his famous fourteen points. The architects of various versions of "strategic management," such as Michael E. Porter, are also professors from U.S. universities such as Harvard Business School. "Reengineering" came from two American management experts, Michael Hammer and James A. Champy, in their book *Re-engineering the Corporation: A Manifesto for Business Revolution* (1993).

Second, the major reform importers of management tools from the private sector are from the Thai business community (in particular the Thailand Management Association (TMA)), consultancy companies, and key individual figures. Because of globalization, knowledge about management tools is transferred quickly, and the Thai business community is well aware of the state of the art. Training sessions and consultancy services are provided by the TMA and other companies involved in management training. Buying and selling management tools is big business in Thailand. It is a big event when a management guru such as Robert S. Kaplan is invited to conduct lectures and training sessions in Thailand. Thai participants are willing to pay a very high entrance fee to attend the special lectures. Of course, the guru is well paid.

How do management tools cross the line from the business world into the world of government? Who are the reform drivers? First, foreign advisors from international organizations such as the UN, the OECD, and the ADB may suggest using them in the public sector. Second, bureaucrats think that using them to improve their organizations will not threaten the status quo: on the contrary, they think those management tools will make them look good and modern. Moreover, the tools may open the doors to new opportunities in their career aspirations. Sometimes, bureaucrats seem to genuinely believe that the management tools can work magic in their organizations, as happened during the 1990s, when management experts were appointed as members of the national reform commissions.

At the same time, certain groups of bureaucrats, usually from the central agencies, will show interest in using a particular management tool and organize conferences, invite experts, conduct training sessions for their staffs, write up blueprints and draft work manuals. When the political boss allows them to use the management tool, they become the focal actor in the reform. The central agencies include, for example, the Civil Service Commission (CSC), the Office of Public Sector Development (OPDC), and the Budget Bureau. The CSC uses "core competencies." The OPDC claims to use the balanced scorecard and TQM. The Budget Bureau uses RBM (results-based budgeting).

The next step in the transfer process is the implementation of the imported tools. Laws, rules, and regulations are issued to give legitimacy to the focal actor in charge of a particular tool. For example, the CSC operates under the new 2008 Civil Servant Act, and the OPDC under the 2003 Royal Decree on Good Governance. The focal actor then devises the forms, manuals, and implementation steps to be administered to the targets of the reform, which usually covers the entire bureaucracy. Reform implementers include the focal actors and government agencies in which the management tool is to be administered.

At this stage, the original version of the management tool is adjusted by the focal actors so that, they claim, the tool will fit the Thai public context. For example, the four goals of the balanced scorecard tool are adjusted to match that context. One wonders how much is left of the original tool if it is substantially changed. Another problem is that the application of the BSC in Thailand focuses more on the search for KPIs (key performance indicators) and ignores the construction of strategic maps. Sometimes, private companies such as the Thai Rating and Information Services (TRIS) are hired to work out the KPIs. Since all government organizations are required to use the BSC, the hiring of consultancy firms is a lucrative business.

The politics of tool choice (Peters, 2002, 553–64) is also interesting. Newcomers tend to disregard the work of their predecessors, ignoring their tools and using new ones of their own. For example, the PSO was buried by administrative reformers of the Thaksin governments, and the United Kingdom's Citizen Charter Award of the Prime Minister, which had been borrowed at one time during previous governments, was replaced with other types of awards, such as the Thai version of the Malcolm Baldrige National Quality Award from the United States (called the PMQA, or Public Sector Management Quality Award).

At the end of the reform diffusion process there are gainers and losers. Among the bureaucrats, the gainers are usually those working for the focal organization that administered the reform. They have increased their control over other government agencies, and they have more work to do, which makes them look good. They can justify their requests to expand their organizations and upgrade their positions. Recently, the status of the OPDC, which split off from the CSC six years ago, was upgraded to a PC–11 organization. The OPDC officials are even thinking of setting up their own representative units in all government organizations. Except for the focal actors, the remaining two million bureaucrats are mostly losers. They have to do more paper work, as required by the management tools. And more control is exercised over them from the center. In short, the "doctors" from the focal actor become better off, but the patients working in government agencies remain sick. The application of management tools does not affect politicians very much. However, some management tools, such as the Thai version of the United Kingdom's "framework agreement," may be applied to politicians.

The three reform ideas, that is, the guiding reform paradigm, the accountability institutions, and the management tools, differ from one another in two interesting ways. First, management tools tend to have short life cycles: they come and go, as was the case with OD (organization development) in the 1970s and reengineering in the 1990s. The guiding reform paradigm, on the other hand, tends to have a longer life cycle. Once accepted, the principles of the chosen paradigm tend to stay for a long time, because they represent basic beliefs and values about the principles of good government. Because of their firm legal status, the accountability institutions also last longer than the management tools.

Second, their orientations are also different. Management tools concentrate directly on the efficiency improvements of the bureaucrats and the bureaucracy from a managerial point of view. The new accountability institutions aim to ensure that the practices of both politicians and bureaucrats are accountable for. Thus, in turn, accountability institutions check and balance the use of discretionary power by politicians and bureaucrats. Under the principles of democratic governance, the belief is that citizens are the owners of government and that their power should be above that of politicians and bureaucrats. This new belief about citizen superiority runs counter to the traditional subjective political culture that has for centuries dominated Thai society and Thai people.

REFORM CONSEQUENCES: HAVE REFORM IDEAS PRODUCED EFFECTIVE CHANGE?

To ask whether reform ideas produce effective change is to pose a value-laden question. With governance, the reform goal is to empower citizens so that they become masters of bureaucrats and politicians.

In a society such as Thailand, where bureaucrats and politicians monopolize political and administrative power and citizens are weak, the task of administrative reform is an elephantine one, since there is stiff resistance from powerful bureaucrats and politicians to changes that may jeopardize their power, privileges, and special status.

Four major consequences flow from the transfer of reform ideas from developed countries into the Thai polity. First, there is an illusion of success once a reform idea is implemented. Establishing a new accountability agency, writing a new constitution based on governance ideas, or launching a new management tool in the bureaucracy can make us believe that the reform has been successful. Outsiders such as delegations from neighboring governments who come for a study tour of administrative reform in Thailand may leave the country with a good impression, since the government agencies they have visited and the state-of-the-art management tools they have been briefed on look good. In this regard, Thailand seems to be ahead of many developing countries, since it has imported many reform ideas from developed countries. Some reform innovations, such as the administrative court system, have not even been put into practice in many developed countries.

However, in spite of all the changes in structure, laws and regulations, and bureaucratic practices, the new reform ideas have not resulted in major changes in the behavior and values of politicians and bureaucrats. For example, the introduction of performance indicators for making promotion decisions has not changed the widespread practice of nepotism and patronage in the Thai bureaucracy. The patron bureaucrat manipulates the system of scoring so that his clients or favorites can be promoted. At the same time, he claims to abide by the new rules of the balanced scorecard. Using the new management tools to justify old bad practices is common. Another example is provided by the transfer of new ideas to combat corruption. New, strong counter-corruption agencies have been created, and revised anti-corruption laws have been enacted. Yet corruption, especially at the top, seems to be rising in the Thai polity. On the streets, the police still commonly demand bribes from traffic violators. In short, the more you try to change, the more things remain the same – or worsen.

Perhaps one should regard the importation of administrative reform ideas as capable of achieving only limited improvement (Peters 1998, 2000; Hood and Peters 2004) in the behavior of bureaucrats and politicians. But, some argue, they are better than nothing. The limits of reform are obvious. First, fundamental changes are almost impossible in the short run. But will major structural changes lead to major changes in values and behavior in the long run? We should adopt a long-term perspective for studying reform change. One way to do so is to regard reform as a phenomenon of cultural transformation (Bowornwathana 2007). Second, we should not be too ambitious or fall into the trap of government practitioners and claim instant success from the reform undertakings. Self-evaluation by the reform agency of its success is not acceptable. We should be more humble in our evaluation. An alternative would be to follow the suggestions of some scholars about "good enough governance." Instead of good governance, good enough governance may become a more realistic goal for many countries faced with reducing poverty (Grindle 2004).

Second, there are also the often forgotten unintended consequences or outcomes that follow much later on after a reform is introduced. The introduction of governance principles has resulted in the blurring of the meaning of the concept of governance. The words "governance" and "good governance" became useless and confusing because they can mean too many things to many Thais. The transfer of accountability institutions did not result in an effective system of neutral and independent agencies. Instead, many have been politicized at one time or another. Politicization has occurred because stakeholder politicians have exerted influence over the new institutions. Bureaucratization has occurred because the new institutions have behaved like a typical public organization with ambitions to expand its domain and increase its authority in the bureaucracy by revising rules and regulations and issuing new ones. The new management tools from the business world contain assumptions in support of a strong chief executive officer (CEO). Once translated into the world of government, they tend to support a single authoritative center of power with the head of public agencies at the top of the pyramid. This central-pull tendency of management tools co-existed well with former prime minister Thaksin's desire to centralize all power in his hands (Bowornwathana 2004a, 2005b, 2006d).

Another unintended consequence that goes unnoticed is the existence of too many management tools. Bureaucrats are asked to do similar things for different focal actors. Each management reform tool requires the victimized bureaucrats to do certain things such as filing reports and collecting information for the focal actor. For example, under the new performance evaluation system, bureaucrats must report their work accomplishments in detail on paper. This time-consuming exercise has meant that they spend less time working on their core functions. To be promoted to a higher-level position in the job classification system, they must also write reports hundreds of pages in length on their achievements. Sometimes, subordinates help their superiors to complete the report with promises from the boss that they will be given salary increases and promotions in the future.

Third, unintended consequences also originate from the problem of the interconnectedness of the imported reform innovations. The questions that arise include, Are the new governance paradigm, the new accountability institutions, and the management tools congruent? Is each accountability institution and each management tool, in principle and practice, really in support of the principles of governance? Are accountability institutions working in harmony with one another, or are they engaging in a fierce fight over bureaucratic turf? And do management tools complement one another so that governance principles are upheld? What follows when too many management tools are enforced and all government agencies and bureaucrats have to comply? Do overloads in management tools slow down the good performance of government agencies and bureaucrats? These are questions that future research on the importation of administrative reform should pursue.

The interconnectedness problem is common when narrow-minded reform implementers become too parochial and too concerned with their own reform turf. It gets worse if they start competing among themselves. The line bureaucrats then become "reform victims" who, for example, have to fill in hundreds of forms about the reform for too many focal actors, especially those from the central agencies, whose successes, ironically, depend on the inputs of the victims.

Fourth, one should also take note of the unchanging nature of the traditional Thai bureaucracy. Why, despite all the efforts to reform it, have things remained almost the same? Some traditional explanations have been given. As Ferrel Heady has mentioned, when others are weak, bureaucrats may stray from their instrumental roles to become the primary wielders of power in the political system (1966, 99). They may form a self-serving interest group because no other groups can check and balance their power. Another explanation, provided by Fred Riggs, is "formalism." He has argued (1966) that while on the surface a developing country such as Thailand has all the formal structures of a developed country, in fact, the behavior and practices of bureaucrats and politicians are contrary to what one sees on paper.

I have argued that one should see government reform as an effort to change the culture of bureaucrats and politicians in Thailand (Bowornwathana 2007). Cultural reform of the Thai bureaucracy takes a long time. There is no instant reform solution. One must remember that at least in the Thai experience, Western reform ideas and models, whatever their good intentions and however diverse they may be, are transformed into completely different animals. In the future, effective change is likely to come from outside, not inside, the government. Factors that facilitate effective reform of bureaucrats and politicians are a much larger educated middle class, increased globalization and democratization, rapid economic development, and success in poverty reduction. It is difficult to reform bureaucrats and politicians if they are in charge of reforming themselves. As an old Thai saying goes, "Don't let the cat guard the grilled fish."

PART SIX

Change and Reform
in a Multinational Context

10

Change and Reform
in the European Union

ALBERTA M. SBRAGIA

The European Union has grown ever more important as its membership has increased along with the range of policy areas under its jurisdiction. It is now a global actor in many areas, as well as a major force in its member states' policy environment. The unique nature of the EU, which differs from both traditional states and traditional international organizations, is such that its features can seem either quite familiar or quite the opposite, depending on the characteristic chosen for analysis. Neither a state nor simply a multilateral institution, it combines the attributes of an intergovernmental organization with those of a diverse, complex, and ever-evolving polity.

The issues linked to reform and change in the EU are therefore necessarily different from those faced by individual nation-states. The process of change, of evolving from primarily a (very distinctive) international organization to one with many of the characteristics of a polity, involves very disparate instruments. Some are grounded in international relations such as those based on treaties, while others are anchored in more traditional state-like dynamics such as administrative reform.

This chapter provides a (necessarily partial) overview of the key instruments that have been used in the extraordinary transformation of an international institution originally designed to create a common market and to act as a unitary negotiator in global trade negotiations. The various strategic steps in the process that has led to the European Union of 2009, once again on the brink of a major recalibration of its institutional dynamics, have involved the participation of the EU's member-states' governments in negotiating new treaty arrangements, each of which has moved the process of integration further. Those states, in turn, have viewed their membership in the European Union as key to their economic health and, more recently, to their internal security. The negotiation of treaties, therefore, is a crucial part of the mosaic by which integration proceeds (Moravscik 1998).

Treaties as formal documents, however, tell only part of the story. The EU's institutional universe is now densely populated. New organizations, as well as administrative instruments, have been created to cope with new challenges and problems as they arise. Some of those challenges have been anchored in the wide-ranging demands of coping with the implementation of a single market, which for its part represents a huge expansion of the powers and problems that now belong to Brussels (Egan 2001). The single market, featuring the liberalization of the movement of capital, goods, services, and labor, transformed the challenge of governance in the European Union, while simultaneously catapulting the EU into the ranks of first-tier economic powers.

The single market, in fact, has triggered the creation of a whole host of new agencies that now extend the EU's reach to many technical areas that previously belonged to national institutions. The rapid growth of such new organizations brought with it new types of relationships with member states, which themselves often created new counterpart agencies that then coordinated their activities with the relevant EU agency.

Just as the single market was beginning to be implemented, the EU faced a major new challenge that in many ways came to overshadow the difficulties intrinsic to the operational features of a single market. The European Union, which consisted of fifteen West European member-states in 1995 – the EU–15 – was thoroughly shaken by the prospect of its enlargement to what eventually became the EU–27. The new applicant states, with the exception of Cyprus and Malta, were all post-communist states, with all that implied in terms of economic structure, the role of law and property rights, democratic institutions, and minority rights. They had been through an economic and political experience totally unknown to any of the EU–15. Even Greece, Spain, and Portugal – which had entered the EU after experiencing dictatorship – had not had to cope with the legacy of a socialist economy.

The EU imposed "conditionality" upon the new aspirants, and the European Commission oversaw the process by which conditionality was imposed and responded to. Although "conditionality" as an instrument had previously been used by international financial institutions such as the International Monetary Fund in its dealings with developing countries (Vreeland 2007), it had not been used by the EU in previous enlargements. It gave the EU a type of leverage over aspirant states that it had not previously demanded or exercised.

As the issue of enlargement loomed in the distance, the EU was faced with the more immediate question of how much further it could centralize power at the EU level. The Treaty of Maastricht, which came into effect in 1993, had moved integration forward a great deal. As the powers of the EU expanded and policy areas such as environmental protection were added to its portfolio, the issue of how deeply the EU was to penetrate core aspects of the political economy of the nation-state became more pressing. The combination of the single market, the commitment to economic and monetary union, which led to the introduction of the euro in 2002, and the expansion of the policy portfolio under the jurisdiction of the EU's institutions led to a re-examination of the EU's traditional method of policy-making. Was the EU to take responsibility for employment, for example? The flexibility of labor markets?

The member-states were not willing to cede sovereignty in those areas, those most critical to the European "social model." However, they did accept that the EU would be involved to some extent. Various types of governance structures were constructed that did not restrict the sovereignty of member-states in sectors such as employment policy but that did try to increase policy convergence across member-states through voluntary means. Such "new modes of governance" added to the EU's toolkit of policy instruments.

While treaty reforms give the member-state governments center stage, the creation of new agencies, the process of enlargement, and the development of new modes of governance all involved the European Commission. While the exact nature of the balance of power among the collectivity of member-states, the European Parliament, and the Commission has varied, the Commission has always been a key actor in the policy-making process. It does not legislate, but its drafting power (Bauer 2008), agenda setting, administrative activity, and oversight of national implementation are essential to the way the EU operates. The Commission is the pivotal administrative arm of the EU and is the institution critical to the Union's capacity for action. The Commission is in many ways the most visible face of supranationality, and it is the institution that more than any other distinguishes the EU from other regional organizations pursuing economic integration.

It is the European Commission that negotiates for the member-states at the WTO. It is included in numerous international venues along with the member-states and holds the monopoly on the initiation of legislation, which is then amended by the Council of Ministers and the European Parliament. It brings member-states to the European Court of Justice for failing to comply with EU legislation. The involvement of the Commission has expanded over time as it has gradually obtained the competence to act in most areas of Justice and Home Affairs (internal security). Although it does not play a key role in the area of foreign and security policy, the European Commission has been defined as the "heart" of the process of European integration outside of foreign and security policy arenas. Although it has had to share its power over time with other institutions, it is clear that in comparative terms the Commission is an exceptionally powerful and pivotal international bureaucracy.

The Commission is therefore an international bureaucracy working within the most integrated, most supranational, and most powerful regional organization in the world. Although it had resisted changes for over two decades, the Commission was forced to undergo a major internal reform in the period 2000–5. The Commission in 2008 functions differently from the way it functioned in 1998 – although the exact parameters of that change are still unknown. The attempt to reform such a unique institution has illuminated many of the tensions between the role of the Commission as a policy actor and its role as an administrative/management arm of the EU.

In line with our discussion, this chapter provides an overview of treaty reforms, the birth and development of agencies, the use of "conditionality" in the historic enlargement of the EU to twenty-seven members in the period 2004–7, the adoption of "new modes of governance," and the reform of the European Commission.

TREATY REFORMS

A key benchmark in marking change in the European Union has been the negotiation of new treaties. While treaties often include practices that have evolved under a pre-existing treaty without that treaty's formal blessing, treaties also involve important changes in the relationship between the EU's supranational institutions and the member-states. The nature and the focus of treaties provide one way of understanding the trajectory of European integration. They represent a crucial response to problems that demand effective change. Such a response involves the unanimous acceptance by the members at that point in time, and the consequent treaty is one that future members will be required to accept in order to gain admission. Furthermore, future members will be required to accept all the legislation that has been adopted under the existing treaties, the EU's *acquis*.

Treaties have defined the role of supranational institutions, those not directly representing the interests of the member-states, and the role of institutions that represent national interests. The tension between the supranational institutions – the European Court of Justice, the European Central Bank, the European Commission, and the European Parliament, on the one hand, and the Council of Ministers, the key intergovernmental policy-making institution representing national interests, on the other, is a constant theme in the narrative of change and reform within the European Union.[1] In a globalizing world, balancing the "European interest" with the interests of individual democratically elected governments, some of which are major world powers, is a never-ending struggle.

.Treaties define the responsibilities of both the EU institutions and of member governments. The EU's decision-making process almost always involves the member-states, but it is treaties that spell out those areas in which the member-states can act unilaterally within their own national boundaries or externally in global affairs, those areas in which they will act collectively as a single unit, and those areas in which they will act collectively but in interaction with the European Commission and the European Parliament. Treaties also define the decision rules that will be operative when the national government is acting in concert with other actors, national or supranational, in Brussels. And finally, treaties define the reach of the two institutions that do not negotiate with either the EU's other supranational institutions or with the member states – the European Court of Justice and the European Central Bank.

It must be remembered that treaties are negotiated by national executives. National parliaments ratify treaties, but it is the political parties in power that are at the negotiating table. Given the structure of parliamentary governments in Europe, ratification by parliaments is nearly always an easy process. Treaty negotiations, therefore, are the most intergovernmental processes in the European Union. National interests and national perspectives are key. National leaders (prime ministers or presidents, depending on the national system), operating as the European Council, are the key actors in treaty reform. In Helen Wallace's words, "the European Council became ... the key forum for determining treaty reforms ... [It] has increasingly become the venue for addressing ... the big and more strategic decisions to do with the core new tasks of the EU and those that define its 'identity' as an arena for collective action" (2000, 20).

FROM ROME TO LISBON

The Treaty of Rome, as the founding Treaty of the European Union, holds a special place in the iconography of European integration. A relatively short treaty, it laid out the principles that were to guide the process of economic integration, as well as the institutional structure that was to oversee this process and the representation of the EU in the General Agreement on Tariffs and Trade (GATT). It also accepted a special relationship for the EU with its then colonies, a relationship that grew in importance after Britain joined in 1973. The special link that the EU still has with the African, Caribbean, and Pacific countries – and that gives it a special (often unrecognized) influence in much of the developing world – was institutionalized in the Treaty of Rome (Holland 2002; Carbone 2007). That relationship in fact has led to transatlantic (U.S.-EU) conflicts that, while they seemed arcane to many, were actually embedded in the birth and evolution of the EU as a regional organization with ties to the developing world.

The key institutions of the Community – with the exception of the European Central Bank and the European Council – were established by the Treaty of Rome. The powers of those original institutions were to be transformed over time, but the basic concern with inter-institutional balance was present. Crucially, however, the DNA of the Treaty of Rome was similar to that of its predecessor the Treaty of Paris in that the process of economic integration was viewed as part of a long-term political process that would gradually lead to some unspecified form of European unification. The EU was never conceptualized as a European NAFTA – it was, by contrast, to be an organization that would bring European governments and European peoples into ever closer cooperation. While the modalities were to be debated and changed over the life of the EU, that core concept has always been present. The methodology chosen to achieve such cooperation was that of a balance between "supranationalism" and "intergovernmentalism." The former was to pursue and protect the "European interest" – that is, the interest of an integrating and cooperative Europe – while the latter was to protect the individual and collective interests of the member-states vis-à-vis each other, as well as relative to the supranational institutions.

The Single European Act (SEA), which came into effect in 1987, provided a major impetus to the process of economic integration, as well as providing the opportunity for the EU to move into such areas as environmental protection, by introducing the ability to make decisions under super-majority rules rather than by unanimity. Pushed by fears that its firms were less competitive than their Japanese and U.S. counterparts, the EU moved to create a single market, one in which non-tariff barriers that serve to keep out goods produced in other EU member states would be reduced and in which capital, services, and labor would be able to move across borders without hindrance (Sandholtz and Zysman 1989; Cameron 1992). The single market is still in the process of actually coming into existence, as it is a politically difficult enterprise. However, sector by sector, the EU has been able to liberalize national economies (Sandholtz 1992; Staniland 2008; Thatcher 1999, Fligstein and Stone Sweet 2001; Young 2005). A key concept, introduced by the European Court of Justice, that enabled this transformation was known as "mutual recognition." In this formulation, regulatory standards accepted by one member-state would be accepted by another with some safe-guards. It opened the door for an increase in trade because it eliminated the necessity of harmonizing national standards, a process that was both arduous and incredibly slow (Egan 2001; Alter and Meunier-Aitsahalia 1994).

The SEA also allowed the EU to move into the area of environmental policy much more easily. By changing the decision rules, the EU was able to move toward environmental protection by using a super-majority voting rule, rather than by using consensus. The EU then began introducing environmental legislation at a rapid pace. As the U.S. pulled back from its previously far-reaching attempts to protect the environment, the EU emerged as a leader in that field. In

2006, the adoption of REACH, a far-reaching piece of legislation that regulates chemicals to an extent never before seen, as well as the coming into force of ROHS, crystallized the EU's reputation as a global leader in the field of environmental protection (Schapiro 2007).[2] Similarly, the EU's decision (fiercely disputed by the rest of the world) to force aviation to abide by the Kyoto Protocol's limits on carbon dioxide represented another example of its "green" credentials (Staniland 2009).

With the fall of the Berlin Wall and the re-emergence of the "German Question," which had propelled the first attempt at integration in 1951, the Union moved beyond market-related integration. The Maastricht Treaty was a turning point in that it brought the EU – although not its supranational institutions – into foreign policy and internal security (known under various terms such as Justice and Home Affairs and Freedom, Security, and Justice). It also increased the power of the European Parliament by giving it equal legislative powers with the Council of Ministers in a significant number of areas, as well as allowing super-majority voting to replace unanimity in many more policy areas within the Council of Ministers. In the economic sphere, the treaty committed the Union to move toward economic and monetary union – that is, toward the creation of a European Central Bank and a common currency, which later became known as the euro. Very narrowly approved by the French electorate in a referendum, the Maastricht Treaty also allowed the EU to begin the still-ongoing process of developing greater capability in its foreign relations.

As the issue of internal security became more pressing, the Treaty of Amsterdam laid out the blueprint for a far-reaching expansion of EU power in the fields of immigration, asylum, and policing. While policing remained under the intergovernmental so-called third pillar of the Maastricht Treaty, issues having to do with immigration, border controls, visas, and asylum were brought under the jurisdiction of the EU's supranational institutions. Again, the power of Parliament was increased by expanding the use of the co-decision procedure and the requirement that the Parliament had to approve the member-states' nominee for commission president (Shackleton 2005; Hix 2002).

The issue of the EU's enlargement had become a topic of discussion shortly after the retreat of the Soviet Union from the Central and

Eastern European countries, which had been in the Soviet sphere. As they began to talk about the "return to Europe," the post-communist states signalled just how much the European Union and Europe had become viewed as one and the same (a formulation of course opposed by Switzerland, Norway, and Iceland, which were not EU members). In 1993, at the Copenhagen Summit, the European Council, made up of the EU–12's heads of state and government, laid out a road map for accession. Known as the "Copenhagen criteria," the leaders emphasized that states wishing to join the EU must develop a working market economy, a democratic system of governance, and respect for minority rights. The European Commission and the European Parliament, as well as individual member states, began working with what would be the new accession states to transform their socialist economies and non-democratic systems into market systems working under the rule of law and governed by democratically elected leaders.

As it became clear that the former socialist regimes were advancing toward meeting the Copenhagen criteria, the issue of how their accession would be accommodated institutionally moved up the political agenda. The Treaty of Nice, negotiated in a manner that left a huge amount to be desired and coming into effect in February 2003, allocated to each member one commissioner until twenty-seven members had joined (after which the Commission's membership would be rotated), changed the number of members of Parliament allocated to each state, changed the formula for calculating how a super-majority was to be defined, and increased the power of the Commission president.

Given the shortcomings of the treaty negotiation process as exemplified by the Treaty of Nice, a new institutional process was adopted for the next treaty reform. A constitutional convention was called, with national government representatives, national parliament representatives, and members of the European Parliament, to draft a treaty to move beyond Nice (Magnette 2003, 2004; Dehousse 2005). After rejections in France and the Netherlands, the Constitutional Treaty was reshaped into the Lisbon Treaty, which retained many of the characteristics as its predecessor but was more traditional in that it did not try to unify the previous treaties and omitted the signs of statehood such as an anthem and a flag (which is in constant use in any case). When the Lisbon Treaty was rejected by the Irish in a referendum in June 2008, however, the EU was left with the question of whether it would find a way to proceed toward further institutionalization, especially in the foreign policy arena. In October 2009, the Irish approved the Lisbon Treaty, and the way seemed clear for a new phase of European integration to begin.

AGENCIES

National systems have experienced the growth of a variety of organizations that are "at arm's length (or further) from the main hierarchical 'spine' of central ministries/departments of state" (Talbot 2004, 5). Although the usage can be fuzzy, depending on the national context, such organizations are often known variously as "agencies" or "quangos" (ibid.), and the OECD has referred to them as belonging to "the wider state sector" (2001, 6). We are using the term, when applied to the EU level, to mean organizations that usually have their own legal personality and are distinct, depending on the policy sector involved, from the European Commission or from the bureaucracy serving the member-states in the area of internal security or foreign and security policy (Groenleer 2006).

The EU has in fact experienced an explosion of the agency phenomenon, so much so that in many policy sectors the relevant agency plays a role ranging from technical standard-setting to certification. None of these agencies has the power of U.S. regulatory agencies, for they do not exercise rule making, as do their U.S. counterparts. Nonetheless, their creation has transformed the institutional space within which many policy practitioners work.

Although they differ in significant ways, agencies can be grouped into five broad categories as to their core function (although there is overlap among functions in some agencies): gathering information, regulating, overseeing the development of common technical standards, coordinating/educating, and carrying out program management activities for the Commission. [3] The information gathering and regulatory agencies, as well as the executive agencies, which carry out program management, mainly operate in those policy areas in which the Commission plays a key role. Most of these agencies are known as Community agencies; they are governed by European public law and have their own legal personality. As of October 2009, there were twenty-two Community agencies. However, the Council

---

BOX 10.1
European Community Agencies

- Community Fisheries Control Agency (CFCA)
- Community Plant Variety Office (CPVO)
- European Agency for Reconstruction (EAR)
- European Agency for Safety and Health at Work (EU-OSHA)
- European Agency for the Management of Operational Cooperation at the External Borders (FRONTEX)
- European Aviation Safety Agency (EASA)
- European Centre for Disease Prevention and Control (ECDC)
- European Centre for the Development of Vocational Training (CEDEFOP)
- European Chemicals Agency (ECHA)
- European Environment Agency (EEA)
- European Food Safety Authority (EFSA)
- European Foundation for the Improvement of Living and Working Conditions (EUROFOUND)
- European Fundamental Rights Agency (FRA) – previously EUMC
- European GNSS Supervisory Authority (GSA)
- European Institute for Gender Equality (under preparation)
- European Maritime Safety Agency (EMSA)
- European Medicines Agency (EMEA)
- European Monitoring Centre for Drugs and Drug Addiction (EMCDDA)
- European Network and Information Security Agency (ENISA)
- European Railway Agency (ERA)
- European Training Foundation (ETF)
- Office for Harmonisation in the Internal Market (Trade Marks and Designs) (OHIM)
- Translation Centre for the Bodies of the European Union (CdT)

Note: A Community agency is a body governed by European public law; it is distinct from the community institutions (council, parliament, commission, etc.) and has its own legal personality. It is set up by an act of secondary legislation in order to accomplish a very specific technical, scientific, or managerial task, in the framework of the European Union's "first pillar."

---

of the European Union (which represents the member-states) established the European Union Satellite Centre in 2002, which also has its own legal personality and produces information. It, like the

European Defense Agency, is situated under the so-called second pillar of the EU, which shapes policy-making in the area of foreign policy, an area for which the member-states acting collectively, rather than the Commission, have primary responsibility.

The birth and growing popularity of regulatory agencies has led to comparisons with the U.S. system, in which regulatory agencies play an important role in regulating the market. As Majone has written, Congress has established "scores of independent regulatory commissions, boards and agencies, and [has delegated] to them all the necessary powers of rule-making, adjudication, and enforcement" (Majone 2002a, 321). The EU, for its part, has followed what superficially seems to be a similar path. That is, a very large number of agencies now exist, many of them at the national level, as a result of EU decisions and policies. However, their formal powers differ from those in the United States.[4] They are not endowed with the powers of rule-making. Furthermore, they vary in their ability to exercise even softer forms of authority.

The growth of EU regulatory agencies was preceded by their appearance at the national level (Majone 1994). However, agencies at the national level wielded more power than did those created at the EU level in the 1990s. The European Environment Agency (established in 1990) and the European Agency for Safety and Health at Work (established in 1994) essentially provided information and created a variety of networks with both national and international organizations. The European Agency for the Evaluation of Medicinal Products (EMEA) was more powerful, but it too had to deliver its opinions to the European Commission, which then made the final decision concerning the safety of new drugs (Majone 2002b).

ENLARGEMENT AND CONDITIONALITY

The accession of twelve new states in the period 2004–7 served as an extraordinary shock to the European Union, which moved from fifteen to twenty-seven members. The new states were, with the exception of Cyprus and Malta, former Communist states that had to move to a market economy and establish an independent judiciary and the rule of law, as well as private property rights; create new political parties; develop a new political class; and in some cases deal with very thorny issues related to minority rights. These states can be thought of as the EU–10 since, even though they differed in many ways, they all faced issues anchored in their Communist past. Previous enlargements, in retrospect, seem fairly mundane affairs in that Greece, Spain, and Portugal had market economies as they moved toward democratization, and the other new members, such as Austria, Sweden, and Finland were all well-established market democracies.

The EU–10 were very different from the EU–15, and that showed in many ways. The Commission was given the task of shepherding them through the various steps that were necessary to prepare them for accession. The process was made more difficult because the EU's *acquis* was very large by the time the new members joined in 2004. The EU, by that time, was a far more rules-bound organization than it had been when, for example, Austria, Sweden, and Finland joined in 1995. These three, in fact, had already aligned much of their legislation with that of the EU once they had joined the European Economic Area, a kind of half-way house for prospective members.

The question of how to ensure that the EU–12, but especially the EU–10, carried out those reforms deemed to be necessary to function in the EU, with its focus on market integration, law and regulations, and the need to ensure that the single market worked properly was a key issue in the enlargement process. The answer was given in the form of conditionality, a term that in practice meant that the applicant state had to meet a variety of conditions and criteria in order to be admitted. The Commission was charged with assessing whether those conditions had been properly met. The breadth and depth of conditionality has been so expansive that "it is possible to claim that a new enlargement method has been developed and a separate 'enlargement *acquis*' has emerged including requirements for horizontal administrative reform, regionalization, reform of the judiciary, ethnic minorities' rights, border treaties, safety of nuclear power plants, and so on." (Steunenberg and Dimitrova 2007, 4; see also Dimitrova 2002; Vachudova 2005; Jacoby 2006; Maniokas 2004).

Many of the EU's priorities were also promoted by international institutions such as the International Monetary Fund and the World Bank (Linden 2002; Epstein 2008). In some cases, such as the acceptance of central bank independence (CBI), all three institutions promoted such independence as "economic 'best practice' ... international institutions, through persuasion, argumentation, and coalition building, cultivated a social consensus in favor of CBI" (Epstein 2006, 1020). Although it was not imposed as a condition as such by the

Table 10.1
Criteria for Accesion to the European Union

Copenhagen criteria
1 The existence of democracy and the observation of human rights and the protection of minorities
2 The existence of a market economy
3 The ability to cope with competitive pressures from the EU
4 The ability to take on the responsibility of membership (to implement the *acquis communautaire*)
5 The capacity of the EU to absorb new members

Madrid Criterion
The Madrid Council conclusions also mentioned "the adjustment of their administrative structures" as being important as a preparation for accession, though not as a condition.

EU, CBI was very much in line with what the EU would eventually want the new entrants to achieve.

Conditionality as such, however, was imposed by the European Union under the rubric of the "Copenhagen criteria," which were formulated at the European Council meeting in 1993, held in Copenhagen, and subsequently reinforced with the Madrid criterion of 1995. Those criteria shaped the entire accession process. "'Political conditionality' – referring to the acceptance of human rights, the development of the institutions of liberal democracy, and the rule of law – in particular was absolutely central to the enlargement process. Those basic elements of democracy had to be in place before the actual accession negotiations took place" (Schimmelfenning, Engert, and Knobel 2005, 29).

Once those negotiations began, the laborious task of transposing over eighty thousand pages of EU codes into the applicant states' legal codes began. The incorporation of the *acquis communautaire* – the entire corpus of EU law that had been adopted since 1958 – represented a monumental transfer of legislation. Accession Partnerships were drawn up, with the applicants committing themselves to changing the policies they had in place and replacing them with those enshrined in the *acquis*. The Commission, for its part, monitored their progress and annually published an assessment of how well each applicant state was faring in its journey toward accession (Hille and Knill 2006).

Although the Commission applied pressure on each applicant, outcomes in terms of implementation varied significantly across countries. Scholarly debate has been intense with regard to explanations for such variation. Historical legacies (both pre-Communist and Communist), the level of economic development, the social context within which pressure was applied, the existence of political competition, the role of norms, the nature of incentives as well as of domestic opposition to the outcome desired by the imposition of conditionality, the density of both international rules and domestic actors, rhetorical action, and the nature of veto players have all been put forth as explanations for variation (Vachudova 2005; Hughes, Sasse, and Gordon 2004; Kelley 2004; Jacoby 2004; Schimmelfennig 2003; Giuliani 2003; Haverland 2000; Hellman 1998; Epstein 2005). Of particular interest is Hille and Knill's finding, which privileges the role of the public administration as a key variable in explaining the implementation of the *acquis*. In their words,

> the functioning and the quality of the domestic bureaucracy constitute crucial preconditions for effective alignment with EU policy requirements. This holds true in particular if the focus is not only on the formal transposition but also on the practical application of EU requirements ... Appeals to achieve political consensus on increasing efforts towards alignment seem to be of less relevance for the success of enlargement than efforts to strengthen administrative structures. (2006, 549)

The use of conditionality gave the Commission a crucial role in the process of enlargement. Its yearly reports were eagerly awaited, and the process of monitoring and assessment highlighted its technocratic capabilities.

NEW MODES OF GOVERNANCE

Understanding how the EU is "governed," inasmuch as it lacks a traditional government while incorporating twenty-seven national governments, has shaped much of the literature on the EU. Although the EU as a regional organization does not posses a "government" in the traditional sense, public authority is exercised over a wide range of policy issues. Many scholars have argued that complex sets of relationships involving subnational, national, and supranational actors have emerged as the process of "international" integration has given way to the "governance" of the unique and complicated

polity-like system that integration has created. The concept of "governance" is used to capture the complex relationships between public
and private actors and among actors at different levels of the EU – at
the subnational, national, and regional levels. In Kohler-Koch and
Rittberger's words, "the 'governance turn' in EU studies takes the
EU polity as a given and 'look[s] at the impact of the Euro-polity on
national and European policies and politics'" (2006, 32; Jachtenfuchs
2001, 50).

Whereas the traditional mode of governing in the EU has involved
the passage of legally binding legislation, various new ways of shaping behavior have been adopted that collectively are known as "the
new modes of governance." This category is quite diverse and has
generated a good deal of research (Citi and Rhodes 2006; Rhodes
and Visser forthcoming), but its components share the characteristic
that they are at best "soft," rather than hard, manifestations of EU
authority. Such modes of governance do not carry with them the
power to legally enforce mandates; they are voluntary and often
have an educational function, although their ultimate objective is to
achieve some type of policy reform. This type of governance relies
on ideas and concepts that were often pioneered in the private sector,
are more familiar to students of the new public management than
they are to students of comparative politics or of EU politics, and
rely on the idea that persuasion and learning can inform policy-
making. Policy learning, policy convergence, and policy transfer are
key concepts in this kind of approach (Casey and Gold 2005).
Caporaso and Wittenbrinck point out that "these modes include
benchmarking, mainstreaming, best practices, and the open method
of co-ordination ... The application of these methods to particular
issue areas ... can be quite specialized and difficult to understand"
(2006, 471).

The European Employment Strategy was the first major example
of this new approach to policy change in the EU, and it was quickly
underpinned by the so-called Open Method of Coordination (OMC).
The OMC was designed to advance the Lisbon Strategy of 2000
(which aimed at making the EU far more competitive economically)
by allowing its application to a wide range of policy areas that were
not subject to supranational law-making but in which some kind of
policy convergence was thought desirable. Employment, research,
pensions, social inclusion and poverty reduction, and health and
long-term care, for example, have all now come under the OMC

umbrella (Casey and Gold 2005; Lodge 2007). Jonathan Zeitlin concludes that the "OMC rapidly became the governance instrument of choice for EU policy making in complex, domestically sensitive areas, where the Treaty base for Community action is weak, where inaction is politically unacceptable, and where diversity among Member States precludes harmonization" (Zeitlin 2007, 4).

The introduction of such new forms of governance has expanded the range of interactions among actors across national boundaries. Although the impact of such new forms of interaction is still unclear, it has expanded the reach of "Europeanization" (Zeitlin and Pochet 2005). In an institution that had relied so heavily on legislation, enforceable through the European Court of Justice, the movement to instruments relying on policy learning and policy transfer represented an important innovation in attitude, if not in results. Actors who are not formally enmeshed in the EU's formal apparatus, who are involved neither in formulating nor in implementing EU laws, have become involved in transnational communication and have subjected themselves to peer review. The ultimate impact of such a process is far from clear, but it is possible that decades from now this new form of governance may be viewed as having been a step toward the building of an "European" identity on the part of many actors who otherwise have little interaction with either EU actors or those from other member-states. The "new modes of governance" in effect may represent one step in the breaching of national insularity.

The "multi-level" nature of the European Union and thus of its governance has also attracted a good deal of attention. In fact, the term "multi-level governance" (Hooghe and Marks 2001) is now widely used in the literature on the European Union and generally indicates that public and private actors are both interconnected and work across subnational, national, and supranational levels of policymaking. In its simplest formulation, multi-level governance symbolizes the move away from the predominant role originally played by the central state in the process of integration and highlights the role played both by subnational and supranational actors in the EU's policy process. Interestingly, this approach (as well as the "governance" perspective in general) to the study of the European Union has varied considerably across national scholarly communities, with British and German scholars being particularly attracted to its use (Kohler-Koch and Larat 2009).

THE COMMISSION'S KINNOCK REFORMS

The European Commission has often been viewed as the "engine" or as the "heart" of European integration (Nugent 1997). A unique institution, it combines a variety of functions including policy initiation, agenda-setting, and overseeing implementation, which are largely carried out by national administrations. It is the EU's administrative/executive arm, and it is widely viewed as giving the EU a unique status among other regional organizations dedicated to regional integration. Its existence and administrative capacity allows the EU to have an impact both within and outside the EU that is unparalleled in other regional institutions. When the term European Union is used, many think immediately of the European Commission. As such, it has been the subject of a great deal of attention and scrutiny. Critics have judged it to be a bloated international bureaucracy, while others have viewed it as suffering from severe overload as the EU has taken on more responsibilities without a commensurate increase in the number of staff (Levy and Stevens 2004; Levy 2006).

The Commission, with its roots in the three Communities whose administrations were merged in 1967, was initially based on the French and German models. Therefore, it had a closed (career-based) system, rather than an open system characteristic of the United Kingdom and Swedish models (Auer et al. 1996; Balint et al. 2008). As the EU increased both in membership and in policy responsibility, the reform of the Commission became the subject of a good deal of discussion as its lack of management capacity became increasingly apparent (Laffan 1997). Various proposals were floated, none of which led to substantial change (Coull and Lewis 2003). However, in 1999 a "policy window" opened that led to non-incremental change (Balint et al. 2008).

In 1999 the Santer Commission was forced to resign, an event that has been characterized as "akin to a major and equally unexpected earthquake which shook the Commission from top to bottom" (Bearfield 2004, 13). As a result, the Commission underwent a historic internal reform process known as the Kinnock Reforms, named after Commissioner Kinnock, who was in charge of the process (Commission of the European Communities 2000). "Reform of human resources, planning and budgeting as well as accountability policies and systems" were at the core of the attempt to transform the organization into a more modern organization (Levy 2006, 426). The reforms were thus multi-dimensional, covering a wide range of areas.

In the area of human resources, the new system was designed to reward performance by promotion and to make promotion a process involving many more steps, thereby maintaining an incentive structure for officials as they gained seniority. Salary structures were aligned accordingly:

> The New Pay Structure ... creates financial incentives for excellent performance ahead of time served. At no stage under the new system is an individual paid less after being promoted, as the highest step (5) of any grade is paid no more than the first step of the next highest grade. Under the old system it was different ... a C3 official in step would actually earn more than an official starting at C1, two grades his senior ... As such the new system encourages better performance and aligns pay rewards with the prestige and demands of higher grades. (Coull and Lewis 2003, 4)

In the area of financial management, the Commission instituted a series of changes linked to international standards in the field, moved to modern accrual accounting, and created two new units – the Central Financial Service and the Internal Audit Service. Kinnock viewed those changes as "the most fundamental overhaul of financial management ever undertaken by an EU Institution or, come to that, most other administrations" (Kinnock 2004, 9).

The reforms were widely viewed as a major attempt at changing the culture and operations of the Commission. Wille argues that

> The Kinnock reforms are ... the most radical and comprehensive program of modernization in the Commission's 50-year history ... The idea was to bring Weber back into the organization – merit based, detached from national differences and expressing a common European interest ... A human resource strategy was brought in as an answer to the lack of anything resembling a personnel policy. A more transparent promotion procedure was introduced and staff performance was to be evaluated by managers on a regular basis. (Wille 2007, 39, 41)

The evaluations of how the reforms (which have gone through several phases) have fared are decidedly mixed, too mixed to conclude that the Commission has been successful in avoiding the failures that other public sector organizations have experienced in the area of management reform. However, the scholarly consensus seems to be that the Commission has indeed changed (Peterson 2008; Kassim 2004, 2008; Ellinas and Suleiman 2008), although change has varied rather dramatically across the services (Schon-Quinlivan 2008). Balint et al. (2008) argue that the Commission has moved away from the Franco-German model to one somewhere in between that model and the Anglo-Scandinavian model, the latter being based on merit rather than seniority. Ellinas and Suleiman, based on two hundred interviews with Commission officials who have lived through the change, argue that the reforms "can best be described as a marriage of NPM [new public management] and 'Weberian-bureaucratic' principles" (2008, 709). While nationality and seniority count less than they did, they still count. The appraisal system is widely criticized on a variety of grounds, including its cumbersome nature (Ellinas and Suleiman 2008; Ban 2008a,b). The increased role of rules, especially in the area of financial management, is a major contributor to the "bureaucratization" of the institution. Thus, Ellinas and Suleiman find two parallel trends – one is based on a more meritocratic Commission, and the other is based on following an ever-increasing number of rules, which are making the Commission less effective (Ellinas and Suleiman 2008).

Pay for performance constituted one element of the Kinnock reforms. Such a system has required appraisals, the allocation of points, and de-emphasizing seniority, while emphasizing promotion (Ban 2008). Some of the reforms were instituted on precisely the day ten new member-states joined, and lower pay, greater difficulty in being promoted, and other differences with the working conditions that officials from the EU–15 had enjoyed led to bitterness on the part of new member-states (Peterson 2008). In general, however, the pay-for-performance system has led to such low morale and has had such perverse effects that by mid–2007 a new "reform of the reform" was in the works (Ban 2008a,b).

CONCLUSION

The European Union has undergone a major transformation along numerous dimensions. Its institutional architecture has become increasingly complex and sophisticated. Some of its changes have been anchored to at least some extent in the new public management, while others have resulted from the extraordinary consequences of the end of the Cold War and the desire of post-communist states to join "Europe." Still others have resulted from the continual expansion of EU tasks – tasks that been confronting the EU with new problems both within and outside the single market. "Reform and change" can be viewed as the emblems of the European Union, for they are instrinsic in many ways to its evolution as a unique form of governance.

The dilemma facing the European Union, and the Commission in particular, has to do with the very success of that evolution. The more integrated the EU becomes, the larger it becomes, and the more powerful it becomes as a "global authority," to use Martin Holland's phrase, the more complex become the problems of coordination, administrative effectiveness, and democratic legitimacy. The EU's institutions are engaged in governance without government, while simulataneously being engaged in governance with governments – twenty-seven of them to be exact. The EU "co-exists with national governments" (Sbragia 2002, 5), and that co-existence shapes how reform and change is conceptualized and pursued.

While the EU is extraordinarily effective within the universe of regional organizations, its very success confuses the metric of evaluation. Should it be compared to, and evaluated by the standards of, highly institutionalized nation-states? Should it be compared to federations? Should the European Commission be viewed as a "core executive" in search of political masters? Should it be viewed as a neutral/nonpartisan elite administrative body that as a collectivity represents opposing functional interests while simultaneously managing to propose and shepherd pioneering legislation through the EU's legislative bodies?

Such questions will not disappear. The EU is, in comparative terms, extremely successful in producing complex policy responses to a variety of challenges faced by a large and very diverse group of states. When faced with environmental problems, illegal immigration, or economic and financial crises, it is able to construct a consensus broad enough to move forward in spite of lacking a government that could give it an explicitly political direction. The European Commission, underpinned by its extensive interaction with national administrations (Hofmann and Turk 2007), is an absolutely essential component of that success. It can claim a significant portion of the credit for the fact that reform and change, rather than stasis and paralysis, continue to characterize the European Union.

. The negotiation of formal treaties that have permitted an expansion of the use of "hard law," the creation of new agencies that expand the reach of the EU while using networks rather than hierarchy, the invention of new modes of governance that use "soft" rather than "hard" instruments in their efforts to shape behavior, and the attempted reform of the European Commission have occurred almost simultaneously with the most historic and difficult project of economic and political integration ever attempted anywhere under the aegis of democracy. The incorporation of the post-communist states into an expanded European Union symbolizes the fact that the European Union not only can change but that it can do so while confronting historic challenges that it could not possibly have foreseen and for which it could not have prepared.

In general, the European Union is facing the contradictions that come with its success as the most advanced form of regional governance the world has known. Regional governance differs intrinsically from national governance, as regions face a host of challenges that differ from those faced by nation-states. The introduction of new public management in the EU's agencies, for example, might well produce problems unknown to national states. In a similar vein, the European Union must coordinate the activities of its member-states very differently from the way a national government coordinates the activities of its subnational governments. If nothing else, the EU has an international presence – co-existing, however, with the international presence of its member-states – which creates issues unknown to national governments that do not need to take account of their subnational governments when acting on the international stage. And yet citizens of democratic nation-states expect to influence regional governance in ways familiar to them as national citizens. Given the cultural and economic diversity of the EU's member-states, such an expectation may be impossible to fulfill, but it exists nonetheless.

Thus, the EU faces a dilemma that probably will define it for a long time to come. That dilemma involves the "triple trinity" of balancing institutional strength, democratic governance, and international flexibility. Most of its member-states have achieved that tripartite balance at the national level to such a degree that it has become the norm. Achieving such a balance will be more difficult for the EU, given the novelty and the complexity of the regional system of governance that has emerged. Just as the nation-state seemed extraordinarily remote and complicated to the residents of the "city-state" about which Max Weber wrote so brilliantly, so too a system of regional governance is viewed as lacking the democratic underpinnings that after several centuries have come to be associated with the democratic state. Ironically, it is precisely the elected leaders of such democratic states who have decided that an increasingly strong regional system of governance is preferable to the standard system of national governance operating in a traditional international environment. The role and shape of regional democratic governance, however, remains to be defined.

NOTES

1 The question of whether the EU's supranational institutions are able to exercise independent power has been a major focus of debate. For interesting perspectives arguing that they are, see Tallberg (2003); Alter (2001); Cram (1997); Stone Sweet and Sandholtz (1997); Pollack (2003).

2 REACH is the acronym for EU legislation entitled Registration, Evaluation, Authorisation, and Restriction of Chemicals. ROHS is the acronym for "The restriction of the use of certain hazardous substances in electrical and electronic equipment."

3 The European Railway Agency (ERA), for example, has the responsibility of overseeing the preparation of an integrated European railway area as a component of the EU's common policy on transportation. The agency will be responsible for the "development and implementation of Technical Specifications for interoperability and a common approach to questions concerning railway safety." http://europa.eu/agencies/community.agencies/era/index.en.htm (accessed 10 December 2007).

4 Majone argues that the difference between the two lies in the importance of the concept of "institutional balance" in the EU. In his analysis, the centrality of that concept makes the EU an example of a "mixed polity" that resembles the types of polities found in medieval Europe before the entrenchment of the monarchy (Majone 2002).

PART SEVEN

Looking Back at Reform Efforts: What Worked?

Success and Failure of Reform: Taking Stock

DONALD J. SAVOIE

We have witnessed numerous attempts at reforming government operations throughout the Western world, but particularly in Anglo-American democracies, during the past thirty years. Some of the reforms were inspired by private sector management practices, others by a desire on the part of the political executive to exert greater authority over the shaping of public policies, others by a willingness to improve the delivery of public services to "clients," and still others by the need to deal with demanding fiscal challenges. This chapter takes stock of the various reform measures from a comparative perspective, but with a focus on Anglo-American democracies. It also seeks to take stock of the success or lack of success of some of the reform measures.

A consensus emerged in the early 1980s that government operations were in urgent need of repair and that the public sector should adopt management procedures or arrangements resembling those of the business community (Kettl 2000). About the same time, politicians in many jurisdictions came to the conclusion that they had lost power to public servants and that there was a need to regain the upper hand, at least on policy (Savoie 1994). Thus, for politicians the problem to be addressed was at the bureaucratic level. In short, politicians concluded that political institutions were operating well but that bureaucracy was in urgent need of repair.

Margaret Thatcher, it will be recalled, launched an ambitious plan to reform bureaucracy. By the time she left office, she had privatized state corporations, introduced a "make or buy" concept, cut a number of public servants, cut some government programs and spending, overhauled the government approach to financial management, empowered front-line managers – and the list goes on. Governments everywhere took note and before long foreign governments came knocking on her door to borrow lessons learned from her government's approach to governing. Geoffrey Howe (2006, 104), a senior Thatcher minister, remembers "making speeches around the world which made it sound as though we had learned to walk upon the water."

It is no exaggeration to suggest that we have witnessed a veritable orgy of reform measures since the likes of Margaret Thatcher, Brian Mulroney, and Ronald Reagan came to power in the late 1970s and the early 1980s. It is not easy, however, to determine if the various measures met with much success. As with many other things, success depends on the eyes of the beholder. Indeed, there are no widely accepted criteria to evaluate the impact of the measures that have been implemented under the new public management, or for that matter under any other heading.

This, however, has not stopped the politicians who followed Thatcher and her colleagues from continuing with a government reform agenda. There seems to be no end to the orgy. John Major, Bill Clinton, and Tony Blair, for example, have also sought to reinvent government and to improve the delivery of public service. They, too, tried their hand at making government operations look like the private sector. Thus, the drive to reform the public sector during the past thirty years or so has been fuelled by political ideology, by a desire by politicians to regain the upper hand in shaping policy, and by a desire to make public bureaucracies more efficient. In this chapter, I take stock by looking at the political and policy environment that led governments to reform their operations. I review briefly a number of reform measures and conclude with observations on the impact of the reforms and speculate on what now.

THE POLITICAL CONTEXT

Government reform measures are never introduced in a political or policy vacuum. Thatcher, who led the way in changing the machinery of government, came to power in the immediate aftermath of Britain having to go, cap in hand, to the International Monetary Fund (IMF) to request a loan. The British economy in the mid-1970s, it will be recalled, was mired in a series of problems ranging from low productivity to large government deficits. Having to turn to the IMF for help held an important message. As Howard Davies (2006, 9) observed, "the IMF's role, surely, was to knock sense into governments in developing countries, such as Argentina or Mexico, lacking the political maturity to solve their own problem unaided, not to bail out one of its founding fathers." In return for agreeing to the loan, it will also be recalled, the IMF required cuts in public spending. Britain, in the eyes of many, had been brought low, and Thatcher believed that government and, in particular, the bureaucrats were part of the problem. She set out to establish a new consensus, one that valued private sector initiatives and individual self-reliance.

Britain, however, was not alone in confronting economic challenges. The oil crisis and a deep recession in the Western world in the mid–1970s gave the world a dreaded new word, "stagflation," which forced the hand of governments to review their expenditure budget. The search was on to make the public sector "lean and more competitive" (Loffler 2007, 478). Keynesian economics had run its course as we discovered that the scope and cost of government kept growing in both good economic times as well as bad. The standard Keynesian response of increasing government spending to deal with rising unemployment appeared ever more inappropriate in the face of inflationary pressure and growing government deficits.

New economic theories came into fashion. The work of Milton Friedman became required readings on university campuses, in think tanks, and in policy circles. Friedman insisted that "a freely functioning market economy results in economic and technological progress, efficient utilization of resources and a rising standard of living that is distributed with reasonable equity" (Friedman 1984; Wolf 1988, 2). Government intervention, Friedman added, not only impedes achieving full employment but also gives rise to large government organizations that invariably "mismanage" their tasks. To be sure, public servants were much more at home with the work of Lord Keynes than with Milton Friedman.

Friedman was hardly the only academic challenging the work of bureaucrats. It will be recalled that we also saw the rise of the public choice school in the 1970s, and its presence is still being felt today. It will also be recalled that Thatcher applauded the work of public choice theorists and made it required reading for senior public servants (Savoie 1994).

The public choice school starts with the premise that the individual is the basic unit of analysis. Thus, individual choice is the basis for organizational or collective action, so that what is usually thought of as collective action is, in reality, the aggregation of individual choices. The individual decision maker is much like the classical economic man and is, as a result, self-interested, rational, and always seeking to maximize his own utilities. Dennis Mueller (1976, 395) defined public choice theory succinctly as "the economic study of non-market decision-making, or simply the application of economics to political science."

Many observers still look to the public choice theory, which has gained considerable popularity in recent years, to explain the behaviour of public servants, and many social scientists believe it to be the most likely explanation for the growth in government spending. One, for example, went so far as to suggest that "government bureaucrats, like any other bureaucrat (or indeed, any other people), are quick to seize on new program possibilities that promise general advancement – again, virtually without regard to likely results. Unless we try massive lobotomies, we are unlikely to change behaviour so rooted in human nature" (Silkerman 1980, 37).

The theory placed the public administration community on the defensive. It stood accused of lacking "both a clear sense of identity and the confidence to deal with increasingly difficult problems" (Denhardt 2004, 142–3). In the United States, two Minnowbrook conferences were sponsored to rescue the public administration discipline from "a kind of wondering relevance to students, practitioners and the future" (Laporte 1971, 21). Curtis Ventriss (1989, 174) concluded in 1989 that the public administration community was "finding itself in an intellectual swamp with only a modicum of theoretical legitimacy." Aaron Wildavsky (1990, xiii), the dean of the public administration community from the 1960s until his untimely death in 1993, wrote about "the schizoid character of the discipline," replete with "contradictory recommendations," which was making "progress difficult." The fact that there has been an ongoing intellectual crisis in the study of public administration was and remains of little comfort to practitioners who themselves are confronting a crisis.

Richard Crossman (1975, 90) published his widely read diaries in 1975, detailing his difficulties in dealing with public servants. The diaries spoke of exasperation with a bureaucratic machine that took on a life of its own, like an uncontrollable monster. He wrote: "Whenever one relaxes one's guard the Civil Service in one's Department quietly asserts itself ... Just as the Cabinet Secretariat constantly transforms the actual proceedings of Cabinet into the form of the Cabinet minutes (i.e., it substitutes what we should have said if we had done as they wished for what we actually did say), so here in my department the civil servants are always putting in what they think I should have said and not what I actually decided."

The Crossman diaries gave rise to the popular BBC television series "Yes, Minister." It attracted some nine million viewers in Britain alone and became the favourite television program of the permanent secretaries. Mrs Thatcher had each episode videotaped and reported that she subscribed to the caricature view of the senior civil service. The series also gained a worldwide audience and became highly popular with many politicians and civil servants in both Canada, Australia, New Zealand, and the United States. The not-so-subtle message of "Yes, Minister" was that public servants were running the country, their deference to politicians was pure pretense, and the Sir Humphreys of the bureaucratic world wielded considerable power. The series actually served to give credence to bureaucrat-bashing.

A good number of politicians bought into the "Yes, Minister" image of the powerful bureaucrat setting policy and running things. It did not seem to matter that, at least on the face of it, they were embracing a contradiction – on the one hand, powerful and efficient bureaucrats but, on the other, inefficient bureaucrats who had brought their countries low.

By the late 1970s politicians began to run against the bureaucracy in Washington, Canberra, London, and Ottawa in their efforts to win election. They were successful as President Carter, Ronald Reagan, and Bill Clinton in the United States, Brian Mulroney and Jean Chrétien in Canada, and Margaret Thatcher and Tony Blair demonstrated. Moreover, the formula still works, as Stephen Harper and Barack Obama can attest.

Bureaucracy stood accused and continues to this day to be accused of many things – being bloated, uncreative, costly, always favouring the status quo, and unable to manage resources with any degree of efficiency. In brief, bureaucracy was perceived in Anglo-American democracies as a barrier against, rather than a vehicle for, progressive change. All of which is to say that by the 1980s public servants had few friends left. Those who argued against tampering with the machinery of government and its "armies" of entrenched officials were dismissed by both political left and right. They became the new reactionaries. Even people who had supported the ideas and social welfare programs of leaders such as Franklin Roosevelt, Clement Attlee, Harold Gaitskell, T.C. Douglas, and Adlai Stevenson were now calling for changes to the apparatus of government (Galbraith 1986, 13).

Public servants came under attack virtually everywhere in the Western world. Even the British civil service, long a role model for other countries, came under heavy fire. The transition from a highly respected institution to a widely criticized one is best exemplified by the work of the Fabian society, an organization devoted to spreading socialist principles. In 1947 the society declared that "we have in Britain what is probably the best civil service in the world" (Parris 1969, 284). By the late 1970s the society had produced a highly critical report and called for major changes (Savoie 1994, 87–8).

Society itself was also changing in a way that would have implications for bureaucracy. Ezra Suleiman (2003, 9) maintains that government and bureaucracy are as much affected by "mores in society as by cultural or sociological changes in society." Richard Wilson, cabinet secretary in Britain between 1998 and 2002, observed in early 2006 that "the public was no longer patient or deferential" (Lord Wilson of Dinton 2006, 7).

Robert Putnam (2000, 104) has documented the decline of social capital, which resonates in many Western countries. Individuals today are better educated, family ties are not as strong, and society is now much more secular than was the case some forty years ago. Individuals may still be interested in pursuing political objectives, but they are more willing to do so through unconventional forms of political action or by joining single-issue groups rather than those with a collective agenda. Individuals are also considerably less loyal to public institutions, including political parties, than was the case thirty years ago.

The rise of market capitalism has reinforced liberal values and the tendency of individuals to act in ways that "reduce our ability to make collective choices" (Bentley 2005, 7). There is nothing to suggest that the pendulum is swinging away from a focus on the individual. Ten years after Tony Blair's Labour party came to power, a study revealed that a majority of United Kingdom citizens now believe that life "is best improved by putting the individual first." As the head of the research project explains, "in 1997 ... almost 70 percent of our respondents opted for the community-first approach. Over the decade, we have seen a fast-moving shift towards people feeling more individualistic. Today, 52 percent feel looking after ourselves will best improve the quality of life ("Generation Y Speaks," 25). It stands to reason that the shift favouring the attributes of individuals over those of the community would also be felt in every corner of our political and administrative institutions.

Added to all of the above was the rise of a right-of-centre political ideology. Less government, fewer bureaucrats, and less public spending were all to the good. If governments were to intervene, the politicians who came on the scene in the 1980s and later would look to tax incentives and to public private partnerships as the instruments of choice.

WHAT TO DO?

Politicians, starting with Margaret Thatcher, concluded that bureaucracy needed fixing on two fronts: management and policy. Politicians from Britain, the United States, Australia, New Zealand, and Canada shared the conviction that most of the perceived inefficiencies in government operations were simply a function of poor management. On policy, politicians also shared the conviction that public servants had both too much influence and their own self-serving agenda.

Politicians would look to the private sector not just to strike new partnerships to deliver public services but also for inspiration to fix the government's boiler room. Business management techniques came into fashion in the 1980s and moved from one country to another with great speed, as if there were no jurisdictional boundaries. Christopher Pollitt (1990, 181) pointed to some of the more important similarities "in the assumption of public sector inefficiency, the recourse to private sector expertise, the stillborn belief in the usefulness of merit pay and the tremendous emphasis on new accounting procedures."

Politicians looked to the business community for inspiration at least in part because public servants and the public administration academic community had little to offer in the way of solutions. What both did have to offer held little appeal to the politicians of the day. Politicians like Margaret Thatcher or Ronald Reagan wanted to introduce sweeping changes and to give the system a tremendous wrench of the wheel. They saw little in the literature or in briefing books prepared by permanent officials that outlined a way forward for their agenda. Gérard Veilleux, former secretary to the Treasury Board in the government of Canada, once observed that "the academic community is excellent at pointing at where and how we go wrong in government but it is either incapable or unwilling to offer solutions to anything about government."[1]

The arrival in office of Margaret Thatcher, Ronald Reagan, and Brian Mulroney in Canada pushed public servants into unchartered territory. Never before had they been asked to welcome a political leadership that was so eager to question what they did and how they did it. Time and again, the new leaders made it clear that they were determined to make the shift from incremental to decremental government. Yet, what role civil servants were expected to play in this shift was never spelled out. And again the civil service was fingered as part of the problem.

When she came to office, Thatcher received briefing books from the Cabinet Office, insisting that the 733,000-strong civil service was already stretched to limit. The books argued that there was no fat in the system and that "even modest" cuts in staff would inhibit departments from functioning effectively (Savoie 1994; Fry 1988, 7). She made it clear to senior public servants that she was not buying what they were telling her. She announced a series of cuts early in her first mandate, and she directed that the civil service be reduced in size by nearly 15 percent. By the time she left office, it had been cut by over 22 percent, down to 569,000. She imposed the cuts by simply outlining targets. Convinced that more could be made without reduction in services, she said that cuts could be absorbed through increased efficiencies in the system and through contracting out to the private sector.

The search was on in all Anglo-American democracies to "do more with less." The onus was on public servants to manage operations and programs more efficiently. In the United States, Vice President Al Gore (1993a) led the charge in "creating a government that works better and costs less." In Canada, the government launched a series of initiatives from Increased Ministerial Authority and Accountability (IMAA) to Public Service 2000. In Britain, senior executives were brought in from the private sector to scrutinize government operations. Governments in Australia, beginning in the

1980s, have sought to move "beyond bureaucracy" by empowering managers (Aucoin 1995).

For politicians, then, the culprit was poor management, and it was the result of senior public servants having over the years shown little interest in management. The glamour of government work for them has been in policy, not in administration. Indeed, it seems that senior officials were happy to live with elaborate rules and regulations, so long as they were free to play a policy role. The thinking in some quarters was that the functional units were there to worry about rules dealing with personnel, administration, and financial matters. The senior official's job was to concentrate on keeping politicians out of trouble and on emerging policy issues. Some go so far as to argue that in government, particularly in parliamentary systems based on Westminster model, managing major departmental programs traditionally has been a job for "junior personnel or *failed* administrative class people who were seen by the mandarins as not being able to make it to the top levels" (Williams 1988).

Governments in many jurisdictions tried to distinguish the role of policy formulation from the role of management, which, it was felt, would upgrade the importance of management. It also provided an opportunity for politicians to carve out a larger role in shaping policy.

The new political class that emerged in the 1980s wanted to control the policy levers right down to "the paper clips" (Willitts 1987, 445). Politicians, then and to this day, see it as their prerogative not only to decide on policy but also to have a hand in shaping policy options. For one thing, they took steps to ensure that they would have a stronger capacity in their own offices to establish board policy directors. They also introduced several measures so that senior public servants would be much more responsive to their policy preferences than in years past.

THE MEASURES

It is not necessary to outline in any detail the various public sector reform measures put in place in Anglo-American democracies since the early 1980s. This has been done elsewhere (Aucoin 1995). Suffice to stress that an overriding objective of the various reform measures was to separate somehow responsibilities for policy and operations. Indeed, governments in all Anglo-American democracies have tried

their hand at separating the two responsibilities and at debureaucratiz-
ing their operations. This, it was assumed, would not only give politicians the upper hand in shaping policy, but it would also lead to much
better management practices. In turn, the belief was that isolating managers would enable policy-makers to better assess their performance.

The authors of a seminal report on public sector management,
which led to Margaret Thatcher's most ambitious reform measure,
called for a break from the past in the machinery of government.
The Next Steps report argued that "most civil servants are very
conscious that senior management is dominated by people whose
skills are in policy formulation and who have relatively little experience of managing or working where services are actually being
delivered. In any large organization, senior appointments are watched
with close attention" (Jenkins et al. 1988, 2). This was true, even
though the report admitted that only 5 percent of the civil service
was directly concerned with policy. The remaining 95 percent was
directly concerned with the delivery of government services.

Too little attention was paid to results and too much was paid to
expenditures and activities in departments, and there were relatively
few external pressures demanding improvement in performance. The
report's most important finding, however, was that the civil service
was "too big and too diverse to manage as a single entity." This had
led to the development of a machinery of government that "fits no
operation effectively." A unified civil service had given rise to all
kinds of uniform controls and rules, so that managers were not free
to manage effectively. Controls, it reported, existed on recruitment,
dismissal, choice of staff, promotion, pay, hours of work, accom-
modation, organization of work, and even on the use of communication equipment. The authors summed up their findings by identifying
five critical issues confronting management in the civil service: first,
a lack of clear and accountable management responsibility and the
self-confidence that goes with it, particularly among the higher ranks
in departments; second, the need for greater precision about the
results expected of people and of organisations; third, a need to focus
attention on outputs as well as inputs; fourth, the handicap of impos-
ing a uniform system in an organisation of the size and diversity of
the present civil service; fifth, a need for sustained pressure for
improvement (Jenkins et al. 1988, 3–4, 7).

The solution was to reorganize the work of individual departments
so that the job to be done received priority, rather than the centrally

conceived rules and controls. The focus in future should be on results, not process. The report revisited the politics-administration dichotomy and put forward a radical proposal: agencies should be established to carry out the executive functions of government within a policy-and-resources framework set by ministers and the relevant department. The managers of the agencies would be given substantial freedom to manage their operations as they saw fit, but they would be held "rigorously to account for the results achieved." The report essentially argued that if government operations were allowed to operate at arm's length from ministers and from the Whitehall culture, then one would soon see a "release of managerial energy." In brief, the goal was nothing short of redefining the way the "business of government" was conducted (Jenkins et al. 1988, 9, 15).

As is well known, the British civil service was re-structured into executive agencies to break down the generalists' emphasis on policy rather than management. The agencies were decentralist, consumer-oriented, and compatible with the business-management model. Thatcher divorced ministerial departments from executive agencies, so that departments set policy and program targets and the agencies implemented policies and delivered the services. This move to decouple policy formulation from operations was also designed to empower managers and to make government operations more businesslike, employees more entrepreneurial, and government more customer focused. By 1997, more than three-quarters of civil servants in the Home Civil Service were working in agencies.

Empowerment became the buzzword of the 1980s. It signalled the search for doers rather than thinkers and emphasized the importance of managers' taking the lead, getting things done, and dealing effectively with customers and their needs. Bureaucracy, red tape, and centrally prescribed rules were to be replaced by a new delegation of authority to managers in line departments, much as in the private sector.

Anglo-American democracies would borrow more than a page from the Thatcher reform. American presidents do not have nearly the scope to reform the machinery of government that prime ministers under the Westminster parliamentary systems have. It will be recalled, for example, that President Reagan did not pursue his announced proposals to eliminate the Departments of Education and Energy, because he knew that Congress would oppose him at every turn (Savoie 1994, 214). Reagan did, however, introduce measures

to shift federal management from direct service provision and production to greater dependence on third-party service providers
(Levine 1986, 198).

President Clinton and his vice-president, Al Gore, would make
empowerment the central feature of their efforts to reinvent government. The efforts focused on reforming governmental processes to
improve customer service and procurement practices. The Gore reinventing exercise also looked to the private sector for inspiration, and
program managers were to be valued like never before (Kettl 1998).

The Clinton-Gore National Performance Review documented the
government's performance problems, which, it argued, had given
rise to "the deepest crisis of faith in government in our lifetimes" (Gore
1993b, 2). The review sought to turn citizens into consumers, insisting
that "taxpayers are customers too" (Kettl 1998, 28). Empowering
managers and front-line employees was a sure way to turn citizens
into consumers and to strengthen the delivery of public services.
Their efforts combined to give rise to a new movement, "the new
public management" which not only swept through Westminster
systems such as those of New Zealand, Australia, and Canada, but
also other countries, such as Sweden.

New Zealand, confronting an economic crisis, deregulated the
economy, sold state enterprises, and shut down many subsidies. It
carefully selected which services its government should deliver and
contracted with government managers to produce and deliver them.
Peter Aucoin (1995, 206) writes that New Zealand reformers
"assumed that better and more transparent management systems
would inevitably lead to improved management and therefore to
improved public service."

The new public management in Australia was different from that in
New Zealand in that its focus was on improving the delivery of public
service, ensuring that the public service was more responsive to ministers and improving the performance of government. It was less concerned than New Zealand about reshaping the state. Australia has also
sought, particularly in more recent years, to strengthen its capacity to
evaluate programs and to find better ways to apply this capacity to the
government's strategic and expenditure budget process.

Canada followed Britain's lead and introduced Special Operating
Agencies (SOAS) to provide, in the words of government officials,
"the first clean break with the traditional control and command

model and to offer concrete evidence of the beginnings of a culture for government services that emphasized the practices of management in place of the systems and processes of program administration" (Roth 1990, 2). The goal again was to introduce business discipline to government operations. The SOAS were followed by numerous other measures, all designed to empower program managers (Savoie 2003).

The call to let government managers manage was accompanied by a call to let politicians decide policy. It is not too much of an exaggeration to write that as politicians were strengthening the hand of front-line government managers, they deliberately set out to undermine the policy role of public servants and check their influence.

Tony Blair not only increased the number of special advisors in No. 10, he also, for the first time, gave two of them the authority to direct the work of senior public servants. Blair was no different from Bush, Mulroney, Harper, and other heads of governments in Anglo-American democracies. They have all looked for a more responsive bureaucracy. The literature suggests that they have been successful (Savoie 2008).

Politicians in many mature democracies have appointed an increasing number of partisan political advisors as a means to check the influence of public servants on policy. Carl Dahlström, through consultations with country experts, has documented the growth in partisan political advisors in eighteen democracies in Europe, North America, Australia, and New Zealand. But this is not all. Politicians can now turn to a growing number of research institutes and think tanks for a second opinion to challenge the advice from their senior officials. Lobbyists have in recent years become an important part of the political process in all mature democracies. Because many of them are politically partisan, they have access to senior politicians. They are always at the ready to offer advice. In brief, they are hired to promote the interests of their corporate customers and paid to sell truth to politicians about government policy, as their customers see it. There are even lobbyists working to promote the interests of the tobacco industry. If nothing else, politicians can now turn to any number of paid lobbyists to get a second opinion on a policy issue. If truth is not absolute, elected politicians now have any number of sources to consult to establish truth as they wish to hear it.

ON THE OUTSIDE LOOKING IN

There is some evidence that citizens or clients of public services today
are better served than was the case thirty years ago. To be sure,
major advances in communications and in managing information
technologies have made public services more accessible and government operations more transparent. In addition, governments everywhere in the Western world have launched sustained efforts to
measure client satisfaction and management practices (Herdan
2006, 6).

It will be recalled, for example, that John Major launched important efforts in Britain to improve service delivery under his Citizen's
Charter. The charter was designed to make bureaucracy more
accountable and citizen friendly. The efforts did not end there. Tony
Blair consistently claimed that improving service delivery was one
of his top priorities. Blair, among his other service delivery initiatives,
announced in November 2005 a Transformational Government
strategy. The strategy, much as the one adopted in Canada, focuses
on delivering a citizen- or business-centric service. It also looks to
IT, specific targets, and the involvement of citizen and local government in implementing the strategy. In Canada, all governments,
starting with the Mulroney government in 1984, have introduced
measures to improve the delivery of public services and to strengthen
the bond between government and clients.

There have been some efforts to evaluate how well governments
have succeeded in strengthening the delivery of public services. A
leading private sector consulting firm, Accenture, has produced an
elaborate report card comparing the performance of national governments. Accenture ranked Canada first and the United States second
in leading the way to improving customer service in the public sector.
These two countries were labelled "trendsetters." Britain was placed
among the "followers" and ranked twelfth among twenty-one countries. The Accenture survey was based on forty-six in-depth interviews with senior officials and 8,600 citizens (Accenture undated,
100–1). However, both Canada and Britain rank poorly when compared with the private sector in terms of promoting innovation in
service delivery. Canadian and British citizens also reported that
private sector business was doing a better job at developing online
services – the perception gap for Canada was established at minus
20 percent in relation to the private sector (ranking sixteenth among

twenty-one countries) and for Britain at minus 24 percent (ranking twentieth out of twenty-one).

It will also be recalled that the British government commissioned an independent review of the Charter Mark Scheme and Measurement of Customer Satisfaction. The review's verdict was that there is a great deal of anecdotal but still limited hard evidence of the Charter Mark's effectiveness. It concluded that "the Charter Mark scheme continues to prosper, but percentage penetration of the whole public sector – and therefore overall impact – remains quite low. There is now a very low level of public awareness of the Charter Mark, and a general scepticism about quality schemes and awards was displayed by members of the public" (Herdan 2006, 6).

An official with the Cabinet Office reflected on Britain's efforts to strengthen service delivery and focus on the "customer." She concluded that the efforts had limited success, claiming that the process had become too "bureaucratic" and had "little customer feedback." These shortcomings persisted, she reports, despite efforts to "devolve more power and responsibility" to those working at the front line. She points out that those working in "public services sometimes feel little sense of ownership" in their work (Tetlow 2004).

LOOKING BACK

Politicians, starting with Margaret Thatcher but continuing to this day, have set out to fix bureaucracy. We have seen a veritable orgy of reform measures introduced over the past thirty years or so, all with the promise of improving government operations. After Thatcher's ambitious reform measures and after John Major's Citizen Charter, Tony Blair pledged to "modernize Britain's unwieldy state bureaucracy." Once in power, Blair tabled a major statement on modernizing government, lamenting the fact that "some parts of the public sector" were not "as efficient, dynamic and effective" as the private sector. He outlined the reasons, including departments and agencies that "tend to look after their own interests, inertia, a focus on inputs rather than results, risk aversion, poor management," and low morale stemming from the "denigration of public servants." Blair was simply echoing the words Margaret Thatcher had voiced some eighteen years earlier. And, like Thatcher, Blair made it clear time and again that the private sector is the key to improving management in government ("The Two Tonys" 1997; United Kingdom 1999, 11).

How, then, is one to assess the success and failure of the various reform measures? Politicians who have run against Washington (every presidential candidate since Jimmy Carter), London (from Thatcher to Blair), and Ottawa (starting with Mulroney) have met with political success. Viewed from the perspective of politicians or aspiring politicians, running against bureaucracy and the status quo in government holds many benefits.

The verdict, however, is less positive from other perspectives. There is evidence to suggest that civil services in Western industrialized countries suffer from a serious morale problem. Survey after survey of public opinion has reported since the early 1980s that morale problems have plagued national civil services, and there is little evidence that things are improving.

Kevin Lynch (2008, 3, 5), Canada's former top civil servant, recently decided to weigh into the debate. He writes, "within the public service, some would argue that we have experienced renewal exercises with depressing regularity over the decades, with little to show for the efforts." He quoted an Ottawa-based policy think tank to write that "policy capacity and agility in response to major challenges is diminishing; the public service is not effective at implementing policy ideas." Lynch labels some of the criticism levelled at the Canadian civil service as "misperceptions" and sets out to set the record straight. It is difficult to imagine that the clerk of the Privy Council would have even felt the need thirty years ago to address "misperceptions" about the public service.

Two questions jump to mind: is the management of government operations now better and is the policy capacity of the civil service stronger than was the case thirty years ago? Definitive answers to both questions are not possible. Our inability to answer these two questions in many ways is what is wrong with our public services.

The call to let managers manage rang hollow for many government managers. Managers were free to manage and much was said about risk management so long as they ran error-free operations. Let the media report on an error, and managers were no longer free to manage. Public servants, notably senior managers, learned very quickly that, no matter the rhetoric, they continue to operate in a highly charged political environment. At the risk of stating the obvious, letting managers manage seeks to empower managers by reducing constraints on the action. However, constraints can go up just as easily as they can come down, as the immediate aftermath of the sponsorship scandal in Canada so clearly showed (Savoie 2008).

No government has been able to let managers manage and make sure that they manage through performance measures. Establishing performance measures continues to be work in progress after forty years. The work has been made even more difficult in recent years as borders and organizational boundaries collapsed.

Have management reforms cut costs? Both Thatcher and Al Gore insist that they did. To be sure, there was downsizing in both civil services. Gore reported that the reforms eliminated 330,000 positions, while Thatcher, as noted earlier, claimed that her reforms reduced the size of the British Civil Service by at least 164,000 (Savoie 2008, 9). Gore claimed that his National Performance Review would generate $177.4 billion in savings, while Don Kettl (1998, 17), in a report for Brookings, reported actual savings of $111.8 billion.

There is mounting evidence, however, that the reforms have not lived up to expectations with respect to cutting cost. For example, executive agencies have fallen out of favour in recent years as the British government seeks to improve control of overhead costs. Hundreds of agencies, each with their own information technology (IT), human resources, and purchasing units are proving to be costly, and efforts are now being made to coordinate common services across government. The Treasury has taken back some of the management authority delegated to the agencies, and there is increasing discussion about integrating some of the agencies back with their home departments (Dunleavy et al. 2006, 467–94).

Peter Drucker went to the heart of the matter when he observed that public service reforms have been more hype than substance. The Clinton-Gore reforms, he argued, were timid, if not trivial, and such efforts in other organizations "would not even be announced, except perhaps on the bulletin board in the hallway." What was announced, he insisted, were things "that even a poorly run manufacturer expects supervisors to do on their own – without getting much praise, let alone any extra rewards" (Drucker 1995, 50, 52; Kettl 1998, 11).

The reforms, however, have strengthened the hand of elected politicians in their dealings with public servants. There is evidence to suggest that senior civil servants have become more responsive to politicians from Bush to Blair to Harper. Political journalist Lawrence

Martin (2006, A1, A6) writes that in Ottawa bureaucrats now either "fall in line or fall out of favour." He quotes a deputy minister as saying, "When you live in a world where options aren't necessary, I suppose you don't need much of a bureaucracy" and makes the point that the "government does not want high level bureaucrats to exercise the challenge function." Jim Travers (2007) writes that the view among senior bureaucrats in Ottawa is that "instead of sous-chefs helping the government prepare the national menu, bureaucrats complain that they are being used as short-order cooks." Shortly after coming to power, Tony Blair told Canadian prime minister Jean Chrétien that "I want to know all about what my ministers are doing" (Goldenberg 2006, 83). History tells us that he gave it a good try. He insisted, for example, that all ministerial "major interviews and media appearances, both print and broadcast, should be agreed with the No. 10 Press Office before any commitments are entered into" (United Kingdom 2001, 8). Indeed, the similarities in how Canadian and British prime ministers have in recent years sought to strengthen the centre are remarkable. In Britain, a journalist coined the phrase "sofa government" after listening to former cabinet secretary Robin Butler describe the current approach to policy and decision making in the United Kingdom government.[2] In Canada, formal cabinet processes no longer apply as they once did, and the prime minister has also adopted a less formal approach to governing. A Chrétien minister described the Cabinet as a focus group for the prime minister (Savoie 1999). The expression "sofa government" captures the situation well in both Britain and Canada.

Former senior British public servants have decided to speak out on the issue. Richard Wilson, cabinet secretary under Blair, summed it all up before the Select Committee on Public Administration when he observed, "I think that Sir Humphrey would be completely lost today if he were here" (United Kingdom Parliament 2003, 2). To be sure, Sir Humphrey would not approve.

On the role of the centre, Richard Wilson told the same committee that "the role of Number 10, the size of Number 10 and the concentration of special advisors in Number 10 are different from what they have been before" (United Kingdom Parliament 2003, 3). Richard Mottram, permanent secretary at Transport, also told the committee that the government now "has a very strong centre and the networks around the centre have a much bigger input from non-civil servants" (United Kingdom Parliament 2002, 1). Robert

Armstrong, a former Cabinet secretary, noted, "There has never, in my experience, been a time when considerations of political spin did not enter into the business of news management, but it seems to me that the balance has now swung too far in that direction" (ibid., 2). On the pervasive presence of partisan political advisers, Armstrong told the *Spectator* that the lines separating partisan political advisers and civil servants "have been blurred" (ibid., 1). Richard Wilson told the committee that the number of special political advisers has increased and, as already noted, two in the Prime Minister's Office now have the authority to direct civil servants (ibid., 2).

All of the above is to make the case that the presence of elected politicians now looms large in shaping public policy but that there is little evidence to suggest that government operations are today better managed than was the case thirty years ago.

NOTES

1 Consultations with Gérard Veilleux, former secretary to the Treasury Board, government of Canada, Montreal, 11 September 2007.
2 Sir Robin Butler told me that contrary to popular belief, it was a journalist, not he, who coined the phrase "sofa government."

12

Conclusions: The Future of Public Management

JON PIERRE

In 1990, the Caidens, reflecting on the state of comparative public administration research, argued that "one thing certain about the future of comparative public administration is that it has one" (Caiden and Caiden 1990, 384). As the chapters in this volume all seem to testify, the same statement could be made about the future of public management as an empirical phenomenon and as a research field; the one thing certain is that it has one. As the preceding chapters also suggest, however, there is much to suggest that the future of public management will look rather different compared to its past or present.

CONTENDING IDEAS OF REFORM

The practice and theory of public management appears to be moving towards a new form, whether it is called neo-Weberianism or post – new public management (Bouckaert and Pollitt 2004; Christensen and Laegreid 2007). In the introduction to this volume, Patricia Ingraham and I suggest that public management has come of age. The overall orientation of public management reform and practice is today more attentive to the values embedded in public sector organizations. There are also more nuances in the international dissemination and adoption of public management in different guises. Several chapters in this volume, primarily those by John Halligan (chapter 6) and Donald Savoie (chapter 11), take stock of what has been achieved so far, and the record is rather disappointing. Many chapters also search for explanations for the success or failure of public management reform, outlining what could be seen as an intriguing research agenda on the macro- and micro-politics of reform.

This concluding chapter will discuss possible next steps in public management both as a practice and as a research field. The discussion is conducted against the backdrop of the findings and arguments presented in the previous chapters. It is important to note the distinction between, on the one hand, public management as a practice where national governments and bureaucracies search for new ways and strategies to increase efficiency and quality in public services and public management as a field of academic research, on the other. While the public management reform movement appears to have lost some momentum over the past several years, public management research appears to some extent to be on the rise. Also, as this book shows, there is now in many countries momentum for change that seeks to address the pathologies generated by the initial wave of public management reform and to restore features of the previous model of administration that were removed but were later found to be integral to good public administration.

Which were those pathologies? Downplaying the role of elected officials and empowering middle-level operative managers clarified roles and helped professionalise public service delivery but led to a deficit of leadership, both in the organizational and in the partisan sense. Performance measurement was instrumental in providing managers with feedback information about performance, but it had severe dysfunctions in prioritising what could be measured and targeted those who were being measured, not the decision makers. Customer choice models and flexibility meant a modernization of public services but they challenged entrenched notions of equal treatment, legality, and accountability. Creating independent agencies enhanced the operative capacity and accountability of government but generated, or exacerbated, problems of coordination. These and other problems related to the early days of new public management are now being addressed, and public service systems are being "rebalanced," as the Australians say.

Most importantly, this "rebalancing" seeks to bring back the public into public administration. The early management reform took aim at public sector idiosyncrasies that were believed to be the root cause of the problems facing the public sector, i.e., political control, hierarchy, input-based budgeting, organizational rigidities, and due process. In the current reform, as John Halligan shows (chapter 6), there is recognition that the public sector specificity matters; it is not a set of structures that lends itself to the same organizational and managerial thinking, as is the case in the private sector.

Also, the role of the public administration in democratic governance has been reaffirmed, and future management reform will have to be conducted with that aspect of the public service in mind (Suleiman 2003). As Halligan concludes, "management's place is secure, but within a broader framework of public governance." If the early versions of management reform were based on the normative assumption that management is a generic phenomenon that should not be tailored to the public sector (Peters 2001), the more recent perspective is essentially a rediscovery that public management must be embedded in public sector values and must recognize the governance role of the public administration.

Alternative ways ahead have been suggested in the debate. Some observers suggest that the road to better administration lies in empowering its clients. Eran Vigoda (2002) argues that public administration must become more interactive by a mobilization of the citizens and that traditional goals of responsiveness should be replaced, or complemented, with a new model of partnership. Robert Denhardt and Janet Denhardt, too, put forward a communitarian model of public administration "in the governance system that places citizens at the center" (2000, 550). In their view, steering society has become an overwhelming task for government to handle and therefore public *service* and engaged and empowered citizens should be the aim.

Others, like Mark Moore (1995) believe that public managers, not politicians or citizens, should be empowered to allow for a production of better "public value." The general idea here is that managers are in the best position to make decisions on public service and to utilize public sector service facilities to create value for the taxpayers' money. The model thus accords politicians an even less significant role than new public management offers them. Instead, the public manager essentially runs the show, albeit with some exchange with elected officials, to the satisfaction of clients and politicians. Although published more than a decade ago, Moore's book has stirred considerable debate recently (see Alford 2008; Rhodes and Wanna 2007; O'Flynn 2007).

A third strategy of reform brought up by Johan Olsen and set against the backdrop of the extensive debate about the blessings and perils of new public management reform is simply to revisit the previous, more traditional form of public administration (Olsen 2006). If the costs of reform balance or outweigh the benefits, there might be reason to go back to the ex ante model of administration that, for all its flaws, was internally consistent and provided unambiguous control and accountability. Thus, for instance, one answer to all those who bemoan the complexities of purchaser-provider models, contract management, and the uncertainties of market-based service provision might simply be to go back and see to what extent in-house service production provides an attractive alternative.

The multitude of ideas for reform is recognition of the importance of public administration in responding to clients' needs. It is also proof of the role that public administration plays not just in delivering services but in the process of governing as well. That said, we also note the wide range of ideas and the differences in terms of the role those ideas define for politicians, public managers and clients, or citizens, or customers.

THE MICRO-POLITICS OF CHANGE

The common theme in this book is public sector change: what drives and obstructs that change, the extent to which seemingly rigid structures like bureaucracies can change, and the more detailed, micro-level mechanisms of change. In chapter 1, Johan Olsen addresses the classical dilemma in institutional analysis between the continuity that characterizes institutions, on the one hand, and their capacity to change, on the other. His main argument is that institutions can and do change; "rules and practices are modified as a result of positive and negative experience, organizational learning and adaptation." Coming from an expert on administration, this observation speaks directly to the current debate about management reform and, more broadly, about public sector change. Some reform advocates seem to argue that any significant change in administrative systems must be driven by exogenous forces. That would be underestimating the capacity of those systems to evaluate their performance, to learn, and to adjust to new challenges.

Alberta Sbragia's chapter on treaty reform in the EU (chapter 10) offers excellent examples of the complexities and intricacies of institutional change. The EU is still in a formative moment; its institutional roles and capabilities are still being defined, and the vertical and horizontal integration of the Union is still very much in motion. However, the integration is a contested issue; popular opinion in several member states is obviously tentative towards the idea of strengthening the capabilities of the EU institutions over member-state governments. There is also a large and heterogeneous cast of actors in EU politics, which adds to the complexity of institutional reform. Finally, there is no precedent to learn from; creating and integrating an international union where member states surrender significant parts of their regulatory autonomy to supranational bodies has never been tried before. The result of all these challenges is that change becomes less predictable and less "linear" than most domestic institutional change. Again, macro-level change can be understood only by observing the micro-level factors that shape actors' preferences. Treaties to replace previous treaties have been negotiated among the member states for several years now. Change almost becomes a permanent feature of the union.

The theme of change is obviously not new. However, the contribution of the present text to our understanding of public sector change and administrative reform lies in the detailed analyses of processes of change. Hood and Margetts (chapter 5) apply a somewhat functional perspective, or a phase model, to change processes, identifying necessary and sufficient conditions for change, in their case the adoption of ICT in the public service. Furthermore, several chapters highlight the differences between the macro-politics and the micro-politics of administrative reform. Systemic needs for reform may play an important role in reform processes but as Bowornwathana, Burns, and Thynne agree (chapters 9, 8, and 3), reform is to a large extent predicated on personal incentives for bureaucrats. In Thailand, as Bidhya Bowornwathana argues, "governance reform is marked by failure and uncertainty." Politicians and bureaucrats assessed reform options in terms of what is in it for them and "reinterpreted the meanings of governance to justify their power supremacy." Little surprise, perhaps, that governance reform that aimed at producing a smaller government that does less instead led to a bigger government doing more.

Thus, the micro-politics of change could also be used to study the process through which Western ideas are inserted into administrative reform programs in developing countries. In Thailand, politicians and bureaucrats seek to claim some ownership of new reform concepts in order to promote their careers. Similarly, Burns shows that in China incentives for organizational leaders are critical to the adoption and success of reform ideas; "the desire for promotion fuels a search for models that can enhance [leaders'] performance credentials." Short of such incentives very little will happen, and, by the same token, reform models may be adopted that are more a reflection of their capacity to support the career development of senior bureaucrats than of the actual problems that the reform is set in place to resolve. In the case of Mexico, major administrative reform drew on an inventory of reform in other countries, as Jose Luis Mendez shows, but there was also a careful assessment of different reform alternatives.

Thus, understanding success and failure in administrative reform is to some degree a matter of uncovering not only the relationship between problems and solutions at the organizational level. It is also a matter of understanding the relationship between reform and intra-organizational, even individual, strategies and calculi. Together, Hood and Margetts' functional framework of the adoption of new concepts and the agency-centred, micro-level analysis of incentives in the reform process provide new insights on the issue of why some reform is successful and others fail.

THE NEW POLITICS OF PUBLIC MANAGEMENT

Several chapters testify to problems in management reform such as insufficient leadership (Bouckaert, chapter 2) or poor design of management models (Halligan) or a lack of criteria for evaluating reform (Savoie) or a reliance on seductive but misleading "hard" international benchmarks of reform (Pollitt, chapter 4), and so on. The fact that public service systems, or public bureaucracies more broadly, are deeply institutionalised systems that are not easily reformed should not come as a surprise to anyone with even moderate expertise in public administration. However, they do change, to reiterate Johan Olsen's previous comment, and a quick glance around the world provides ample evidence of the extensive, if not dramatic, change that has characterized public administration in many countries in the past two decades.

This book is both a stock-taking and a forward-looking enterprise. It seems as if we are now at an impasse in public management development where previous reform is critically assessed and new reform models are considered. We saw earlier that there is no shortage of ideas about how to proceed with reform. The previous chapters bring out two distinct themes of future reform.

First, a key aspect of this next wave of public management reform is leadership. It is no coincidence that several of the chapters devote substantive attention to leadership issues. Geert Bouckaert outlines a "new public leadership" and sees it as "a condition and a consequence of reform itself." This "new political leadership" has three interacting components – politics, administration, and citizen leadership – that should form public sector leadership. There is an emphasis on coordination, strategic views, internationalisation, legitimacy, and responsiveness. Previous management reform emphasised managerial leadership, with politicians as goal-setters with no operative role. That idea tended to define away the top leadership of the public sector and rejects the defining feature of public organizations as operating under political leadership (Christensen et al. 2007). The result was a leadership deficit that has manifested itself in growing problems of coordination. Almost regardless of what other features future administrative reform will display, leadership will have to be a key issue.

Second, public management will have to consider the larger picture of public administration, public value, deliberation, the public interest, the specificity of the public sector, legality, and accountability. In other words, public management should be less concerned with the art and craft of doing more with less but more engaged in playing its role as an integral part of governance, or what Halligan refers to as "integrated governance." Public administration cannot be divorced from the process of governance, and therefore major managerial reform and public administration restructuring will have ramifications for democratic governance. Public management must become less of a problem and more of the solution in that perspective.

The notion of "integrated governance" could, ideally, be shorthand for a wedding between public management and democratic governance in which public management ensures public sector efficiency, low costs, and the empowerment of clients, while a democratic network provides political leadership and accountability. If traditional democratic government placed too much emphasis on political control and if the early NPM reform sought to rectify that problem by downplaying the role of politics and denying any public sector specificity, then perhaps "integrated governance" is the point of balance that promotes both goals of democratic governance and of high-quality public management.

This holy grail of management and governance has been sought on both sides of the Atlantic, as well as in the Antipodes. Guy Peters recently suggested that one of the differences between the United States and Europe was that in the United States public management comes first and legality second, whereas in Europe it is the other way around (Painter and Peters 2010). In that view, his work on public management has more of a European than an American inflection. In publications like *The Future of Governing* (2001) and *The Politics of Bureaucracy* (2008) Guy Peters cautions against overlooking the public nature of the bureaucracy and the significance that has in the context to legitimising collective action. Indeed, defining and integrating "publicness" into public management models is an important aspect of contemporary reform, as several chapters in this book have shown.

This turn in defining the agenda of reform is happening also in foreign aid and in supporting developing countries. The World Bank, previously an aggressive promoter of "good governance" with a distinct neo-liberal "bent," now appears to be much more aware of the need to build robust government institutions to foster democratic governance. The Bank seems to acknowledge that the main problems facing developing countries are not only economic problems but also governance problems. A group of scholars on democracy recently delivered a powerful assessment of the quality of democracy, particularly in the developing countries: "There is a spectre haunting democracy in the world today. It is bad governance. Governance that serves only the interests of a narrow ruling elite. Governance that is drenched in corruption, patronage, favoritism, and abuse of power" (Carothers et al. 2007, 119).

This analysis obviously does not suffer from the exigencies and ambiguities in World Bank indices discussed by Christopher Pollitt (chapter 4). Rather, it should serve as a reminder that most of the "big" problems facing us today are in fact not problems of knowledge or resources but of governance. Environmental experts insist that the solutions to global warming are available, just as poverty and development experts argue that there is no immediate shortage of resources. The problem is a lack of governance to organize and implement the programs necessary to address the problems effectively.

Contributors

GEERT BOUCKAERT   Katholieke Universiteit Leuven

BIDHYA BOWORNWATHANA   Chulalongkorn University

JOHN P. BURNS   The University of Hong Kong

JOHN HALLIGAN   University of Canberra

CHRISTOPHER HOOD   Oxford University

PATRICIA INGRAHAM   Binghamton University

HELEN MARGETTS   Oxford University

JOSÉA LUIS MÉNDEZ   El Colegio de México

JOHAN P. OLSEN   University of Oslo

JON PIERRE   University of Gothenburg

CHRISTOPHER POLLITT   Katholieke Universiteit Leuven

DONALD J. SAVOIE   Université de Moncton

ALBERTA M. SBRAGIA   University of Pittsburgh

IAN THYNNE   Charles Darwin University, Australia

References

INTRODUCTION

Christensen, T.P., P.G. Roness Laegrid, and K.A. Rovik. 2007. *Organization Theory and the Public Sector*. London: Routledge.

Kettl, D.F. 2002. *The Transformation of Governance: Public Administration for 21st Century America*. Baltimore: The Johns Hopkins University Press.

Peters, B.G. 2001. *The Future of Governing: Four Emerging Models*. Lawrence, KS: University Press of Kansas.

– 2007. *American Public Policy*. 7th ed. Washington, DC: Congressional Quarterly Press.

Peters, B.G., and D. Savoie. 1995. *Governance in a Changing Environment*. Ottawa: Canadian Centre for Management Development.

Pollitt, C., and G. Bouckaert. 2004. *Public Management Reform: A Comparative Analysis*. 2d ed. Oxford: Oxford University Press.

CHAPTER ONE

Ágh, A. 2003. "Public Administration in Central and Eastern Europe." In B.G. Peters and J. Pierre, eds., *Handbook of Public Administration*, 526–48. London: Sage.

Allison, G.T. 1971. *Essence of Decision: Explaining the Cuban Missile Crisis*. Boston: Little, Brown.

Arthur, W.U. 1989. "Competing Technologies and Lock-in by Historical Events. *The Economic Journal* 99: 116–31.

Axelrod, R., and M.D. Cohen. 1999. *Harnessing Complexity: Organizational Implications of a Scientific Frontier*. New York: Free Press.

Bartolini, S. 2005. *Re-Structuring Europe: Centre Formation, System Building, and Political Structuring between the Nation State and the European Union*. Oxford: Oxford University Press.

Bátora, J. 2005. "Does the European Union Transform the Institution of Diplomacy?" *Journal of European Public Policy* 12 (1):1–23.

Berger, P.L., and T. Luckmann. 1967. *The Social Construction of Reality*. New York: Doubleday, Anchor Books.

Broderick, A., ed. 1970. *The French Institutionalists: Maurice Hauriou, Georges Renard, Joseph T. Delos*. Cambridge, MA: Harvard University Press.

Brunsson, N., and J.P. Olsen. 1998. "Organization Theory: Thirty Years of Dismantling, and Then ...?" In N. Brunsson and J.P. Olsen, eds., *Organizing Organizations*, 13–43. Oslo: Fagbokforlaget.

Calvert, R. 1995. Rational Actors, Equilibrium, and Social Institutions. In J. Knight and I. Sened, eds., *Explaining Social Institutions*, 57–95. Ann Arbor: University of Michigan Press.

Caporaso, J. 2007. "The Promises and Pitfalls of an Endogenous Theory of Institutional Change: A Comment." *West European Politics* 30 (2): 392–415.

Clemens, E.S., and J.M. Cook 1999. "Politics and Institutionalism: Explaining Durability and Change." *Annual Review of Sociology* 25: 441–66.

Christensen, T., and P. Lægreid, eds. 2007. *Transcending New Public Management: The Transformation of Public Sector Reforms*. Aldershot, England: Ashgate.

Cohen, M.D., J.G. March, and J.P. Olsen. 1972. "A Garbage Can Model of Organizational Choice." *Administrative Science Quarterly* 17: 1–25.

– 2007. "The Garbage Can Model." In S. Clegg and J.R. Bailey, eds., *International Encyclopedia of Organization Studies*: 534–7. London: Sage.

Cyert, R.M., and J.G. March 1963. *A Behavioral Theory of the Firm*. Englewood Cliffs, NJ: Prentice Hall. 2d ed. 1992. Oxford: Basil Blackwell.

Dahl, R.A. 1998. *On Democracy*. New Haven: Yale University Press.

DiMaggio, P.J., and W.W. Powell. 1991. "Introduction." In W.W. Powell and P.J. DiMaggio, eds., *The New Institutionalism in Organizational Analysis*, 1–38. Chicago: University of Chicago Press.

Di Palma, G. 1990. *To Craft Democracies*. Berkeley: University of California Press.

Egeberg, M., ed. 2006. *Multilevel Union Administration: The Transformation of Executive Politics in Europe*. Houndmills: Palgrave Macmillan.

Eisenstadt, S.N. 1965. "Bureaucracy, Bureaucratization, Markets, and Power Structure." In S.N. Eisenstadt, *Essays in Comparative Institutions*, 175–215. New York: Wiley.

Fagerberg, J., D.C. Mowery, and R.R. Nelson, eds. 2005. *The Oxford Handbook of Innovation*. Oxford: Oxford University Press.

Farrell, H., and A. Héritier. 2007. "Conclusion: Evaluating the Forces of Interstitial Institutional Change. *West European Politics* 30 (2):405–15.

Goodin, R.E. 1996. "Institutions and Their Design." In R.E. Goodin, ed., *The Theory of Institutional Design*, 1–53. Cambridge: Cambridge University Press.

Goodin, R.E., M. Rein, and M. Moran. 2006."The Public and Its Policies." In M. Moran, M. Rein, and R.E. Goodin (eds.) *The Oxford Handbook of Public Policy*: 3–35. Oxford: Oxford University Press.

Gorges, M.J. 2001. "Blind Alley: New Institutionalist Explanations for Institutional Change; A Note of Caution." *Politics* 21: 137–45.

Greif, A., and D.D. Laitin. 2004. "Theories of Endogenous Institutional Change." *American Political Science Review* 98 (4):633–52.

Habermas, J. 1996. *Between Facts and Norms*. Cambridge, MA: MIT Press.

Hamilton, A., J. Jay, and J. Madison, eds. 1964 [1787–88]. *The Federalist Papers*. New York: Pocket Books.

Hanson, R.L. 1987. "Democracy." In T. Ball, J. Farr, and R.L. Hanson, eds., *Political Innovation and Conceptual Change*, 68–89. Cambridge: Cambridge University Press.

Heper, M., A. Kazancigil, and B.A. Rockman, eds. 1997. *Institutions and Democratic Statecraft*. Boulder, CO: Westview Press.

Héritier, A. 2007. *Explaining Institutional Change in Europe*. Oxford: Oxford University Press.

Holland, J.H. 1995. *Hidden Order: How Adaptation Builds Complexity*. Reading, MA: Helix Books, Addison-Wesley.

– 1998. *Emergence: From Chaos to Order*. Redwood City, CA: Addison-Wesley.

Huntington, S.P. 1968. *Political Order in Changing Societies*. New Haven: Yale University Press.

Hurrelmann, A., S. Leibfried, K. Martens, and P. Mayer. 2007. *Transforming the Golden-Age Nation State*. Houndmills: Palgrave Macmillan.

Immergut, E.M. 2006. "Historical Institutionalism in Political Science and the Problem of Change." In A. Wimmer and R. Kossler, eds., *Understanding Change: Models, Methodologies and Metaphors*, 237–59. New York: Palgrave Macmillan.

Kaufman, H. 1976. *Are Government Organizations Immortal?* Washington, DC: Brookings.

Knight, F. 1992. *Institutions and Social Conflict.* Cambridge: Cambridge University Press.

Krasner, S. 1984. "Approaches to the State: Alternative Conceptions and Historical Dynamics." *Comparative Politics* (1): 223–46.

Lægreid, P., and J.P. Olsen. 1978. *Byråkrati og beslutninger.* Bergen: Universitetsforlaget.

Laffan, B. 1999. "Becoming a 'living institution': The Evolution of the European Court of Auditors." *Journal of Common Market Studies* 37 (2): 251–68.

Lathrop Gilb, C. 1981. "Public or Private Governments?" In P. C. Nystrom and W.H. Starbuck, eds., *Handbook of Organizational Design*, vol. 2, 464–91. Oxford: Oxford University Press.

Lindblom, C.E. 1965. *The Intelligence of Democracy: Decision Making through Mutual Adjustment.* New York: Free Press.

Lipset, S.M., and S. Rokkan, eds. 1967. *Party Systems and Voter Alignment.* New York: Free Press.

Long, N.E. 1962a. "Public Policy and Administration." In N.E. Long, *The Polity*, 77–93. Chicago: Rand McNally. Reprinted from "Public policy and Administration: The Goals of Rationality and Responsibility," *Public Administration Review* 1954, vol. 14 (1): 22–41.

– 1962b. "Power and Administration." In N.E. Long, *The Polity*. Chicago: Rand McNally. Reprinted from "Power and Administration," *Public Administration Review*, 1949, vol. 9 (4): 257–64.

Mair, P. 2007. "Party Systems and Alternation in Government, 1950–2000: Innovation and Institutionalization." In S. Gloppen and L. Rakner, eds., *Globalization and Democratization: Challenges for Political Parties*, 135–53. Bergen: Fagbokforlaget.

Majone, G. 1996. *Regulating Europe.* London: Routledge.

March, J.G. 1981. "Footnotes to Organizational Change." *Administrative Science Quarterly* 26: 563–77.

– 1991. "Exploration and Exploitation in Organizational Learning." *Organization Science* 2: 71–87.

– 1999. "A Learning Perspective on the Network Dynamics of Institutional Integration." In M. Egeberg and P. Lægreid, eds., *Organizing Political Institutions*, 129–55. Oslo: Scandinavian University Press.

– 2004. "Parochialism in the Evolution of a Research Community: The Case of Organization Studies." *Management and Organization Review* 1 (1): 5–22.

March, J.G., and J.P. Olsen. 1983. "Organizing Political Life: What
Administrative Reorganization Tells Us about Government." *American
Political Science Review* 77: 281–97.

March, J.G., and J.P. Olsen. 1984. "The New Institutionalism:
Organizational Factors in Political Life." *American Political Science
Review* 78: 734–49.

– 1986. "Popular Sovereignty and the Search for Appropriate
Institutions." *Journal of Public Policy* 6: 341–70.

– 1989. *Rediscovering Institutions.* New York: Free Press.

– 1995. *Democratic Governance.* New York: Free Press.

– 1998. "The Institutional Dynamics of International Political Orders."
International Organizations 52 (4): 943–69.

– 2006a. "The Logic of Appropriateness." In M. Rein, M. Moran, and
R.E. Goodin, eds. *The Oxford Handbook of Public Policy,* 689–708.
Oxford: Oxford University Press.

– 2006b. "Elaborating the 'New Institutionalism.'" In R.A.W. Rhodes,
S. Binder, and B. Rockman, eds., *The Oxford Handbook of Political
Institutions,* 3–20. Oxford: Oxford University Press.

March, J.G., and H.A. Simon. 1958. *Organizations.* New York: Wiley.
(2d ed., Cambridge MA: Blackwell 1993).

March, J.G., M. Schultz, and X. Zhou. 2000. *The Dynamics of Rules:
Change in Written Organizational Codes.* Stanford, CA: Stanford
University Press.

Maassen, P., and J.P. Olsen, eds. 2007. *University Dynamics and
European Integration.* Dordrecht: Springer.

Merton, R.K. 1942. "Science and Technology in a Democratic Order."
Journal of Legal and Political Sociology 1: 115–26.

Meyer, J.W., and B. Rowan. 1977. "Institutionalized Organizations:
Formal Structure as Myth and Ceremony." *American Journal of
Sociology* 83: 340–63.

Mill, J.S. 1962 [1861]. *Considerations on Representative Government.*
South Bend, IN: Gateway Editions.

Moore Jr., B. 1966. *Social Origins of Dictatorship and Democracy: Lord
and Peasant in the Making of the Modern World.* Boston: Beacon Press.

Moran, M. 2006. "Economic Institutions." In R.A.W. Rhodes, S. Binder,
and B. Rockman, eds. *The Oxford Handbook of Political Institutions,*
144–62. Oxford: Oxford University Press.

Nef, J. 2003. "Public Administration and Public Sector Reform in Latin
America." In B.G. Peters and J. Pierre, eds., *Handbook of Public
Administration:* 523–35. London: Sage.

Nystrom, P.C., and W.H. Starbuck 1981. "Designing and Understanding Organizations." In P.C. Nystrom and W.H. Starbuck, eds., *Handbook of Organizational Design;* vol.1, *Adapting Organizations to their Environments*, ix-xxii. Oxford: Oxford University Press.

Oakeshott, M. 1991 (new and expanded edition) [1962]. *Rationalism in Politics and Other Essays.* Indianapolis: Liberty Press.

Offe, C. 2001. "Institutional Design." In P.B. Clarke and J. Foweraker, eds., *Encyclopedia of Democratic Thought*, 363–9. London: Routledge.

Olsen, J.P. 1983. *Organized Democracy.* Bergen: Universitetsforlaget.

– 1997. "Institutional Design in Democratic Contexts." *The Journal of Political Philosophy* 5: 203–9.

– 2001. "Garbage Cans, New Institutionalism, and the Study of Politics." *American Political Science Review* 95: 191–8.

– 2003. "Coping with Conflict at Constitutional Moments." *Industrial and Corporate Change* 12 (4):815–42.

– 2004. "Survey Article: Unity, Diversity and Democratic Institutions: Lessons from the European Union." *The Journal of Political Philosophy* 12 (4): 461–95.

– 2007. *Europe in Search for Political Order: An Institutional Perspective on Unity/Diversity, Citizens/Their Helpers, Democratic Design/ Historical Drift, and the Co-existence of Orders.* Oxford: Oxford University Press.

– 2008a. "Understanding Institutions and Logics of Appropriateness: Introductory Essay. In J.G. March, *Understanding Organizations*, 189–99. Stanford: Stanford University Press.

– 2008b. "The Ups and Downs of Bureaucratic Organization." *Annual Review of Political Science* 11: 13–37. Palo Alto, CA: Annual Reviews.

Olsen, J.P., and B.G. Peters, eds. 1996. *Lessons from Experience: Experiential Learning in Administrative Reforms in Eight Countries.* Oslo: Scandinavian University Press.

Orren, K., and S. Skowronek. 2004. *The Search for American Political Development.* Cambridge: Cambridge University Press.

Peters, B.G. 1996. "Learning from Experience about Administrative Reform." In J.P. Olsen and B.G. Peters, eds., *Lessons from Experience: Experiential Learning in Administrative Reforms in Eight Countries*, 113–45. Oslo: Scandinavian University Press.

– 1999a. *Institutional Theory in Political Science: The "New Institutionalism."* London and New York: Pinter.

Peters, B.G. 1999b. "Institutional Theory and Administrative Reform."
    In M. Egeberg and P. Lægreid, eds., *Organizing Political Institutions*,
    331–55. Oslo: Scandinavian University Press.
Peters, B.G., and J. Pierre, eds. 2003. *Handbook of Public Administration.*
    London: Sage.
– 2005. "The Politics of Path Dependency: Political Conflict in Historical
    Institutionalism." *The Journal of Politics* 67 (4):1275–1300.
Pierson, P. 1996. "The Path to European Integration: A Historical
    Institutionalist Analysis." *Comparative Political Studies* 29 (2):123–63.
– 2000. "The Limits of Design: Explaining Institutional Origins and
    Change." *Governance* 13 (4):475–99.
– 2004. *Politics in Time: History, Institutions, and Social Analysis.*
    Princeton: Princeton University Press.
Pierson, P., and T. Skocpol. 2002. "Historical Institutionalism in Contemp-
    orary Political Science." In I. Katznelson and H.V. Miller, eds., *Political
    Science: State of the Discipline*, 693–721. New York: Norton.
Pitkin, H.F. 1972 [1967]. *The Concept of Representation.* Berkeley:
    University of California Press.
Polsby, N.W. 1975. "Legislatures." In F. Greenstein and N.W. Polsby,
    eds., *Handbook of Political Science;* vol. 5, *Governmental Institutions
    and Processes*, 257–319. Reading, MA: Addison-Wesley.
Powell, W.W., and P.J. DiMaggio, eds. 1991. *The New Institutionalism
    in Organizational Analysis.* Chicago: University of Chicago Press.
Przeworski, A. 2006. "Self-enforcing democracy." In B.R Weingast and
    D.A. Wittman, eds., *The Oxford Handbook of Political Economy*,
    312–28. Oxford: Oxford University Press.
Rokkan, S. 1966. "Norway: Numerical Democracy and Corporate
    Pluralism." In R.A. Dahl, ed., *Political Oppositions in Western
    Democracies*, 70–115. New Haven: Yale University Press.
– 1999. *State Formation, Nation-Building and Mass Politics in Europe:
    The Theory of Stein Rokkan*, 1–191. Edited by P. Flora, with
    S. Kuhnle and D. Urwin. Oxford: Oxford University Press.
Rothstein, B. 1996. "Political Institutions: An Overview." In R.E. Goodin
    and H-D. Klingemann, eds., *A New Handbook of Political Science*,
    133–66. Oxford: Oxford University Press.
Sait, E. 1938. *Political Institutions: A Preface.* New York: Appleton-
    Century-Crofts.
Sartori, G. 1969. "From the Sociology of Politics to Political Sociology."
    In S.M. Lipset, ed., *Politics and the Social Sciences*, 65–100. New York:
    Oxford University Press.

Schattschneider, E.E. 1960. *The Semi-Sovereign People*. New York: Holt, Rinehart and Winston.

Scott, W.R. 1995. *Institutions and Organizations*. Thousand Oaks, CA: Sage.

Scott, R.R., J.W. Meyer, and Associates. 1994. *Institutional Environments and Organizations: Structural Complexity and Individualism*. Thousand Oaks, CA: Sage.

Schumpeter, J.A. 1994. paperback ed. [1942], *Capitalism, Socialism and Democracy*. London: Allen and Unwin.

Searle, J.R. 1995. *The Construction of Social Reality*. London: Penguin.

Selznick, P. 1957. *Leadership in Administration*. New York: Harper & Row.

Shepsle, K.A. 2006. "Old Questions and New Answers about Institutions: The Riker Objection Revisted." In B.R Weingast and D.A. Wittman, eds., *The Oxford Handbook of Political Economy*, 1031–49. Oxford: Oxford University Press.

Simon, H.A. 1953. "Birth of an Organization: The Economic Cooperation Administration." *Public Administration Review* 13: 227–36.

– 1957. *Administrative Behavior*. 2d ed. New York: Macmillan.

Steinmo, S., K. Thelen, and F. Longstreeth. 1992. *Structuring Politics: Historical Institutionalism in Comparative Analysis*. Cambridge: Cambridge University Press.

Stinchcombe, A.L. 2001. *When Formality Works: Authority and Abstraction in Law and Organizations*. Chicago: University of Chicago Press.

Streeck, W., and K. Thelen, eds. 2005. *Beyond Continuity: Institutional Change in Advanced Political Economies*. Oxford: Oxford University Press.

Thelen, K. 1999. "Historical Institutionalism in Comparative Politics." *Annual Review of Political Science* 2: 369–404.

– 2004. *How Institutions Evolve*. New York: Cambridge University Press.

Tolbert, P.S., and L.G. Zucker. 1983. "Institutional Sources of Change in the Formal Structure of Organizations: The Diffusion of Civil Service Reform, 1880–1935." *Administrative Science Quarterly* 25: 22–39.

Viroli, M. 1992. *From Politics to Reason of State: The Acquisition and Transformation of the Language of Politics 1250–1600*. Cambridge: Cambridge University Press.

Weaver, R.K., and B.A. Rockman, eds. 1993. *Do Institutions Matter? Government Capabilities in the United States and Abroad*. Washington, DC: Brookings.

Weber, Max 1978. *Economy and Society*. Edited by G. Roth and C. Wittich. Berkeley: University of California Press.

Wright Mills, C. 1956. *The Power Elite*. New York: Oxford University Press.

Wrong, D.H. 1961. "The Oversocialized Conception of Man in Modern Sociology." *American Sociological Review* 26 (2): 183–93.

CHAPTER TWO

Adams G.B., and D.L. Balfour. 2008. "Ethical Leadership and Administrative Evil: The Distorting Effects of Technical Rationality." In L.W. Huberts, Jeroen Maesschalck, and Carole L. Jurkiewicz, eds., *Ethics and Integrity of Governance: Perspectives across Frontiers*. Edward Elgar Publishing, 85–100.

Bass, B.M. 1985. *Leadership and Performance beyond Expectations*. New York: Free Press.

Blake, R.R., and J.S. Mouton. 1977. *The Managerial Grid*. Houston: Gulf Publishing.

Boin, A., P. 't Hart, E. Stern, and B. Sundelius. 2006. *The Politics of Crisis Management: Public Leadership under Pressure*. Cambridge: Cambridge University Press.

Boin, A., and T. Christensen. 2008. "The Development of Public Institutions: Reconsidering the role of Leadership." *Administration & Society* 40, no.3 (2008): 271–97.

Bouckaert, G. 2003. "Renewing Public Leadership: The Context for Public Service Delivery Reform." In J. Finlay and M. Debicki, eds., *Delivering Public Services in CEE Countries: Trends and Developments*, 15–26. Bratislava: NISPAcee.

Bouckaert, G., and J. Halligan. 2008. *Managing Performance: International Comparisons*. Routledge: London.

Bouckaert, G., D. Ormond,and B.G. Peters. 2000. *A Potential Governance Agenda for Finland*. Research Reports number 8 (2000) Ministry of Finance, Helsinki, 83.

Bryson, J. and B. Crosby. 2005. *Leading in a Shared Power World*. San Fransisco: Jossey-Bass Publishers.

Burns J.M. 1978. *Leadership*. New York: Harper & Row.

Christensen, T. 2001. "Administrative Reform: Changing Leadership Roles." *Governance* 14(4): 457–80.

Christensen, T., and P. Laegreid, eds. 2001. *New Public Management: The Transformation of Ideas and Practice*. Aldershot: Ashgate.

Dansereau, F., G.G. Graen, and W. Haga. 1975. "A Vertical Dyad
Linkage Approach to Leadership in Formal Organizations."
Organizational Behaviour and Human Performance 13: 46–78.

Denhardt, R.B., and J.V. Denhardt. 2006. *The Dance of Leadership:
The Art of Leading in Business, Government, and Society.* Armonk,
NY: M.E. Sharpe.

Denis, J.L., A. Langley, and L. Rouleau. 2005. "Rethinking Leadership
in Public Organizations." In E. Ferlie, L.E. Lynn, and C. Pollitt, eds.,
The Oxford Handbook of Public Management, 446–7. Oxford:
Oxford University Press.

Ergun, T. 2006. "Public Sector Leadership Capacity Building through
Education and Training." In A. Rosenbaum and J.M. Kauzya, eds.,
*Excellence and Leadership in the Public Sector: The Role of Education
and Leadership,* 157–9. IASIA/UN: Brussels/New York: IASIA/UN.

Fairholm, M.R. 2004. "Different Perspectives on the Practice of
Leadership." *Public Administration Review* 64(5): 577–90.

Fernandez, S. 2008. "Examining the Effects of Leadership Behavior on
Employee Percpetions of Performance and Job Satisfaction." *Public
Performance & Management Review* 32(2): 175–205.

Gibbs-Springer, C. 2007. "Leaving a Leadership Legacy." *PA Times,*
ASPA, Washington, DC, May 2007, 7.

Gore, A. 2004. "The Politics of Fear." *Social Research* 71(4): 779–98.

Graen, G.B., and J. Cashman. 1975. "A Role-Making Model of
Leadership in Formal Organizations: A Development Approach."
In J.J. Hunt and L.L. Larson, eds., *Leadership Frontiers,* 143–66.
Kent, OH: Kent State University Press.

Halligan, J. 2003. "Leadership and the Senior Service from a Comparative
Perspective." In B.G. Peters and J. Pierre, eds., *Handbook of Public
Administration,* 98–108. Sage: London.

Hambleton, R., and D. Sweeting. 2004. "U.S.-Style Leadership for
English Local Government?" *Public Administration Review* 64(4):
474–88.

Hersey, P., K. Blanchard. 1977. *Management of Organizational Behavior.*
Englewood Cliffs, NJ: Prentice-Hall.

Horton, S., and D. Farnham. 2006. "Turning Individual Leadership
into Improved Staff and Organisational Performance," 17. Unpublished paper.

House, R.J. 1976. "A Theory of Charismatic Leadership." In J.J. Hunt
and L.L. Larson, eds., *Leadership: The Cutting Edge,* 189–207.
Carbondale: Southern Illinois Press.

Ingraham, P. 2001. "Linking Leadership to Performance in Public Organisations." OECD PUMA/HRM, HRM Working Party Meeting, Paris, 25–26 June 2001, 16.

Ingraham, P., S.C. Selden, and D.P. Moynihan. 2000. "People and Performance: Challenges for the Future Public Service; The Report from the Wye River Conference." *Public Administration Review* 60(1):54–60.

Javidan, M., and D.A. Waldman. 2003. "Exploring Charismatic Leadership in the Public Sector: Measurement and Consequences." *Public Administration Review* 63(2): 229–42.

Kymlicka, W., and W. Norman. 1995. "Return of the Citizen: A Survey of Recent Work on Citizenship Theory." In Ronald Beiner, ed., *Theorizing Citizenship*, 283–322. Albany, NY: SUNY Press.

Minzberg, H. 1973. *The Nature of Managerial Work*. New York: Harper & Row.

Moynihan, D.P. 2008. *The Dynamics of Performance Management: Constructing Information and Reform*. Washington, DC: Georgetown University Press.

National Commission on the Public Service. 1989. *Leadership for America: Rebuilding the Public Service*. Lexington, MA: Lexington Press.

Newman, M.A., M.E. Guy, and S.H. Mastracci. 2009. "Beyond Cognition: Affective Leadership and Emotional Labor." *Public Administration Review* (January/February): 6–20.

Northouse, P.G. 2003. *Leadership: Theory and Practice*. Thousands Oaks, CA: Sage.

OECD. 1996. *L'Administration à l'écoute du public: Initiatives relatives à la qualité du service*. Paris: OECD.

– 2000. *Government of the Future*. Paris: OECD.

– 2001a. *Citizens as Partners: Information, Consultation and Public Participation in Policy-making*. Paris: OECD.

– 2001b. *Public Sector Leadership for the 21st Century*. Paris: OECD.

– 2005. *Modernising Government: The Way Forward*. Paris: OECD.

Paarlberg, L.E., J.L. Perry, and A. Hondeghem. 2008. "From Theory to Practice: Strategies for Applying Public Service Motivation." In J.L. Perry and A. Hondeghem, eds., *Motivation in Public Management: The Call of Public Service*, 268–93. Oxford: Oxford University Press.

Perry, J.L., and A. Hondeghem, eds. 2008. *Motivation in Public Management: The Call of Public Service*. Oxford University Press: Oxford.

Peters, B.G. 1996. *The Future of Governing: Four Emerging Models.*
Lawrence, KS: University Press of Kansas.

Pollitt, C., and G. Bouckaert. 2002. "Evaluating Public Management
Reforms: An International Perspective." *International Journal of
Political Studies* (spring): 167–92.

– 2004. *Public Management Reform: An International Comparison.*
Oxford: Oxford University Press.

Pollitt, C., G. Bouckaert, and E. Löffler. 2006. "Making Quality
Sustainable: Co-Design, Co-Decide, Co-Produce, and Co-Evaluate."
4Q Conference Paper, Tampere.

Rainey, H.G. 2003. *Understanding and Managing Public Organizations.*
San Francisco: Jossey-Bass.

Stogdill, R.M. 1974. *Handbook of Leadership: A Survey of Theory and
Research.* New York: Free Press.

Vandenabeele, W. 2008. *Toward a Public Administration Theory of
Public Service Motivation.* Leuven: Faculteit sociale wetenschappen.

Van de Walle, S., and G. Bouckaert. 2003. "Public Service Performance
and Trust in Government: The Problem of Causality." *International
Journal of Public Administration* 26 (8–9): 891–913.

Van Slyke, D.M., and R.W. Alexander. 2006. "Public Service Leadership:
Opportunities for Clarity and Coherence." *American Review of Public
Administration* 36: 362–74.

Van Wart, M. 2003. *Dynamics of Leadership in Public Service: Theory
and Practice.* Armonk, NY: M.E. Sharpe.

– 2005. *Dynamics in Leadership in Public Service: Theory and Practice.*
Armonk, NY: M.E. Sharpe.

Verhoest, K., and G. Bouckaert. 2005. "Machinery of Government and
Policy Capacity: The Effects of Specialization and Coordination."
In M. Painter and J. Pierre, eds., *Challenges of State Policy Capacity:
Global Trends and Comparative Perspectives.* Basingstoke: Palgrave.

Vinzant, J.C., and L. Crothers. 1998. *Street-Level Leadership: Discretion
and Legitimacy in Front-Line Public Service.* Washington, DC:
Georgetown University Press.

Wallis, J.L., B. Dollery, and L. McLoughlin. 2007. *Reform and
Leadership in the Public Sector.* Cheltenham, England: Edward Elgar.

Yukl, G. 2006. *Leadership in Organizations.* New Jersey: Pearson
Prentice Hall.

Zaleznik, A. 1977. "Managers and Leaders: Are They Different?"
Harvard Business Review 55(3): 67–78.

CHAPTER THREE

Aberbach, J.D., R.D. Putnam, and B.A. Rockman (with T.J. Anton,
    S.H. Eldersveld, and R. Inglehart). 1981. *Bureaucrats and Politicians
    in Western Democracies.* Cambridge, MA: Harvard University Press.
Boston, Jonathan, ed. 1995. *The State under Contract.* Wellington:
    Bridget Williams Books.
Downs, Anthony. 1967. *Inside Bureaucracy.* Boston: Little, Brown
    and Company.
Hall, Peter A., and Rosemary C.R. Taylor. 1996. "Political Science and
    the Three New Institutionalisms." *Political Studies* 44(4): 936–57.
Hay, Colin, and Daniel Wincott. 1998. "Structure, Agency and Historical
    Institutionalism." *Political Studies* 46(4): 951–7.
Hogwood, B.W., and L.A. Gunn. 1984. *Policy Analysis for the Real
    World.* Oxford: Oxford University Press.
Hood, Christopher. 1976. *The Limits of Administration.* London: Wiley.
– 1997. "Which Contract State? Four Perspectives on Over-outsourcing
    for Public Services." *Australian Journal of Public Administration*
    56(3): 120–31.
Kettl, Donald. 2000. *The Global Public Management Revolution.*
    Washington, DC: Brookings Institution.
Lane, Jan-Erik. 2000. *New Public Management.* London: Routledge.
– 2005. *Public Administration and Public Management: The Principal-
    Agent Perspective.* London: Routledge.
Lienhard, Andreas. 2006. "Public-Private Partnerships (PPPS) in
    Switzerland: Experiences-Risks-Potentials." *International Review of
    Administrative Sciences* 72(4): 547–63.
Lindblom, Charles E. 1959. "The Science of Muddling Through." *Public
    Administration Review* 19(2): 78–88.
– 1979. "Still Muddling, Not Yet Through." *Public Administration
    Review* 39(6): 517–26.
Mulgan, Richard. 2003. *Holding Power to Account: Accountability in
    Modern Democracies.* London: Palgrave Macmillan.
Osborne, David, and Ted Gaebler. 1992. *Reinventing Government: How
    the Entrepreneurial Spirit Is Transforming the Public Sector.* Reading,
    MA: Addison-Wesley.
Peters, B. Guy. 2001. *The Future of Governing.* 2d ed., revised.
    Lawrence: University Press of Kansas.
Pierson, Christopher. 1996. *The Modern State.* London: Routledge.

Pollitt, Christopher. 2001. "Clarifying Convergence: Striking Similarities and Durable Differences in Public Management Reform." *Public Management Review* 3(40): 471–92.

Pollitt, Christopher, and Geert Bouckaert. 2004. *Public Management Reform: A Comparative Analysis.* 2d ed. Oxford: Oxford University Press.

Powell, Walter W., and Paul J. DiMaggio, eds. 1991. *The New Institutionalism in Organizational Analysis.* Chicago: University of Chicago Press.

Pressman, Jeffery L., and Aaron Wildavsky. 1974. *Implementation.* Berkeley: University of California Press.

Raadschelders, Jos. C.N., Theo A.J. Toonen, and Frits M. Van der Meer, eds. 2007. *The Civil Service in the 21st Century: Comparative Perspectives.* London: Palgrave Macmillan.

Schmidt, Vivien. 2006. "Institutionalism." In Colin Hay, Michael Lister, and David Marsh, eds. *The State: Theories and Issues,* 98–117. Basingstoke: Palgrave Macmillan.

Selznich, Philip. 1949. *TVA and the Grass Roots.* Berkeley: University of California Press.

– 1957. *Leadership in Administration: A Sociological Interpretation.* New York: Harper and Row.

– 1996. "Institutionalism 'Old' and 'New'." *Administrative Science Quarterly* 41(2): 270–7.

Thynne, Ian. 1994. "The Incorporated Company as an Instrument of Government: A Quest for a Comparative Understanding." *Governance* 7(1): 59–82.

– 1998. "'One Country' or 'Two Systems': Integration and Autonomy in Perspective." In Ian Scott, ed., *Institutional Change and the Political Transition in Hong Kong,* 234–47. London: Macmillan, in association with the Asia Research Centre on Social, Political and Economic Change, Murdoch University.

– 2000. "The State and Governance: Issues and Challenges in Perspective." *International Review of Administrative Sciences* 66(2): 227–40.

– 2003a. "Making Sense of Public Management Reform: 'Drivers' and 'Supporters' in Comparative Perspective." *Public Management Review* 5(3): 449–59.

– 2003b. "Making Sense of Organizations in Public Management: A Back-to-Basics Approach." *Public Organization Review* 3(3): 317–32.

– 2006a. "Statutory Bodies: How Distinctive and In What Ways?" *Public Organization Review* 6(3): 171–84.

– 2006b. "Privatization by Divestment." In B. Guy Peters and Jon Pierre, eds., *Handbook of Public Policy*, 381–93. London: Sage.

– 2006c. "Statutory Bodies as Instruments of Government in Hong Kong: Review Beginnings and Analytical Challenge Ahead." *Public Administration and Development* 26(1): 45–53.

Thynne, Ian, and Roger Wettenhall. 2004. "Public Management and Organizational Autonomy: The Continuing Relevance of Significant Earlier Knowledge." *International Review of Administrative Sciences* 70(4): 609–21.

Tsebelis, George. 2000. "Veto Players and Institutional Analysis." *Governance* 13(4): 441–74.

Weber, M. 1973. "Legitimate Authority and Bureaucracy." In D.S. Pugh, ed., *Organization Theory*, 15–29. Harmondsworth, England: Penguin Education.

Wettenhall, Roger. 1984. *Architects of Departmental Systems: Five Profiles*. Canberra Series in Administrative Studies, Occasional Paper 3. Canberra: School of Administrative Studies, Canberra College of Advanced Education.

Yesilkagit, Kutsal. 2004. "The Design of Public Agencies: Overcoming Agency Costs and Commitment Problems." *Public Administration and Development* 24(2):119–27.

CHAPTER FOUR

Alonso, W., and P. Starr, eds. 1986. *The Politics of Numbers*. New York, Russell Sage Foundation.

Arndt, C. 2008. "The Politics of Governance Ratings." *International Public Management Journal* 11(3): 1–23.

Arndt, C., and C. Oman. 2006. *Uses and Abuses of Governance Indicators*. Paris: OECD, Development Centre Studies.

Bannister, F. 2007. "The Curse of the Benchmark: An Assessment of the Validity and Value of e-government Comparisons." *International Review of Administrative Sciences* 73(2): 171–88.

Batley, R., and G. Larbi. 2004. *The Changing Role of Government: The Reform of Public Services in Developing Countries*. Basingstoke: Palgrave-Macmillan.

Besançon, M. 2003. *Good Governance Rankings: The Art of Measurement*. WPF Reports no.36. Cambridge, MA: World Peace Foundation.

Bevan, G., and C. Hood. 2006. "What's Measured Is What Matters: Targets and Gaming in the English Public Health Care System." *Public Administration* 84(3): 517–38.

Bevir, M. 2005. "How Narratives Explain." In D. Yanow and P. Schwartz-Shea, eds., *Interpretation and Method: Empirical Research Methods and the Interpretive Turn,* 281–90. Armonk, NY: M.E. Sharpe.

Bouckaert, G., and J. Halligan. 2008. *Managing Performance: International Comparisons.* London and New York: Routledge/Taylor and Francis.

Bovaird, T., and E. Löffler. 2003. "Evaluating the Quality of Public Governance: Indicators, Models, and Methodologies." *International Review of Administrative Sciences* 69(3): 313–28.

Boyle, D. 2004. *The Sum of Our Discontents: Why Numbers Make Us Irrational.* New York: Thomson Texere.

Boyne, G., K. Meier, L. O'Toole Jr, and R. Walker, eds. *Public Service Performance: Perspectives on Measurement and Management.* Cambridge: Cambridge University Press.

Daily Mail. 2007. "Why Our Schools Have Plunged in World League Tables Despite Billions Being Spent." http://dailymail.co.uk/pages/live/articles/news/news.html (accessed 6 December 2007).

Frederickson, H.G. 2005. "Whatever Happened to Public Administration? Governance, Governance Everywhere." In E. Ferlie, L. Lynn Jr, and C. Pollitt, eds., 282–304. *The Oxford Handbook of Public Management.* Oxford: Oxford University Press.

Gaster, L., and A. Squires, eds. (2003) *Providing Quality in the Public Sector: A Practical Approach to Improving Public Services.* Maidenhead: Open University Press.

Goldstein, H. 2004. "International Comparisons of Student Attainment: Some Issues Arising from the PISA Study." *Assessment in Education,* 11(3).

Guha, K., and R. McGregor. 2007. "World Bank Directors Test Zoellick," *Financial Times,* 13 July (www.ft.com/cms/s/0/fe1d7ece-30d8-11dc-0a81-0000779fd2ac.html; accessed 23 November 2007).

Hawkesworth, M. 2005. "Contending Conceptions of Science and Politics: Methodology and the Constitution of the Political." In D. Yanow and P. Schwartz-Shea, eds., *Interpretation and Method: Empirical Research Methods and the Interpretive Turn,* 29–49. Armonk, NY: M.E. Sharpe.

Hofstede, G. 2001. *Culture's Consequences: Comparing Values, Behaviors, Institutions, and Organizations across Nations.* 2d ed. Thousand Oaks, CA: Sage.

Hood, C. 2007a. "Public Service Management by Numbers: Why Does It Vary? Where Has It Come From? What Are the Gaps and the Puzzles?" *Public Money and Management* 27:2, 95–102.

– 2007b. "What Happens When Transparency Meets Blame-Avoidance?" *Public Management Review* 9(2): 191–210.

Hood, C., and C. Beeston. 2005. "How Does Britain Rank and How Do We Know? International Rankings of Public Service Performance." Paper presented to the ESRC Public Services Programme and the ESRC Centre for Market and Public Organization Conference, Where Does Britain Rank? International Public Service Rankings," One Great George Street, London, 13 December.

Inter-American Development Bank (IADB). 2007. Datagob: Governance Indicator Database (http://www.iadb.org/datagob/ accessed 01/09/08).

Islam, R. 2003. *Do More Transparent Governments Govern Better?* World Bank Policy Research Working Paper 3077, June. Washington, DC.

Jacobs, R., M. Goddard, and P. Smith. 2006. *Public Services: Are Composite Measures a Robust Reflection of Performance in the Public Sector?* University of York, Centre for Health Economics Research Paper 16, June.

Jenei, G., and L. Gulácsi. 2004. "Do Western Quality Models Work in CEE Countries? Some Insights from the Hungarian Perspective." In E. Löffler and M. Vintar, eds., *Improving the Quality of East and West European Public Services.* Aldershot: Ashgate.

Johnson, D., and T. Zajonc. 2006. "Can Foreign Aid Create an Incentive for Good Governance? Evidence from the Millenium Challenge Corporation." Conference paper, Harvard University, 11 April.

Kaufmann, D., A. Kraay, and M. Mastruzzi. 2004. *Governance Matters III: Governance Indicators for 1996–2002.* World Bank Policy Research Working Paper 3106. Washington, DC.

– 2007. *Governance Matters VI: Aggregate and Individual Governance Indicators, 1996–2006.* World Bank Policy Research Working Paper 4280, July.

Kaufmann, D., A. Kraay, and Zoido-Lobatón. 1999. "Aggregating Governance Indicators." Policy Research Working Paper 2195. Washington, DC: World Bank.

Maxwell, R. 1981. *Health and Wealth: An International Study of Health-Care Spending.* Lexington, MA: Lexington Books.

Next Steps Team. 1998. *Towards Best Practice: An Evaluation of the First Two Years of the Public Sector Benchmarking Project, 1996–98.* London: Efficiency and Effectiveness Group, Cabinet Office.

Osborne, D., and T. Gaebler. 1992. *Reinventing Government: How the Entrepreneurial Spirit Is Transforming the Public Sector.* Reading, MA: Addison-Wesley.

Peters, G.B. 1988. *Comparing Public Bureaucracies: Problems of Theory and Method.* Tuscaloosa, AL: University of Alabama Press.

Pierre, J., ed. 2000. *Debating Governance.* Oxford: Oxford University Press.

Pollitt, C., and G. Bouckaert, eds. 1995. *Quality Improvement in European Public Services: Concepts, Cases, and Commentary.* London: Sage.

Pollitt, C., G. Bouckaert, and E. Löffler. 2007. *Making Quality Sustainable: Co-design, Co-decide, Co-produce, and Co-evaluate.* Helsinki: Ministry of Finance.

Porter, T. 1995. *Trust in Numbers: The Pursuit of Objectivity in Science and Public Life.* Princeton: Princeton University Press.

The Programme for International Student Assessment (PISA). 2007. *Executive Summary.* Paris: OECD. (http://www.pisa.oecd.org/document/2/o, accessed 22 January 2008).

Rice, N., S. Robone, and P. Smith. 2008. *The Measurement and Comparison of Health System Responsiveness.* University of York, HEDG Working Paper 08/05, March.

Rothstein, B., and J. Teorell. 2008. "What Is Quality of Government? A Theory of Impartial Government Institutions." *Governance* 21(2): 165–90.

Rowe, G., and G. Wright. 1999. "The Delphi Technique as a Forecasting Tool: Issues and Analysis." *International Journal of Forecasting* 15(4), October.

– 2001. "Expert Opinions in Forecasting: Role of the Delphi Technique." In Armstrong, J., ed., *Principles of Forecasting: A Handbook of Researchers and Practitioners,* 125–44. Boston: Kluwer Academic.

Schedler, K., and I. Proeller, eds. 2007. *Cultural Aspects of Public Management Reform.* Amsterdam: Elsvier.

Social and Cultural Planning Office. 2004. *Public Sector Performance: An International Comparison of Education, Health Care, Law and Order and Public Administration.* The Hague: SCP.

Stiglitz, J. 2003. "Democratizing the International Monetary Fund and the World Bank: Governance and Accountability." *Governance: An International Journal of Policy, Administration and Institutions.* 16(1): 111–39.

Streeck, W., and K. Thelen, eds. 2005. *Beyond Continuity: Institutional Change in Advanced Political Economies.* Oxford: Oxford University Press.

Tsoukas, H. 1997. "The Tyranny of Light: The Temptations and Paradoxes of the Information Society." *Futures* 29(9): 827–43.

Van de Walle, S. 2005. "Peut-on mesurer la qualité publiques grâce aux indicateurs de gouvernance?" *Revue française d'administration publique* 3(115): 435–61.

– 2006. "The State of the World's Bureaucracies." *Journal of Comparative Policy Analaysis* 8(4): 437–48.

Van De Walle, S., and S. Roberts. 2008. "Publishing Performance Information: An Illusion of Control?" In W. Van Dooren and S. Van De Walle, eds, *Performance Information in the Public Sector: How It Is Used*. Basingstoke: Palgrave.

Van Dooren, W., and S. Van De Walle, eds. 2008. *Performance Information in the Public Sector: How It Is Used*. Basingstoke: Palgrave.

Van Dijk, J., R. Manchin, J. Van Kesteren, S. Nevala, and G. Hideg. 2005. *The Burden of Crime in the EU*. Research Report: A Comparative Analayis of the European Crime and Safety Survey (EU ICS) Brussels.

Van Roosbroek, S. 2007. *Re-thinking Governance Indicators: What Can Quality Management Tell Us about the Debate on Governance Indicators?* Paper presented at the European Group for Public Administration Conference, Madrid, 19–22 September.

West, D. 2006. *Global e-government, 2006*. Centre for Public Policy, Brown University (http://www.insidepolitics.org/egovto6int.pdf).

Wilson, D., and A. Piebalga. 2007. *Accurate Performance Measure but Meaningless Ranking Exercise? An Analysis of the English School League Tables*. CMPO Working Paper Series No. 07/176, CMPO, University of Bristol.

Woods, N. 2001. "Making the IMF and the World Bank More Accountable." *International Affairs* 77(1): 83–100.

World Health Organization Europe. 2005. *The European Health Report 2005: Public Health Action for Healthier Children and Populations*. Denmark: WHO Regional Office for Europe.

– 2006. *Highlights on Health in the United Kingdom, 2004*. Denmark: WHO Regional Office for Europe.

CHAPTER FIVE

Ashby, W Ross. 1956. *An Introduction to Cybernetics*. London: Chapman and Hall.

Avgerou, Christina. 1989. *Information Systems in Social Administration: Factors Affecting the Success*. PHD diss., London School of Economics.

Beer, Stafford. 1966. *Decision and Control*. London: Wiley.

Benkler, Yochai. 2006. *The Wealth of Networks: How Social Production Transforms Markets and Freedom*. New Haven: Yale University Press.

Bentham, Jeremy. 1983. *Constitutional Code*. Oxford: Clarendon Press.

Besley, Tim. 2006. *Principled Agents? The Political Economy of Good Government*. Oxford: Oxford University Press.

Cahir, John. 2004. "The Withering Away of Property: The Rise of the Internet Information Commons." *Oxford Journal of Legal Studies* 24(4): 619–41.

Charlesworth, James C., ed. 1968. *Theory and Practice of Public Administration*. Philadelphia, PA: American Academy of Political and Social Science/American Society for Public Administration.

Coase, Ronald. 1937. "The Nature of the Firm." *Economica* 4: 386–405.

Collingridge, David. 1992. *The Management of Scale*. London: Routledge.

Collingridge, David, and Helen Margetts, 1994. "Can Government Information Systems Be Inflexible Technology? The Operational Strategy Revisited." *Public Administration* 72 (1):55–72.

Douglas, Mary. 1982. "Cultural Bias." In Mary Douglas, ed., *In the Active Voice*, 183–254. London: Routledge and Kegan Paul.

– 1990. "Risk as a Forensic Resource." *Daedalus* 119(4):1–16.

– 1992. *Purity and Danger*. London: Routledge.

Dowding, Keith. 1995. *The Civil Service*. London: Routledge.

Dunleavy, Patrick J. 1991. *Democracy, Bureaucracy and Public Choice*. Brighton: Harvester-Wheatsheaf.

Dunleavy, Patrick, Helen Margetts, Simon Bastow, and Jane Tinkler. 2006. *Digital-Era Governance: IT Corporations, the State and e-government*. Oxford: Oxford University Press.

Dunsire, Andrew. 1978. *Control in a Bureaucracy*. Oxford: Martin Robertson.

– 1986. "A Cybernetic View of Guidance, Control and Evaluation in the Public Sector." In Franz-Xaver Kaufmann, Giandomenico Majone, and Vincent Ostrom, eds., *Guidance, Control and Evaluation in the Public Sector*, 327–46. Berlin: de Gruyter.

– 1990. "Holistic Governance." *Public Policy and Administration* 5(1):179–91.

– 1992. "Modes of Governance." In Jan Kooiman, ed., *Modern Governance*, 21–34. London: Sage.

Durkheim, Emile. 1954 (orig 1912). *The Elementary Forms of the Religious Life*. Tr. Joseph Swain. Glencoe: Free Press.

Foster, Christopher D. 1992. *Privatization, Public Ownership and the Regulation of Monopoly.* Oxford: Blackwell.

Hart, Oliver. 1989. "An Economist's Perspective on the Theory of the Firm." *Columbia Law Review* 89(7):1757–74.

Holstrom, Bengt R., and Jean Tirole. 1989. "The Theory of the Firm." In Richard Schmalensee and Robert D. Willig, eds., *Handbook of Industrial Organization.* Vol 2. Amsterdam: North-Holland.

Hood, Christopher. 1996. "Where Extremes Meet: 'SPRAT' versus 'SHARK' in Public Risk Management." In Christopher Hood and David K.C. Jones, eds., *Accident and Design*, 208–27. London: UCL Press.

Hood, Christopher, and Margetts, Helen. 2007. *The Tools of Government in the Digital Age.* Basingstoke: Palgrave Macmillan.

Kraemer, Kenneth L., and John Leslie King. 1986. "Computing and Public Organizations." *Public Administration Review* 46:488–96.

Leibenstein, Harvey. 1976. *Beyond Economic Man: A New Foundation for Microeconomics.* Cambridge, MA: Harvard University Press.

1991. "The Computerisation of Social Security: The Way Forward or a Step Backwards?" *Public Administration* 69(3): 325–43.

Margetts, Helen Z., and Patrick Dunleavy. 2003. *Cultural Barriers to e-Government.* HC 704-III, Academic Report to Accompany the VFM Report, *Better Public Services through e-Government* (HC 704). London: HMSO.

Matthews, L. Harrison. 1952. *Sea Elephant. The Life and Death of the Elephant Seal.* London: MacGibbon & Kee.

Miller, Gary. 2000. "Above Politics: Credible Commitment and Efficiency in the Design of Public Agencies." *Journal of Public Administration Research and Theory* 10(2):289–328.

National Audit Office. 2007. *Government on the Internet* (HC 529). London: HMSO.

National Performance Review. 1993. *From Red Tape to Results: Creating a Government That Works Better and Costs Less.* Washington, DC: Government Printing Office.

Niskanen, William. 1971. *Bureaucracy and Representative Government.* Chicago: Aldine Atherton.

Osborne, David, and Ted Gaebler. 1992. *Reinventing Government.* Reading, MA: Addison-Wesley.

Pepperday, Michael E. 2009. "Way of Life Theory: The Underlying Structure of Worldviews, Social Relations and Lifestyles." PHD Diss., Australian National University, Canberra.

Perrow, Charles. 1999. *Normal Accidents: Living with High Risk Technologies*. Princeton: Princeton University Press.

– 2007. *The Next Catastrophe: Reducing Our Vulnerabilities to Natural, Industrial and Terrorist Disasters*. Princeton: Princeton University Press.

Pollitt, Christopher. 1993. *Managerialism and the Public Services*. 2d ed. Oxford: Blackwell

Power, Michael and Laughrin, Richard. 1992. "Critical Theory and Accounting." In Nils Alvesson and Hugh Wilmott, eds., *Critical Management Studies*, 113–35. London: Sage.

Sawer, Marian. 1990. *Sisters in Suits*. Sydney, NSW: Allen and Unwin.

Sisson, Charles H. 1976. "The Civil Service after Fulton." In William J. Stankiewicz, ed. *British Government in an Era of Reform*, 252–62. London: Collier-Macmillan.

Steinmo, Sven, Kathleen Thelen, and Frank Longstreth, eds. 1992. *Structuring Politics*. Cambridge: Cambridge University Press.

Thompson, Michael, Richard Ellis, and Aaron Wildavsky. 1990. *Cultural Theory*. Boulder, CO: Westview.

Verweij, Marco, and Michael Thompson. 2006. *Clumsy Solutions for a Complex World: Governance, Politics and Plural Perceptions*. London, Palgrave.

Weidenbaum, Murray. 1969. *The Modern Public Sector*. New York: Basic Books.

Wildavsky, Aaron. 1985. "The Logic of Public Sector Growth." In Jan-Erik Lane, ed., *State and Market*, 231–70. London: Sage.

– 1990. "Introduction: Administration without Hierarchy? Bureaucracy without Authority?" In Naomi B. Lynn and Aaron Wildavsky, eds., *Public Administration: The State of the Discipline*, xiii-xix. Chatham, NJ: Chatham House.

Williamson, Oliver E. 1975. *Markets and Hierarchies*. London: Collier-Macmillan.

Wilson, James Q. 1980. *The Politics of Regulation*. New York: Basic Books.

CHAPTER SIX

Aucoin, P. 1990. "Administrative Reform in Public Management: Paradigms, Principles, Paradoxes, and Pendulums." *Governance* 3 (2): 115–37.

Boston, J., and C. Eichbaum. 2007. "State Sector Reform and Renewal in New Zealand: Lessons for Governance." In Gerald E. Caiden and Tsai-Tsu Su, eds., *The Repositioning of Public Governance: Global Experience and Challenges*. Taipei: Best-Wise Publishing.

Bouckaert, G., and J. Halligan. 2008. *Managing Performance: International Comparisons*. London: Routledge.

Bouckaert, G., and B.G. Peters. 2002. "Performance Measurement and Management: The Achilles' Heel in Administrative Modernization." *Public Performance and Management Review* 25(4):359–62.

Bovaird, T. 2003. "Understanding Public Management and Public Governance." In T. Bovaird and E. Loffler, eds., *Public Management and Governance*. London: Routledge.

Boyne, George A., Catherine Farrell, Jennifer Law, Martin Powell, and Richard M.Walker. 2003. *Evaluating Public Management Reforms*. Buckingham: Open University Press.

Christensen, T., and P. Lægreid. 2001. "New Public Management: Undermining Political Control?" In T. Christensen and P. Laegreid, *New Public Management*. Aldershot: 2001.

– 2008. "NPM and Beyond: Structure, Culture and Demography." *International Review of Administrative Sciences* 74(1): 7–23.

– eds. 2006. *Autonomy and Regulation: Coping with Agencies in the Modern State*. Cheltenham: Edward Elgar.

Christensen, T., P. Lægreid, P.G. Roness, and K.A. Rovik. 2007. *Organization Theory and the Public Sector: Instrument, Culture and Myth*. London: Routledge.

Ferlie, E., A. Pettigrew, L. Ashburner, and L. Fitzgerald. 1996. *The New Public Management in Action*. Oxford: Oxford University Press.

Flynn, N. 2007. *Public Sector Management*. 5th ed. London:Sage.

Gregory, Robert. 1998. "New Zealand as the 'New Atlantis': A Case Study in Technocracy." *Canberra Bulletin of Public Administration*, no. 90: 107–12.

Gunn, L. 1987. "Perspectives on Public Management." In Jan Kooiman and Kjell A. Eliassen, eds., *Managing Public Organizations: Lessons from Contemporary European Experience*. London: Sage.

Halligan, J. 2001. "Politicians, Bureaucrats and Public Sector Reform in Australia and New Zealand." In B.G. Peters and J. Pierre, eds., *Politicians, Bureaucrats and Administrative Reform*, 157–68. London: Routledge.

– 2008. "Australian Public Service: Combining the Search for Balance and Effectiveness with Deviations on Fundamentals." In C. Aulich and R. Wettenhall, eds., *Howard's Fourth Government*. Sydney: University of New South Wales Press.

– 2009. "The Fate of Administrative Tradition in Anglophone Countries during the Reform Era." In M. Painter and B. Guy Peters, eds., *Administrative Traditions: Inheritances and Transplants in Comparative Perspective*, in press.

Halligan, J., and J. Power. 1992. *Political Management in the 1990s*. Melbourne: Oxford University Press.

Haque, M.S. 2001. "The Diminishing Publicness of Public Service under the Current Mode of Governance." *Public Administration Review* 61(1):65–82.

Hood, C. 2005. "Public Management: The Word, the Movement, the Science." In E. Ferlie, L.E. Lynn, and C. Pollitt, eds., *The Oxford Handbook of Public Management*. Oxford: Oxford University Press.

Hood, C., and M. Lodge. 2006. *The Politics of Public Service Bargains: Reward, Competency, Loyalty – and Blame*. Oxford: Oxford University Press.

Hood, C., and B.G. Peters. 2004. "The Middle Aging of New Public Management: Into the Age of Paradox?" *Journal of Public Administration Research and Theory*, 14(3): 267–82.

Ingraham, P.W. 2007. "Studying State and Local Government Management Systems." In P.W. Ingraham, ed., *In Pursuit of Performance: Management Systems in State and Local Government*, 1–14. Baltimore: John Hopkins University Press.

Ingraham, P.W., P.G. Joyce, and A.K. Donahue. 2003. *Government Performance: Why Management Matters*. Baltimore: John Hopkins University Press.

Keeling, D. 1972. *Management in Government*. London: George Allen and Unwin.

Kickert, W. 2007. "Public Management Reforms in Countries with a Napoleonic State Model: France, Italy and Spain." In Pollitt, C., S. van Thiel, and V. Homburg, eds., *New Public Management in Europe: Adaptation and Alternatives*, 52–70. Basingstoke: Palgrave Macmillan.

Kickert, W., ed. 2008. *The Study of Public Management in Europe and the U.S.: A Comparative Analysis of National Distinctiveness*. Abingdon: Routledge.

Lange, D. 1998. "With the Benefit of Foresight and a Little Help from Hindsight." *Australian Journal of Public Administration* 57(1): 12–18.

Learmouth, M. 2005. "Doing Things with Words: The Case of 'Management' and 'Administration.'" *Public Administration* 83(3): 617–37.

Lynn, L.E. 2006. *Public Management: Old and New*. New York: Routledge.

– 2008. "The Study of Public Management in the United States: Management in the New World and a Reflection on Europe." In W. Kickert, ed., *The Study of Public Management in Europe and the U.S.: A Comparative Analysis of National Distinctiveness*, 233–62. Abingdon: Routledge.

Moynihan, D. 2007. "The Reality of Results." in P.W. Ingraham, ed., *In Pursuit of Performance: Management Systems in State and Local Government*. Baltimore: John Hopkins University Press.

– 2008. *The Dynamics of Performance Management: Constructing Information and Reform*. Washington, DC: Georgetown University Press.

Painter, M., and J. Pierre, ed. 2005. *Challenges to State Policy Capacity: Global Trends and Comparative Perspectives*. London: Palgrave.

Peters, B.G. 1984. *The Politics of Bureaucracy*. New York: Longman.

– 1987. "Politicians and Bureaucrats in the Politics of Policy-making." In J. Lane, ed., *Bureaucracy and Public Choice*. London: Sage.

– 1996a. *The Policy Capacity of Government*. Ottawa: Canadian Centre for Management Development.

– 1996b. *The Future of Governing: Four Emerging Models*. Lawrence: University Press of Kansas.

– 2003. "Administrative Traditions and the Anglo-American Democracies." In J. Halligan, ed., *Civil Service Systems in Anglo-American Countries*, 10–27. Cheltenham: Edward Elgar.

– 2008. "The Napoleonic Tradition." *International Journal of Public Sector Management* 21(2): 118–32.

– Peters, B.G., and J. Pierre. 1998. "Governance without Government? Rethinking Public Administration," *Journal of Public Administration Research and Theory*, 8(2), 223–43.

– 2003. "Introduction: The Role of Public Administration in Governing." In B.G. Peters and J. Pierre, *Handbook of Public Administration*, 1–13. London: Sage.

– eds. 2004. *Politicisation of the Civil Service in Comparative Perspective: The Quest for Control*. London: Routledge.

Pierre, J. 2008. "Stealth Economy? Exploring the Limits of Market Arrangements in the Public Sector." Paper presented at the conference Economics and Democracy, Australian National University, 8–10 December.

Pollitt, C. 1990. *Managerialism and the Public Services.* Oxford: Basil
   Blackwell.
– 1998. "Managerialism Revisited." In B.G. Peters and D. Savoie, eds.,
   Taking Stock: Assessing Public Sector Reforms, 45–77. Montreal and
   Kingston: Canadian Centre for Management Development and McGill-
   Queen's University Press.
– 2007a. "Convergence or Divergence: What Has Been Happening
   in Europe?" In C. Pollitt, S. van Thiel, and V. Homburg, eds. *New
   Public Management in Europe: Adaptation and Alternatives,* 10–25.
   Basingstoke: Palgrave Macmillan.
– 2007b. *Time, Policy, Management: Governing with the Past.* Oxford:
   Oxford University Press.
Pollitt, C., and G. Bouckaert. 2001. "Evaluating Public Management
   Reforms: An International Perspective." *International Journal of
   Political Studies* (September): 167–92.
– 2004. *Public Management Reform: A Comparative Analysis* 2d ed.
   Oxford: Oxford University Press.
Poocharoen, O., and P. Ingraham. 2007. "Integration of Management
   Systems in State and Local government." In P.W. Ingraham, ed.,
   *In Pursuit of Performance: Management Systems in State and Local
   Government.* Baltimore: Johns Hopkins University Press.
Radin, B.A. 2006. *Challenging the Performance Movement: Accountability,
   Complexity and Democratic Values.* Washington, DC: Georgetown
   University Press.
Richards, D. 2008. *New Labour and the Civil Service: Reconstituting
   the Westminster Model.* Basingstoke: Palgrave Macmillan.
Richards, D., and M. Smith. 2006. "The Tensions of Political Control
   and Administrative Autonomy: From NPM to a Reconstituted
   Westminster Model." In T. Christensen and P. Laegreid, eds.,
   Autonomy and Regulation: Coping with Agencies in the Modern State.
   Cheltenham: Edward Elgar.
Saint-Martin, D. 2004. *Building the New Managerialist State:
   Consultants and the Politics of Public Sector Reform in Comparative
   Perspective.* Oxford: Oxford University Press.
Savoie, D. 2006. "What Is Wrong with the New Public Management?"
   In E.E. Otenyo and N.C. Lind, eds., *Comparative Public
   Administration: The Essential Readings,* 593–602. Amsterdam:
   Elsevier.

Wettenhall, R. 1997. "Public Administration and Public Management: The Need for a Top-Quality Public Service." In M. Considine and M. Painter, eds., *Managerialism: The Great Debate*, 224–38. Melbourne: Melbourne University Press.

Yesilkagit, K., and J. de Vries. 2004. "Reform Styles of Political and Administrative Elites in Majoritarian and Consensus Democracies: Public Management Reforms in New Zealand and the Netherlands." *Public Administration* 82(4): 951–74.

CHAPTER SEVEN

Arellano, David. 2003a. "Profesionalización de la administración pública en México 'de un sistema autoritario a un sistema meritocrático rígido.'" In David Arellano, Rodrigo Egaña, Oscar Oszlak, and Regina Pacheco, eds., *Retos de la profesionalización de la función pública*. Caracas, Venezuela: Centro Latinoamericano para el Desarrollo.

– 2003b. "Retos y posibilidades del servicio civil en México." In *Memorias del seminario Profesionalización del Servicio Público en México*, ed. Red Mexicana del Servicio Profesional. México, D.F.: Red Mexicana de Servicio Profesional

Auditoria Superior de la Federación. 2000. *Informe del resultado de la revisión y fiscalización Superior de la Cuenta Pública 2000*. México, D.F.: Auditoria Superior de la Federación.

– 2005. *Informe del resultado de la revisión y fiscalización Superior de la Cuenta Pública 2005*. México, D.F.: Auditoria Superior de la Federación.

Bouckaert, Geert, and John Halligan. 2008. *Managing performance; international comparisons*. New York, NY: Routledge.

Butcher, Jacqueline, coord. 2007. *México solidario. Participación ciudadana y voluntariado en México*. México, D.F.: Centro Mexicano de Filantropía.

Carrillo, Laura, and Juan Pablo Guerrero. 2002. *Los salarios de los altos funcionarios en México desde una perspectiva comparativa*. México, D.F.: CIDE.

Dussauge, Mauricio. 2007. "Paradojas de la reforma administrativa en México." *Buen Gobierno* 3.

Echebarría, Koldo, ed. 2006. *Informe sobre la situación del servicio civil en América Latina*. Washington, DC: Inter American Development Bank.

Geddes, Barbara. 1994. *Politicians Dilemma: Guiding State Capacity in Latin America*. Los Angeles, CA: University of California Press.

Grindle, Merilee S. 2003. "The Good, the Bad and the Unavoidable: Improving the Public Service in Poor Countries." In John D. Donahue and Joseph S. Nye Jr, eds., *For the People: Can We Fix Public Service?* Washington, DC: Brookings.

Guerrero, Juan Pablo. 2001. *Un estudio de caso de la reforma administrativa en México: Los dilemas de la instauración de un servicio civil a nivel federal*. Mexico, D.F.: CIDE.

Hood, Christopher. 1991. "A Public Management for All Seasons?" *Public Administration* 69.

Heredia, Blanca. 2002. *La economía política de la creación de servicios civiles de carrera: La experiencia de México en los años noventa*. Document prepared for the Inter American Development Bank.

Iacoviello, Mercedes, and Ana Laura Rodríguez. 2006. "La burocracia en México desde una perspectiva comparada." *Servicio Profesional de Carrera* 6.

Ingraham, Patricia W. 1995. *The Foundation of Merit: Public Service in American Democracy*. Baltimore, MA: The Johns Hopkins University Press.

Ingraham, Patricia W., and Heather Getha-Taylor. 2005. "Flexibilizar la gestión de los recursos humanos en el gobierno federal de los Estados Unidos ¿lo que ordenó el doctor o una receta equivocada?" *Foro Internacional* 182.

Kingdon, John W. 2003. *Agendas, Alternatives and Public Policies*. New York, NY: Longman.

Konig, Klaus. 1977. "Entrepreneurial Management of Executive Administration: The Perspective of Classical Public Administration." In Walter Kickert, ed., *Public Management and Administrative Reform in Western Europe*. Cheltenham, UK: Edward Elgar.

Martínez Puón, Rafael. 2005. *Servicio profesional de carrera ¿para que?*. México, D.F.: Fundación Mexicana de Estudios Políticos y Administrativos-Miguel Angel Porrúa.

Méndez, José Luis. 1995. "La profesionalización del Estado mexicano: ¿Olvidando o esperando a Godot?." *El Cotidiano* 72.

– 2004. "Propuesta de reglamento de la ley del servicio profesional de carrera." Presented at Consejo Consultivo del Servicio Profesional de Carrera, 18 February, México, D.F.

– 2007a. "La reforma del estado en México ¿Hacia un régimen semi-presidencial?" In Gustavo Vega, coord., *México: Los retos ante el futuro*. México, D.F.: El Colegio de México-Fundación Konrad Adenauer.

– 2007b. "Toward More Balanced Approaches in the Reform of the State." In Jorge I. Domínguez and Anthony Jones, eds., *The Construction of Democracy: Lessons from Practice and Research*. Baltimore, MA: The Johns Hopkins University Press.

Osborne, David, and Ted Gaebler. 1992. *Reinventing Government*. Reading, MA: Addison-Wesley.

Pardo, María del Carmen. 1991. *La Modernización Administrativa en México*. México, D.F.: El Colegio de México.

– 1995. "El servicio civil de carrera en México: Un imperativo de la modernización." *Gestión y Política Pública* 4(2).

– 2005. "El servicio profesional de carrera en México: De la tradición al cambio." *Foro Internacional* 182.

Peters, B. Guy. 2004. "Cambios en la naturaleza de la administración pública: De las preguntas sencillas a las respuestas difíciles." In María del Carmen Pardo, comp., *De la administración pública a la gobernanza*. México, D.F.: El Colegio de México.

Pollitt, Christopher, and Geert Bouckaert. 2004. *Public Management Reform: A Comparative Analysis*. Oxford: Oxford University Press.

Ramió, Carles, and Miguel Salvador i Serna. 2007. "Revisando impactos: Una visión neoinstitucionalista de los intentos de reforma de los sistemas de servicio civil." *Buen Gobierno* 3.

Red mexicana de servicio profesional. 2003. *Profesionalización del servicio público en México; hacia la innovación y la democracia; memorias*. México, D.F.: Red mexicana de servicio profesional.

Romero, Eduardo. 2005. "Avances y resultados del servicio profesional de carrera." *Servicio Profesional de Carrera* 4.

Sabatier, Paul A., and Hank Jenkins-Smith, eds. 1993. *Policy Change and Learning: An Advocacy Coalition Approach*. Boulder, CO: Westview.

Secretaría de la Función Pública. 2005. *Informe anual sobre el servicio de carrera profesional 2004*. México, D.F.: Secretaría de la Función Pública.

– 2006a. *Informe de rendición de cuentas 2000–2006: Primera etapa*. México, D.F.: Secretaría de la Función Pública.

– 2006b. *Informe de rendición de cuentas 2000–2006: Segunda y tercera etapa*. México, D.F.: Secretaría de la Función Pública.

– 2006c. *Informe de rendición de cuentas 2000–2006: Libro Blanco. Servicio Profesional de Carrera.* México, D.F.: Secretaría de la Función Pública.

– 2007. *Primer Informe de Labores.* México, D.F.: Secretaría de la Función Pública.

– 2008a. *Segundo Informe de Labores.* México, D.F.: Secretaría de la Función Pública.

– 2008b. *Programa para el servicio profesional de carrera en la administración pública federal, 2008–2012.* México, D.F.: Secretaría de la Función Pública.

– 2008c. *Programa para la Mejora de la Gestión.* México, D.F.: Secretaría de la Función Pública.

Uvalle, Ricardo. 2000. *Institucionalidad y profesionalización del servicio público en México: Retos y perspectivas.* México, D.F.: Plaza y Valdés.

CHAPTER EIGHT

Asian Development Bank. 1995. *Governance: Sound Development Management,* at website http://www.adb.org/documents/policies/governance.

Barnett, A. Doak. 1967. *Cadres, Bureaucracy, and Political Power.* New York: Columbia University Press.

Bian, Yanjie. 1994. *Work and Inequality in Urban China.* Albany: State University of New York Press.

Bo, Zhiyue. 2002. *Chinese Provincial Leaders: Economic Performance and Political Mobility since 1949.* Armonk, NY: M.E. Sharpe.

Brady, Anne-Marie. 2003. *Making the Foreign Serve China: Managing Foreigners in the People's Republic.* Lanham, MD: Rowman & Littlefield.

Brown, John. 1993. "Evaluating the Performance of Central Government." In Christopher Pollitt and Shirley Harrison, eds., *Handbook of Public Services Management.* Oxford: Blackwell.

Burningham, David. 1993. "An Overview of the Use of Performance Indicators in Local Government." In Christopher Pollitt and Shirley Harrison, eds., *Handbook of Public Services Management.* Oxford: Blackwell.

Burns, John P. 1989. *The Chinese Communist Party's Nomenklatura System.* Armonk, NY: M.E. Sharpe.

– 1994a. "Renshi dang'an: China's Cadre Dossier System." In John P. Burns, ed., *Chinese Law and Government* 27:2 (March–April), 5–104.

– 1994b. "Strengthening Central CCP Control of Leadership Selection: The 1990 Nomenklatura." *The China Quarterly* 138 (June): 458–91.

– 1999. "Changing Environmental Impacts on Civil Service Systems: The Cases of China and Hong Kong." In H.K. Wong and H.S. Chan, eds., *Handbook of Comparative Public Administration in the Asia-Pacific Basin*, 179–218. New York: Marcel Dekker.

– 2003. "Downsizing the Chinese State: Government Retrenchment in the 1990s." *The China Quarterly* 175 (September): 775–802.

Burns, John P., and Jean-Pierre Cabestan, eds. 1990–91. "Provisional Chinese Civil Service Regulations." *Chinese Law and Government* 23(4):10–23.

Burns, John P., and Wang Xiaoqi. Forthcoming. "Civil Service Reform in China: Impacts on Civil Servants' Behavior." *The China Quarterly*.

Cao, Zhi, ed. 1985. *Outline of Foreign Civil Service Systems (Guowai renshi zhidu gaiyao)*. Beijing: Beijing daxue chubanshe (Peking University Press).

Chang, Tianle. "Open Government: A Step Forward, but with Sideways Shuffles Too." *China Development Brief* (May 24), at website http://www.chinadevelopmentbrief.com/node/1111, accessed 18 August 2008.

Chowdhury, N., with C.E. Skarstedt. 2005. "The Principle of Good Governance" Center for International Sustainable Development Law Working Paper, Oxford, March, at website http://www.cisdl.org/pdf/sdl/sDL_Good_Governance.pdf, accessed 18 August 2008.

Dai, Guangqian. 1990–91. "Proposing a Reform of the Cadre and Personnel System and the State." In John P. Burns and Jean-Pierre Cabestan, eds., *Chinese Law and Government* 23(4): 61–73.

Dao, Minh Chau. 1996. "Administrative Concepts in Confucianism and Their Influence on Development in Confucian Countries." *The Asian Journal of Public Administration* 18(1): 45–69.

Deng, Xiaoping. 1984. "On the Reform of the System of Party and State Leadership." *Selected Works of Deng Xiaoping 1975–1982*, 302–25. Beijing: Foreign Languages Press.

Doornbos, Martin R. 2003. "Good Governance: The Metamorphosis of a Policy Metaphor." *Journal of International Affairs*, 22 September.

Downs, Anthony, 1967. *Inside Bureaucracy* Boston: Little Brown.

Ebrey, Patrica B. 1999. *The Cambridge Illustrated History of China*. Cambridge: Cambridge University Press.

Hood, Christopher, and D. Heald, eds. 2006. *Transparency: The Key to Better Governance?* Oxford: Oxford University Press.

Horn, Murray J. 1995. *The Political Economy of Public Administration.*
Cambridge: Cambridge University Press.

Horsley, Jamie P. 2003. "China's Pioneering Foray into Open Government: A Tale of Two Cities." *Freedominfo.org* (14 July), at website http://
www.freedominfo.org/news/20030714.htm, accessed 18 August 2008.

– 2007. "China Adopts First Nationwide Open Government Information
Regulations." *Freedominfo.org* (9 May) at website http://www.
freedominfo.org/features/ 20070509.htm, accessed 18 August 2008.

Hu, N.S. 1998. *Strategic Images of China's Government.* Beijing: Central
Party School Press [in Chinese].

Kingdon, John W. 2003. *Agendas, Alternatives, and Public Policy.* 2d ed.
New York: Longman.

Li, Cheng, and Lynn White. 1990. "Elite Transformation and Modern
Change in Mainland China and Taiwan: Empirical Data and the
Theory of Technocracy." *The China Quarterly* 121 (March): 1–35.

Lieberthal, Kenneth. 2004. *Governing China from Revolution through
Reform* 2d ed. New York: Norton.

Lin, Tingjin. 2008. *Explaining Intra-Provicial Inequality in Education in
China: The Roles of Institutions and Provincial Leaders,* unpublished
PHD diss., University of Hong Kong.

Milgrom, Paul, and John Roberts. 1992. *Economics, Organization and
Management,* Upper Saddle River, NJ: Prentice Hall.

Ministry of Personnel. 1993. "Provisional Regulations on Civil Servants."
Beijing: mimeo.

Nanda, V.P. 2006. "The 'Good Governance' Concept Revisited." *Annals
of the American Academy of Political and Social Science* 603:269–83.

National People's Congress. 2005. *Civil Servants Law,* on website
http://www.gov.cn/ziliao/flfg/2005–06/21/content_8249.htm, accessed
27 July 2008.

Pollitt, Christopher, and Geert Bouckaert. 2000. *Public Management
Reform: A Comparative Analysis.* Oxford: Oxford University Press.

Pollitt, Christopher, and Stephen Harrison, eds. 1993. *Handbook of
Public Services Management.* Oxford: Blackwell.

Pye, Lucian W. 1995. "An Introductory Profile: Deng Xiaoping and
China's Political Culture." In David Shambaugh, ed., *Deng Xiaoping:
Portrait of a Chinese Statesman,* xx. Oxford: Oxford University Press.

Robinson, Thomas W. 1971. *The Cultural Revolution in China.* Berkeley:
University of California Press.

Strauss, Julia. 1998. *Strong Institutions in Weak Polities: State Building
in Republican China, 1927–1940.* Oxford: Oxford University Press.

Whiting, Susan. 2001. *Power and Wealth in Rural China: The Political Economy of Institutional Change*. Cambridge: Cambridge University Press.

World Bank. 1994. *Governance: The World Bank's Experience*. Washington, DC: The World Bank.

Yu, Keping. 2000. *Governance and Good Governance (zhili yu shanzhi)*. Beijing: Shehui kexueyuan chubanshe (Academy of Social Sciences Press) [in Chinese].

Zhang, Chunlin. 2007. World Bank, personal communication, 23 October.

Zhou, Zhiren. 1995 "Public Organization Performance Evaluation: UK Practice for China." *New Vision (xin shiye)* 38–41 [in Chinese].

– 1996. "The 'Service Promise System' in China: Some Reflections from a Theoretical Perspective." *Chinese Public Administration* 14–24.

– 2006. "Public Sector Performance Measurement in China: An Overview and Critique." Paper prepared for the 5th Asian Forum on Public Management, University of Hong Kong, Hong Kong, 14–15 January.

– 2007. Peking University, personal communication, 23 October.

Zou, Ran. 1994a. "Central Government Work Evaluation" [A translation of John Brown (1993)]. *Research Review (yanjiu zonglan)*, 15–16 [in Chinese].

– 1994b. "Overview of the Use of Performance Indicators in English Local Government" [A translation of David Burningham (1993)] *Administrative Personnel Management (xingzheng renshi guanli)* no. 1, 32–3 [in Chinese]

CHAPTER NINE

Aberbach, Joel D., Robert D. Putnam, and Bert A. Rockman. 1981. *Bureaucrats and Politicians in Western Democracies*. Cambridge, MA: Harvard University Press.

Bowornwathana, Bidhya. 2008. "Importing Governance into the Thai Polity: Competing Hybrids and Reform Consequences." In Bidhya Bowornwathana and Clay Wescott, eds., *Comparative Governance Reform in Asia: Democracy, Corruption, and Government Trust*, 5–20. Oxford: JAI Press, Emerald.

– 2007. "Governance Reform Outcomes through Cultural Lens: Thailand." In Kuno Schedler and Isabella Proeller, eds., *Cultural Aspects of Public Management Reform*, 275–98. Oxford: JAI Press, Elsevier.

– 2006a. "Autonomisation of the Thai State: Some Observations." *Public Administration and Development* 26:27–34.

– 2006b. "Government Reform under Thaksin: The Return of the Authoritarian Perspective." *Asian Review of Public Administration* 18:93–126.

– 2006c. "The Thai Model of Rewards for High Public Office." In Daniel H. Unger and Clark D. Neher, eds., *Bureaucracy and National Security in Southeast Asia: Essays in Honor of M. Ladd Thomas*, 33–55. Naperville, IL: Publishers' Graphics.

– 2006d. "Transforming Bureaucracies for the Twenty-First Century: The New Democratic Governance Paradigm." In Eric Otenyo and Nancy Lind, eds., *Comparative Public Administration: The Essential Readings*, 667–80. Oxford: Elsevier.

– 2005a. "Dynamics and Effectiveness of the NCC Commission and the New Counter Corruption Network in Thailand: The Story of the Struggling Tiger." Paper presented at the National University of Singapore's Centennial Conference on Asian Horizons: Cities, States and Societies, The National University of Singapore, Singapore, 1–3 August.

– 2005b. "Administrative Reform and Tidal Waves from Regime Shifts: Tsunamis in Thailand's Political and Administrative History." *The Asian Pacific Journal of Public Administration* 27:37–52.

– 2005c. "State Capture, Conflict of Interest, Business Empires and the Super Patron: Comparison of Big Businessman Thaksin and Berlusconi in Power." Paper presented at the 9th International Research Symposium on Public Management (IRSPM), Bocconi University, Milan, Italy, 6–8 April.

– 2004a. "Putting New Public Management to Good Use: Autonomous Public Organizations in Thailand." In Christopher Pollitt and Colin Talbot, eds., *Unbundled Government: A Critical Analysis of Global Trends in Agencies, Quangos, and Contractualisation*, 247–63. London and New York: Routledge.

– 2004b. "Thaksin's Model of Government Reform: Prime Ministerialisation through 'A Country is My Company' Approach." *Asian Journal of Political Science* 12:133–51.

– 2002a. "Hidden Agendas in Administrative Reform: Thailand." Paper presented at the International Conference on Governance in Asia: Culture, Ethics, Institutional Reform and Policy Change, Governance in Asia Research Centre, City University of Hong Kong, Hong Kong, 5–7 December.

– 2002b. "Joined at the Top and Structural Reform of Thai Ministries: More Government, Not Governance." In Mark Considene, ed., *Knowledge, Networks and Join-Up Government: Conference Proceedings*, 77–93. Melbourne: Centre for Public Policy, University of Melbourne.

– 2001a. "Bureaucracy under Coalition Governments: Thailand." In John P. Burns and Bidhya Bowornwathana, eds., *Civil Service Systems in Asia*, 281–318. Cheltenham: Edward Elgar.

– 2001b. "The Politics of Governance Reform in Thailand." In Ali Farazmand, ed., *Handbook of Comparative and Development Public Administration*, 2d ed., 421–43. New York: Marcel Dekker.

– 2000. "Governance Reform in Thailand: Questionable Assumptions, Uncertain Outcomes." *Governance: An International Journal of Policy, Administration and Institutions*. Also in Ron Hodges, ed. (2005), *Governance and the Public Sector*, 550–71 (Cheltenham: Edward Elgar).

– 1999. "Administrative Reform and the Politician-Bureaucrat Perspective: Vision, Processes, and Support for Reform." In Hon S. Chan, ed. *Handbook of Comparative Public Administration in Asia-Pacific Basin*, 69–77. New York: Marcel Dekker.

– 1997. "The Governance of the Bangkok Metropolitan Administration: The Old System, the New City, and Future Governance." In J.S. Edralin, ed., *Local Governance and Local Economic Development: A New Role of Asian Cities*, 87–114. Nagoya: United Nations Centre for Regional Development.

1996a. "The Phenomenon of New Ministries and the Politician-Bureaucrat Perspective." *Asian Review of Public Administration* 8:23–32.

– 1996b. "Thailand: The Politics of Reform of the Secretariat of the Prime Minister." *Australian Journal of Public Administration*. 55:53–63.

Christensen, T., and P. Laegried, eds. 2001. *New Public Management: The Transformation of Ideas and Practice*. Aldershot: Ashgate.

Collins, David. 2000. *Management Fads and Buzzwords: Critical-Practical Perspectives*. London and New York: Routledge, Taylor and Francis Group.

Deming, W. Edward. 1986. *Out of the Crisis*. Boston, MA: MIT Press.

Grindle, Merilee S. 2004. "Good Enough Governance: Poverty Reduction and Reform in Developing Countries." *Governance: An International Journal of Policy, Administration and Institutions* 17: 525–48.

Hammer, Michael, and James A. Champy. 1993. *Re-engineering the Corporation: A Manifesto for Business Revolution.* New York: Harper Business Press.

Heady, Ferrel. 1966. *Public Administration: A Comparative Perspective.* Englewood Cliffs, NJ: Prentice-Hall.

Hood, Christopher. 1991. "A Public Management for All Seasons" *Public Administration* 69: 3–19.

Hood, Christopher, and Guy Peters. 2004. "The Middle Aging of New Public Management: Into the Age of Paradox?" *Journal of Public Administration Research and Theory* 14:267–82.

Jackson, Brad. 2001. *Management Gurus and Management Fashions.* London and New York: Routledge, Taylor and Francis Group.

Kaplan, Robert S., and David P. Norton. 1996. *The Balanced Scorecard.* Boston, MA: Harvard Business School Press.

Laegrid, Per, Paul G. Roness, and Kristin Rubecksen. "Modern Management Tools in State Agencies: The Case of Norway." *International Public Management Journal* 10:387–413.

Painter, Martin. 2004. "The Politics of Administrative Reform in East and Southeast Asia: From Gridlock to Continuous Self-Improvement?" *Governance: An International Journal of Policy, Administration and Institutions* 17:361–86.

Peters, B. Guy. 2002. "The Politics of Tool Choice." In Lester M. Salamon, ed., *The Tools of Government: A Guide to the New Governance,* 552–64. New York: Oxford University Press.

– 2000. "The Future of Reform." In B. Guy Peters and Donald J. Savoie, eds., *Governance in the Twenty-first Century: Revitalizing the Public Service,* 427–36. Montreal: McGill-Queen's University Press.

– 1998. "What Works? The Antiphons of Administrative Reform." In B.G. Peters and D.J. Savoie, eds., *Taking Stock,* 78–107. Montreal: McGill-Queen's University Press.

Peters, B. Guy, and Jon Pierre, eds. 2001. *Politicians, Bureaucrats and Administrative Reform.* New York: Routledge, Taylor & Francis Group.

Pierre, Jon, and B. Guy Peters. 2000. *Governance, Politics and the State.* New York: St Martin's Press.

Pollitt, Christopher. 2004. "From There to Here, from Now till Then: Buying and Borrowing Public Management Reforms." CLAD Ninth International Conference, Madrid, 3 November.

– 2002. "Clarifying Convergence: Striking Similarities and Durable Differences in Public Management Reform." *Public Management Review* 3:471–92.

– 1995. "Management Techniques in Public Organizations: Pulpit and Practice." In B.G. Peters and D.J. Savoie eds., *Governance in a Changing Environment,* 202–38. Montreal: McGill Queen's University Press.

Pollitt, Christopher, and Geert Bouckaert. 2004. *Public Management Reform: A Comparative Analysis.* Oxford: Oxford University Press.

Porter, Michael E. 1980. *Competitive Strategy: Techniques for Analyzing Industries and Competitors.* New York: Free Press.

Prahald, C. K., and Gary Hamel. 1990. "The Core Competence of the Corporation." *Harvard Business Review,* May–June, 68: 79–91.

Riggs, Fred. 1966. *Thailand: The Modernization of a Bureaucratic Polity.* Honolulu: East-West Center.

Senge, P. M. 1990. *The Fifth Discipline: The Art and Practice of the Learning Organization.* London: Random House.

CHAPTER TEN

Alter, Karen J. 2001. *Establishing the Supremacy of European Law: The Making of an International Rule of Law in Europe.* Oxford: Oxford University Press.

Alter, Karen J., and Sophie Meunier-Aitsahalia. 1994. "Judicial politics in the European Community: European Integration and the Pathbreaking *Cassis de Dijon* Decision." *Comparative Political Studies* 26(4):535–61.

Auer, Astrid, Christoph Demmke, and Robin Polet. 1996. *Civil Services in the Europe of Fifteen: Current Situation and Prospects.* Maastricht: European Institute of Public Administration.

Balint, Tim, Michael W. Bauer, and Christoph Knill. 2008. "Bureaucratic Change in the European Administrative Space: The Case of the European Commission." *West European Politics* 31:677–700.

Ban, Carolyn. 2008a. *The Challenge of Linking Organizational and Individual Accountability in the European Commission.* Working Paper. http://carolynban.net.

– 2008b. "Pay Reform in the European Commission: Pointing in the Wrong Direction." Working paper. http://carolynban.net.

Bauer, Michael W. 2008. "Diffuse Anxieties, Deprived Entrepreneurs: Commission Reform and Middle Management." *Journal of European Public Policy* 15:691–707.

Bearfield, Nicholas David. 2004. "Reforming the European Commission: Driving Reform from the Grassroots." *Public Policy and Administration* 19(3):13–24.

Cameron, David. 1992. "The 1992 Initiative: Causes and Consequences."
In Alberta M. Sbragia, ed., *Euro-Politics: Institutions and Policymaking
in the "New" European Community*, 23–75. Washington, DC: The
Brookings Institution.

Caporaso, James A., and Joerg Wittenbrinck. 2006. "The New Modes
of Governance and Political Authority in Europe. *Journal of European
Public Policy* 13(4): 471–80.

Carbone, Maurizio. 2007. *The European Union and International
Development: The Politics of Foreign Aid.* London: Routledge.

Casey, B.H, and M. Gold. 2005. "Labour Market Programmes in the
EU." *Journal of European Public Policy* 12(1): 23–43.

Citi, Manuele, and Martin Rhodes. 2006. "New Modes of Governance
in the European Union: A Critical Survey and Analysis." In Knud Erik
Jorgensen, Mark A. Pollack, and Ben Rosamond, *Handbook of
European Union Politics*, 463–82. Thousand Oaks, CA: SAGE.

– 2007. "New Modes of Governance in the EU: Common Objectives
versus National Preferences." *European Governance papers
(EUROGOV)* No. N–07–01. http://www.connex-network.org/eurogov/
pdf/egp-newgov-N–07–01.pdf.

Commission of the European Communities. 2000. *Reforming the
Commission: A White Paper; Part I, Communication from Mr Kinnock
in agreement with the President and Mrs Shreyer.* Brussels: European
Commission.

Coull, Janet, and Charlie Lewis. 2003. "The Impact Reform of the Staff
Regulations in Making the Commission a More Modern and Efficient
Organisation: An Insider's Perspective." *Eipascope* 3: 1–9.

Cram, Laura. 1997. *Policy-Making in the EU: Conceptual Lenses and
the Integration Process.* London: Routledge.

Dehousse, Renaud. 2005. "We the States: Why the Anti-Federalists
Won." In Nicolas Jabko and Craig Parsons, eds., *With US or against
US? European Trends in American Perspective*, 105–22. Oxford:
Oxford University Press.

Dimitrova, Antoaneta. 2002. "Governance by Enlargement? The Case
of the Administrative Capacity Requirement in the EU's Eastern
Enlargement." *West European Politics* 25: 171–90.

Egan, Michelle. 2001. *Constructing a European Market: Standards,
Regulation, and Governance.* Oxford: Oxford University Press.

Ellinas, Antonis, and Ezra Suleiman. 2008. "Reforming the Commission:
Between Modernization and Bureaucratization." *Journal of European
Public Policy* 15:708–25.

Epstein, Rachel. 2005. "European Dilemmas: The Paradoxes of Enlargement." *European Political Science* 4:384–94.

– 2006. "Cultivating Consensus and Creating Conflict: International Institutions and the (De)politicization of Economic Policy in Postcommunist Europe." *Comparative Political Studies* 39(8):1019–41.

– 2008. In *Pursuit of Liberalism: The Power and Limits of International Institutions in Postcommunist Europe*. Baltimore: Johns Hopkins University Press.

Fligstein, Neil, and Alec Stone Sweet. "Constructing Politics and Markets: An Institutionalist Account of European Integration." *American Journal of Sociology* 197(5).

Giuliani, Marco. 2003. "Europeanization in Perspective: Institutional Fit and Adaptation." In Kevin Featherstone and Claudio M. Radaelli, eds., *The Politics of Europeanization*. Oxford: Oxford University Press, 57–80.

Groenleer, Martijn. 2006. "The European Commission and Agencies." In David Spence, ed., *The European Commission*. 3d ed., 156–72. John Harper.

Hellman, Joel S. 1998. "Winners Take All: The Politics of Partial Reform in Post-communist Transitions." *World Politics* 50:203–34.

Hille, Peter, and Christoph Knill. 2006 "It's the Bureaucracy, Stupid: The Implementation of the Acquis Communautaire in EU Candidate Countries, 1999–2003." *European Union Politics* 7:531–52.

Hix, Simon. 2002. "Constitutional Agenda-Setting through Discretion in Rule Interpretation: Why the European Parliament Won at Amsterdam." *British Journal of Political Science* 32: 259–80.

Hofmann, Herwig C.H., and Alexander Turk. 2007. "The Development of Integrated Administration in the EU and Its Consequences." *European Law Journal* 13:253–71.

Holland, Martin. 2002. *The European Union and the Third World*. Palgrave.

Hooghe, Liesbet, and Gary Marks. 2001. *Multi-Level Governance and European Integration*. Rowman & Littlefield.

Hughes, James, Gwendolyn Sasse, and Claire Gordon. 2004. *Europeanization and Regionalization in the EU's Enlargement to Central and Eastern Europe: The Myth of Conditionality*, Basingstoke: Palgrave Macmillan.

Jabko, Nicholas, and Craig Parsons. 2005. *With U.S. or against U.S.? European Trends in American Perspective*. Oxford: Oxford University Press.

Jacoby, Wade. 2006. *The Enlargement of the European Union and NATO: Ordering from the Menu in Central Europe.* Cambridge: Cambridge University Press.

Jachtenfuchs, M. 2001. The Governance Approach to European Integration. *Journal of Common Market Studies* 29: 245–64.

Jorgensen, Knud Erik, Mark A. Pollack, and Ben Rosamond, eds. 2006. *Handbook of European Union Politics.* Thousand Oaks, CA: SAGE.

Kassim, Hussein. 2004. "A Historic Accomplishment: The Prodi Commission and Administrative Reform." In Dionyssis G. Dimitrakopoulos, ed., *The Changing European Commission,* 33–62. Manchester: Manchester University Press.

– 2008. "Mission Impossible, but Mission Accomplished: The Kinnock Reforms and the European Commission." *Journal of Euroepan Public Policy* 15:648–68.

Kelley, Judith G. 2004. *Ethnic Politics in Europe: The Power of Norms and Incentives.* Princeton: Princeton University Press.

Kinnock, Neil. 2004. "Reforming the European Commission: Organisational Challenges and Advances." *Public Policy and Administration* 19(3):7–12.

Kohler-Koch, B., and Fabrice Larat, eds. Forthcoming 2009. *European Multi-Level Governance: Contrasting Images in National Research.* Cheltenham: Edward Elgar.

Kohler-Koch, B., and B. Rittberger. 2006. "The 'Governance Turn' in EU Studies." *Journal of Common Market Studies* 44: 27–49.

Laffan, Brigid. 1997. "From Policy Entrepreneur to Policy Manager: The Challenge Facing the European Commission." *Journal of European Public Policy* 4(3): 422–36.

Levy, Roger P. 2006. "European Commission Overload and the Pathology of Management Reform: Garbage Cans, Rationality and Risk Aversion." *Public Administration* 84(2):423–39.

Levy, Roger P., and Anne Stevens. 2004. "The Reform of EU Management: Taking Stock and Looking Forward." *Public Policy and Administration* 19(3): 1–6.

Linden, Ronald H., ed. 2002. *Norms and Nannies: The Impact of International Organizations on the Central and East European States.* New York: Rowman & Littlefield.

Lodge, Martin. 2007. "Comparing Non-hierarchical Governance in Action: The Open Method of Co-ordination in Pensions and Information Society." *Journal of Common Market Studies* 45(2): 343–65.

Magnette, P. 2003. "Coping with Constitutional Incompatibilities: Bargains and Rhetoric in the Convention on the Future of Europe." *NYU Law School Jean Monnet Working Paper Series*, 14/03.

– 2004. "La Convention europeenne: Argumenter et negocier dans une assemblee constituante multinationale." *Revue francaise de science politique* 54(1):5–42.

Maniokas, Klaudijus. 2004. "The Method of the European Union's Enlargement to the East: A Critical Appraisal." In *Driven to Change: The European Union's Enlargement Viewed from the East*, ed. Antoaneta L. Dimitrova, 17–37. Manchester: Manchester University Press.

Majone, Giandomenico. 2002a. "Delegation of Regulatory Powers in a Mixed Polity." *European Law Journal* 2(3):319–39.

– 2002b. "Functional Interests: European Agencies." In John Peterson and Michael Shackleton, eds., *The Institutions of the European Union*, 299–325. Oxford: Oxford University Press.

Mayhew, Alan. 2000. "Enlargement of the European Union: An Analysis of the Negotiations with Central and Eastern European Candidate Countries." SEI Working Paper No. 39, Sussex European Institute.

Moravscik, Andrew. 1998. *The Choice for Europe: Social Purpose and State Power from Messina to Maastricht.* Ithaca: Cornell University Press

Nugent, Neil, ed. 1997. *At the Heart of the Union: Studies of the European Commission.* Basingstoke: MacMillan

OECD. 2001. *Distributed Public Governance: Agencies, Authorities and Other Autonomous Bodies.* Preliminary Draft.

Peterson, John. 2008. "Enlargement, Reform, and the European Commission: Weathering a Perfect Storm?" *Journal of European Public Policy* 15:761–80.

Pollack, Mark A. 2003. *The Engines of European Integration: Delegation, Agency, and Agenda Setting in the EU.* Oxford: University Press.

Pollitt, Christopher, and Colin Talbot, eds. 2004. *Unbundled Government: A Critical Analysis of the Global Trend to Agencies, Quangos and Contractualisation.* London: Routledge.

Rhodes, Martin, and Jelle Visser. Forthcoming. "Seeking Commitment, Effectiveness and Legitimacy: New Modes of Socio-Economic Governance in Europe." In *New Modes of Governance in Europe: Governing in the Shadow of Hierarchy.*

Sandholtz, Wayne 1992. "High-Tech Europe: The Politics of International Cooperation." Berkeley: University of Calfornia Press.

Sandholtz, Wayne, and John Zysman. 1989. "1992: Recasting the European Bargain." *World Politics* (October).

Schapiro, Mark. 2007. *Exposed: The Toxic Chemistry of Everyday Products: Who's at Risk and What's at Stake for American Power.* White River Junction, VT: Chelsea Green.

Schimmelfennig, Frank. 2003. *The EU, NATO and the Integration of Europe: Rules and Rhetoric.* Cambridge: Cambridge University Press.

Schimmelfennig, Frank, Stefan Engert, and Heiko Knobel. 2005. "The Impact of EU Political Conditionality." In Frank Schimmelfennig and Ulrich Sedelmeier, eds., *The Europeanization of Central and Eastern Europe,* 29–50. Ithaca, NY: Cornell University Press.

Schimmelfennig, Frank, and Ulrich Sedelmeier, eds. 2005. *The Europeanization of Central and Eastern Europe.* Ithaca, NY: Cornell University Press.

Schon-Quinlivan, Emmanuelle. 2008. "Implementing Organizational Change: The Case of the Kinnock Reforms." *Journal of European Public Policy.*

Shackleton, Michael. 2005. "Parliamentary Government or Division of Powers: Is the Destination Still Unknown?" In Nicolas Jabko and Craig Parsons, eds., *With U.S. or against U.S.? European Trends in American Perspective,* 123–41. Oxford: Oxford University Press.

Staniland, Martin. 2008. *A Europe of the Air? Air Transport and Regional Integration.* Rowman & Littlefield.

– 2009. "Air Transport and the EU's Emissions Trading Scheme." EU Center of Excellence, University of Pittsburgh, http://www.ucis.pitt.edu/euce.

Steunenberg, Bernard, and Antoaneta Dimitrova. 2007. "Compliance in the EU Enlargement Process: The Limits of Conditionality." *European Integration Online Papers (EIOP),* 11, no. 5, June 22.

Stone Sweet, Alec, and Wayne Sandholtz. 1997. "European Integration and Supranational Governance." *Journal of European Public Policy* 4(3):297–317.

Talbot, Colin. 2004. "The Agency Idea: Sometimes Old, Sometimes New, Sometimes Borrowed, Sometimes Untrue." In Christopher Pollit and Colin Talbot, eds., *Unbundled Government: A Critical Analysis of the Global Trend to Agencies, Quangos and Contractualisation,* 3–21. London: Routledge.

Tallberg, Jonas. 2003. *European Governance and Suprational Institutions: Making States Comply.* London: Routledge.

Thatcher, Mark. 1999. *The Politics of Telecommunications: National Institutions, Convergence and Change*. Oxford: Oxford University Press.

Vachudova, Milada Anna. 2005. *Europe Undivided: Democracy, Leverage and Integration after Communism*. Oxford: Oxford University Press.

Vreeland, James R. 2007. *The International Monetary Fund: Politics of Conditional Lending*. London: Routledge.

Wallace, Helen. "The Institutional Setting." In H. Wallace and W. Wallace, eds., *Policy-Making in the European Union*, 3–38. 4th ed. Oxford: Oxford University Press, 2000.

Wille, Anchrit. 2007. "Senior Officials in a Reforming European Commission: Transforming the Top?" In Michael W. Bauer and Christoph Knill, eds., *Management Reforms in International Organizations*, 37–50. Nomos.

Young, Alasdair. 2005. "The Single Market." In Helen Wallace, William Wallace, and Mark Pollack, eds., *Policy-Making in the European Union*. 5th ed. Oxford: Oxford University Press.

Zeitlin, Jonathan. 2007. "A Decade of Innovation in EU Governance: The European Employment Strategy, the Open Method of Coordination, and the Lisbon Strategy." Paper prepared for the conference of the Portuguese Presidency of the EU, Employment in Europe: Prospects and Priorities Lisbon, 8–9 October.

Zeitlin, Jonathan, and Philippe Pochet, eds. 2005. *The Open Method of Coordination in Action: The European Employment and Social Inclusion Strategies*. Brussels: Peter Lang.

CHAPTER ELEVEN

Accenture. n.d. *Leadership in Customer Service: Building the Trust*. 7th report, 100–1.

Aucoin, Peter. 1995. *Canada: The New Public Management in Comparative Perspective*. Montreal: IRRP.

Bentley, Tom. 2005. *Everyday Democracy: Why We Get the Politicians We Deserve*. London: Demos.

Crossman, Richard. 1975. *The Diaries of a Cabinet Minister*. Vol. 1. London: Hamilton and Cape.

Davies, Howard, ed. 2006. *The Chancellors' Tales: Managing the British Economy*. Cambridge: Polity.

Denhardt, Robert B. 2004. *Theories of Public Organization* Monterey, CA: Books Cole Publishing.

Drucker, Peter. 1995. "*Really* Reinventing Government." *Atlantic Monthly*, February, 50, 52.

Dunleavy, Patrick, H. Margetts, S. Bastow, et al. 2006. "New Public Management Is Dead – Long Live Digital-Era Government." *Journal of Public Administration Research and Theory* 16(3):467–94.

Friedman, Milton. 1984. *Tyranny of the Status Quo*. New York: Harcourt Brace Jovanovich.

Fry, Geoffrey K. 1988. "The Thatcher Government, the Financial Management Initiative and the New Civil Service." *Public Administration* 66(2):7.

Galbraith, John Kenneth. 1986. *Dimension* (winter).

"Generation Y Speaks: It's All Me, Me, Me." 2007. *Sunday Times*, 4 February, 25.

Goldenberg, Eddie. 2006. *The Way It Works: Inside Ottawa*. Toronto: McClelland and Stewart.

Gore, Al. 1993a. *From Red Tape to Results: Creating a Government that Works Better and Costs Less*. Washington: U.S. Government.

– 1993b. *Gore Report on Reinventing Government: Creating a Government That Works Better and Costs Less*. New York: Three Rivers Press.

Herdan, Bernard. 2006. *The Customer Voice in Transforming Public Services: Independent Report from the Review of the Charter Mark Scheme and Measurement/Customer Satisfaction with Public Services*. London: Cabinet Office.

Jenkins, Kate, Karen Caines, and Andrew Jackson. 1998. *Improving Management in Government: The Next Steps*. London: Her Majesty's Stationery Office.

Kettl, Donald F. 1998. *Reinventing Government: A Fifty-Year Report Card*. Washington, DC: Brookings Institution.

– 2000. *The Global Public Management Revolution: A Report on the Transformation of Governance*. Washington, DC: Brookings Institution.

Laporte, Todd. 1971. "The Recovery of Relevance in the Study of Public Organization." In Frank Marini, ed., *Toward a New Public Administration: The Minnowbrook Perspective*. Scranton, PA: Chandler.

Levine, Charles H. 1986. "The Federal Government in the Year 2000: Administrative Legacies of the Reagan Years." *Public Administration Review*, 46(3):198.

Loffler, Elke. 2007. "The Administrative State in Western Democracies." In B. Guy Peters et al., eds., *Handbook of Public Administration*. London: Sage Publications.

Lord Howe of Aberavon. 2006. "Can 364 Economists All Be Wrong?" In Howard Davies, ed., *The Chancellors' Tales: Managing the British Economy*. Cambridge: Polity.

Lord Wilson of Dinton. 2006. "The Mandarin Myth." Fourth lecture in a series, *Tomorrow's Government*. London: BBC, 1 March.

Lynch, Kevin G. 2008. "The Public Service of Canada: Too Many Misperceptions." Ottawa: Privy Council Office.

Martin, Lawrence. 2006. "The Unwritten Bylaw of Bytown: Fall in Line or Fall out of Favour." *Globe and Mail*, 9 August, A1, A6.

Mueller, Dennis L. 1976. "Public Choice: A Survey." *Journal of Economic Literature* 14(2):395.

Parris, Henry. 1969. *Constitutional Bureaucracy*. London: George Allen & Unwin.

Pollitt, Christopher. 1990. *Managerialism and the Public Services: The Anglo-American Experience*. Oxford: Blackwell.

Putnam, Robert D. 2000. *Bowling Alone: The Collapse and Revival of American Community*. New York: Simon & Schuster.

Roth, David. 1990. "Innovation in Government: The Case of Special Operating Agencies." Department of Supply and Services, Consulting and Audit Canada, Ottawa.

Savoie, Donald J. 1994. *Thatcher, Reagan, Mulroney: In Search of a New Bureaucracy*. Pittsburgh: University of Pittsburgh Press.

– 1999. *Governing from the Centre: The Concentration of Power in Canadian Politics*. Toronto: University of Toronto Press.

– 2003. *Breaking the Bargain: Public Servants, Ministers, and Parliament*. Toronto: University of Toronto Press.

– 2008. *Court Government and the Collapse of Accountability in Canada and the United Kingdom*. Toronto: University of Toronto Press.

Silkerman, Lawrence H. 1980. "Policy Analysis: Boom or Curse for Politicians?" In Robert A. Goodwin, ed., *Bureaucrats, Policy Analysts, Statesmen: Who Leads?* Washington, DC: American Enterprise Institute for Public Policy Research.

Suleiman, Ezra. 2003. *Dismantling Democratic States*. Princeton: Princeton University Press.

Tetlow, Mary. 2004. "The Canadian Experience," www.publicfinance.co.uk, 30 January.

"The Two Tonys." 1997. *New Yorker,* 6 October.

Travers, Jim. 2007. "Branding Team Harper," www.thestar.com, 6 February.

United Kingdom. 1999. *Modernising Government.* A document presented to Parliament by the prime minister and the minister for the Cabinet Office.

– Cabinet Office. 2001. *Ministerial Conduct.* London: Her Majesty's Stationery Office.

– 2002. Select Committee on Public Administration, *Minutes of Evidence,* questions 300–19, 7 March.

– Parliament. 2003. Select Committee on Public Administration. *Minutes of Evidence,* questions 352–9, 14 March.

Ventriss, Curtis. 1989. "Toward a Public Philosophy of Public Administration: A Civic Perspective of the Public." *Public Administration Review* 49(2), special issues (March-April):174.

Wildavsky, Aaron. 1990. "Introduction: Administration without Hierarchy? Bureaucracy without Authority." In Naomi B. Lynn and Aaron Wildavsky, eds., *Public Administration: The State of the Discipline.* Chatham, NJ: Chatham House.

Williams, Walter. 1988. *Washington, Westminster and Whitehall.* Cambridge: Cambridge University Press.

Willitts, Dave. 1987. "The Role of the Prime Minister's Policy Unit." *Public Administration* 65(4):445.

Wolf, Charles, Jr. 1988. *Markets or Government: Choosing between Imperfect Alternatives.* Cambridge, Ma: MIT Press.

CHAPTER TWELVE

Alford, J. 2008. "The Limits to Traditional Public Administration, or Rescuing Public Value from Misrepresentation." *Australian Journal of Public Administration* 67:357–66.

Caiden, G., and N. Caiden. 1990. "Towards the Future of Comparative Public Administration." In O.P. Dwivedi and K.M. Henderson, eds., *Public Administration in World Perspective,* 363–99. Ames, IA: Iowa State University Press.

Carothers, T., J.B. Elshtain, L. Diamond, A. Ibrahim, and Z.H. Bangura. 2007. "A Quarter-Century of Promoting Democracy." *Journal of Democracy* 18:112–26.

Christensen, T., and P. Laegreid, eds. 2007. *Transcending New Public Management: The Transformation of Public Sector Reforms.* Aldershot: Ashgate.

Christensen, T., P. Laegreid, P.G. Roness, and K.A. Rövik. 2007. *Organization Theory and the Public Sector.* London: Routledge.

Denhardt, R.B., and J.V. Denhardt. "The New Public Service: Serving rather than Steering." *Public Administration Review* 60:549–59.

Moore, M.H. 1995. *Creating Public Value: Strategic Management in Government.* Cambridge, MA: Harvard University Press.

O'Flynn, J. 2007. "From New Public Management to Public Value: Paradigmatic Change and Managerial Implications." *Australian Journal of Public Administration* 66:353–66.

Olsen, J.P. 2006. "Maybe It Is Time to Rediscover Bureaucracy." *Journal of Public Administration Research and Theory* 16:1–24.

Painter, M., and B.G. Peters. 2010. *Administrative Traditions in Comparative Perspective.* Basingstoke: Palgrave.

Peters, B.G. 2001. *The Future of Governing: Four Emerging Models.* 2d ed. Lawrence, KS: University of Kansas Press.

– 2008. *The Politics of Bureaucracy.* 6th ed. London: Routledge.

Rhodes, R.A.W., and J. Wanna. 2007. "The Limits to Public Value, or Rescuing Responsible Government from the Platonic Guardian." *Australian Journal of Public Administration* 66: 406–21.

Suleiman, E. 2003. *Dismantling Democratic States.* Princeton: Princeton University Press.

Vigoda, E. 2002. "From Responsiveness to Collaboration: Governance, Citizens, and the Next Generation of Public Administration." *Public Administration Review* 62:527–40.

Index